A Field Guide to Gay & Lesbian Chicago

By Kathie Bergquist

and

Robert McDonald

First Edition

LAKE C www.lak(

A Field Guide to Gay & Lesbian Chicago

Kathie Bergquist
and
Robert McDonald

Published June 2006 by:

lcp@lakeclaremont.com
www.lakeclaremont.com

Publisher's Cataloging-In-Publication Data
(Prepared by The Donohue Group, Inc.)

Bergquist, Kathie.
   A field guide to gay & lesbian Chicago / by Kathie Bergquist and Robert McDonald. -- 1st ed.

   p. : ill., maps ; cm.

   Includes index.
   ISBN-13: 978-1-893121-03-4
   ISBN-10: 1-893121-03-8

1. Gay men--Travel--Illinois--Chicago--Guidebooks. 2. Lesbians--Travel--Illinois--Chicago--Guidebooks. 3. Chicago (Ill.)--Guidebooks. I. McDonald, Robert (Robert Earl) II. Title.

HQ75.26.C45 B47 2006
306.76/6/09773   2006924520

**Printed in the United States of America
by United Graphics in Mattoon, Illinois.**

20 10 09 08 07 06   10 9 8 7 6 5 4 3 2 1

Contents

Publisher's Credits

Edited by Laura R. Gabler. Proofreading by Elizabeth Daniel, Diana Runge, and Sharon Woodhouse. Indexing by Elizabeth Daniel, Diana Runge, and Sharon Woodhouse. Cover design by Timothy Kocher. Interior design and layout by Patti Corcoran.

Introduction

H owdy, homo! (Or, for the politically correct: Greetings, fellow homosexuals and those who explore nontraditional gender/sex mores and roles including but not limited to same-sex attraction!) Oh, "Howdy, homo!" will do for a start.

Thank you for picking up our field guide to gay and lesbian Chicago. Assembling this book has been a labor of love, and we hope that you will find our affections well spent. For years, both of us have worked within Chicago's GLBT community, and in the midst of our work and play, we have appreciated the diversity of its offerings. As book clerks in gay- and lesbian-identified shops, we both have also served many years on the information front lines for visitors to Chicago, answering, with witty frankness, their questions about where to stay, play, or pray, where to two-step, or where to 12-step. "What is a good bar to take a date?" "Is there a place where both my girlfriend and my mother can feel comfortable?" "Hey, I'm straight, but my out-of-the-closet-like-a-bullet queer-boy cousin is coming to town—what can I tell him?" "Where can I meet a girl just as charming as you, Kathie?" "Robert, where do gay gents who share your sterling qualities keep themselves in this wonderful town?"

Frankly, we got sick of it—sick *and* tired.

If only there were a single resource that had this information—and more—compiled in one slim, portable volume. Something we could put in the hands of the information seekers, to guide them as a best friend or chatty book clerk would guide them through the myriad of Chicago's gay community offerings. Something filled with the type of off-the-cuff insights and tongue-in-cheek observations that we had so long provided while leaning over a Chicago map spread across a bookshop counter.

And the startling fact is that up until now, this resource did not exist. Sure, a handful of advertising-driven "phone books" have been published over the years, and naturally, Chicago is mentioned in all the major national gay travel guides, but we have often found these resources inaccurate, misleading, or so slanted to advertisers as to be fairly useless for anything other than leveling a crooked table. "Who compiled that information, and do they live on Uranus?" we would ask ourselves when reading that the Closet, a tiny lesbian (but very boy-friendly) bar, has a pool table or, even more laughable, a dance floor. These listings were clearly not doing anyone any service.

And yet, Chicago's gay and lesbian cultural scene has so much to offer the visitor (or resident, for that matter). Chicago has two active neighborhoods that are so strongly gay and lesbian identified that even the straight denizens of these hoods admit that they live in a gay neighborhood. These areas are filled with gay-oriented shops, services, restaurants, gyms, bars . . . gay everything. But these two communities, vibrant though they are, are not the be-all and end-all of Chicago's culture and nightlife. Gay life in Chicago spreads from the city's farthest reaches on the North and Northwest Sides to the south shore and Far Southwest Side. Our community includes numerous churches encompassing virtually every denomination, a comprehensive health center, several gay weekly papers, two competitive sports leagues, a chamber of commerce, and a marching band. Every year thousands of gays and lesbians visit Chicago for several annual events, including tIML, the Lesbian Community Cancer Project's Coming Out Against Cancer Ball, the Northalsted Market Days, and, of course, Chicago Pride, which attracted more than 440,000 participants and spectators in 2005. And thousands more come to the city for non-gay-specific reasons: to visit family and friends, to sightsee, to attend conventions at McCormick Place, the world's biggest (and perpetually expanding) convention center, or to take in a trade show at the Merchandise Mart.

All this culture, yet no way to disseminate it. All these visitors, but no one to tell them where to go. It became clear that we had a mission, and a calling. And, not to put too fine a point on it, a contract.

This is our field guide to the lesbian and gay Chicago that we know and love. It contains the field notes we have accrued in our many, many collective years in the homosexual midst and queer fringes of this city. Some of the knowledge we gained in the school of hard knocks and bitter experience (not to mention extension courses in naughty delights and delighted excess). Some of it we begged and borrowed from friends, exes, acquaintances, and the occasional beautiful stranger. We offer it to you, dear reader, the way we would if you were standing across the counter from us at a bookstore or sitting catty-corner from us at the Closet, where we both have been known to grab an after-work drink or five, and where we know from experience that there is no pool table—and certainly no dance floor. It's our guide, filled with our own predilections, biases, opinions, experience, and advice. We love Chicago, and frankly, while we don't know everything, we do know a lot.

This is our guide, and we hope you will make it your guide, too.

☀ *Chicago's Pride Parade.*
~Photo by Kathie Bergquist

A Field Guide to

Gay & Lesbian

CHICAGO

In Chicago even some of the dogs are homosexuals.
~Photo by Jon Peterson

Part 1

GETTING STARTED: WHAT TO KNOW BEFORE YOU GO-GO

We've both done quite a bit of traveling, and whenever we tell people that we are from Chicago, it becomes perfectly clear that there are two things nearly everybody in the world knows about our fair city. They are Michael Jordan and Al Capone. If we talk with fellow queers abroad, we may add a couple more things to this list. Halsted Street, for one—epicenter of Chicago's gay (male) nightlife. And Kathie remembers the lesbian couple she met in Paris whose bra cups ranneth over at the mention of the lesbian flick *Go Fish*, which was filmed here—especially when she told them that she kind of knew one of the stars (in a friend-of-a-friend-who-sleeps-with-friend's-girlfriend-and-breaks-up-friend's-relationship kind of way—and anyway, that was a long time ago). At another point, she was talking to a Parisian lesbian and the issue came up of whether French girls would date Americans.

Welcome to Chicago.
~Photo by Jon Peterson

Lakefront recreation.
~Photo by Mel Ferrand

"Sure!" Mademoiselle Lesbienne exclaimed. "We love girls from Miami, New York, and San Francisco." "Suppose the girl is from Chicago?" Kathie queried, with purely academic interest. The woman turned away disdainfully and, without skipping a beat, replied, "Lie."

The bottom line is, what people don't know about Chicago could fill a book.

A Taste of Chicago History, Queer Flavored

The history of Chicago as we know it began in 1779, when Haitian native Jean Baptiste Point DuSable established a trading post at the mouth of the Chicago River, which was known as Checagou by the local native tribes. The city of Chicago, with a population of 4,170, was incorporated 58 years later, and the gates of the infamous Union Stockyards opened 28 years after that (in 1865), inspiring Upton Sinclair's socialist novel *The Jungle* as well as Carl Sandburg's description of Chicago as the "Hog Butcher for the World."

In 1869 Chicago's historic Water Tower was completed. Later, the tower would become the namesake for "Towertown," a thriving gay ghetto in the 1920s and '30s. In 1871 the Great Chicago Fire, allegedly started when Mrs. O'Leary's cow kicked over a lantern in her barn, decimated central Chicago and nearly 100 years of urban development. In the city center, only the Water Tower remained standing. (The descendants of Mrs. O'Leary's unjustly maligned bovine finally received vindication in 1997, when the City Council absolved the cow of guilt for the devastating blaze.) Chicago became the focal point for international labor struggles in 1886, when the Haymarket Riots ignited the fuse that exploded tensions between industrialists and workers.

Meanwhile, nearby, Jane Addams and her lesbian girlfriend Ellen Starr were laying the foundation for Hull House, which officially opened its doors to the public in 1889. Hull House, a settlement house nestled in the poor immigrant community on Chicago's Near West Side, served thousands of immigrants, helping them settle into their new lives. Eventually, the complex included a dining hall, a school, public baths, a nursery, a library, and one of the nation's first gymnasiums. In addition to being a social worker, Addams was also an activist for social reform. She started the Women's International League for Peace and Freedom and was a founding member of both the ACLU and the NAACP.

In the early 1900s, Addams began what was to be her most enduring lesbian relationship (with Mary Rozet Smith), which lasted for more than three decades, until Smith's death in 1934. In 1931 Jane Addams became the first woman to be awarded the Nobel Peace Prize. Addams died in 1935, a year after Smith. Ellen Starr eventually retired to a convent, where she passed away in 1940.

Two other lesbians made waves in the beginning of the twentieth century: Margaret Anderson and Jane Heap. Anderson, from Indianapolis, met Heap while

FIELD HISTORY: WHAT WERE THE HAYMARKET RIOTS?

The riots began as a series of worker strikes for an eight-hour workday. When on May 3, 1886, a melee ensued between striking workers and scab strike breakers, police moved in with unprecedented violence, beating strikers with clubs and shooting and killing at least one striker. Strike organizers called a general meeting the next day to organize a protest against the police violence. The meeting, which was attended by the mayor of Chicago, remained peaceful until about 10 P.M., when heavy rains caused strikers to disperse. With only about 200 workers remaining, and without any incitement, a police force nearly matching the number of strikers moved in on the peaceful demonstration with their clubs raised, ordering the remaining participants to disperse. Just then, an unknown perpetrator released a bomb into the throngs of police. Eight police officers were killed in the explosion, and several more were injured.

This caused an outpouring of antiworker hysteria. Raids against suspected anarchist or socialist activity terrorized the fledgling labor movement. The raids ended with the arrest of eight anarchists perceived to be leaders of the movement. Seven of the eight were sentenced to death, and the other to 15 years in prison, despite the fact that no links were made between the bomb and the convicted, and at least two of those found guilty were not even present that night in Haymarket Square. Internationally, the arrests and convictions were seen as a knee-jerk reaction against workers organizing, thus strengthening workers' commitment to band together. Ultimately, four of those arrested were hanged, and one committed suicide in his cell on the day before he was to meet the same fate.

Then, in 1893, the governor of Illinois, citing hysteria, packed juries, and a biased judge, officially pardoned the three strikers who remained imprisoned. To this day, May 1 (May Day) is recognized worldwide as International Workers' Day.

Heap attended classes at the Art Institute of Chicago. Anderson worked at the time as an editor of a small literary review called *The Dial*. Heap introduced her to modernist ideas, and in 1914 the couple began the influential literary journal *The Little Review*. The *Review*, operating from its office in the Fine Arts Building (410 S. Michigan Ave.) published a veritable who's who of modern letters, including Ezra Pound, Gertrude Stein, and, most famously, James Joyce. *The Little Review* serialized Joyce's *Ulysses* when no book publisher would touch it. Eventually the duo moved to New York and then, in 1922, on to Paris, where they joined the vibrant lesbian expatriate community that thrived there between the wars.

Margaret Anderson was in the audience when Edith Lee Ellis, wife of sexologist Havelock Ellis, gave a speech titled "Sexuality and Eugenics" to a crowd of 1,500 at Orchestra Hall in 1915. This speech was arguably the first public call for the acceptance of homosexuals and homosexuality. Anderson, it is reported, found the content of the speech rather tame.

The Times They Are a Changin': 1920s to 1960s

The 1920s and '30s in Chicago may have been the golden era of organized crime, but these decades were also a bit of a golden era for gay and lesbian life in the city. In 1924 Chicago postal worker Henry Gerber started the first official gay organization in the United States, the Society for Human Rights. The society lasted less than a year. Gerber was subsequently jailed and lost his job due to antigay bigotry but remained an activist and crusader for tolerance toward gays. Gay men and women lived relatively openly in the '20s and early '30s. Popular hangouts included what is today the Magnificent Mile stretch of Michigan Avenue, then called Towertown because of its proximity to the old Water Tower. The Michigan Avenue Bridge was a well-known gay cruising and parading ground. On the South Side, clubs like the 7-11 featured African-American drag revues, starring artists such as the "Sepia Mae West." The Dil Pickle Club was a popular watering hole for radicals—gays and lesbians among them—and their lecture series (which eventually trickled out into the soapbox debates at nearby Bughouse Square) dabbled in gay and lesbian subjects (for example, a certain Miss Elizabeth Davis once spoke on the theme "Will Amazon Women Usurp Men's Sphere?").

In 1925, responding to a noise complaint, police broke up an all-female party, where they cited nudity and women in "intimate situations," and arrested its hostess, the "mother of the blues," Ma Rainey. Rainey was known for her racy songs, including "Sissy Boy Blues," in which a woman laments her husband leaving her for a sissy boy, and the "Prove It on Me Blues," which includes the line "Sure I wear a collar and a tie, I like to watch the women passing by." Blues legend Bessie Smith, a Rainey protégé who was known for her bisexuality, bailed Ma Rainey out of jail the next day.

Then in 1935, Chicago's Mayor Kelly outlawed male drag performance. It was a move that can be seen as a beginning to the end of that age of tolerance. This didn't stop a performance by the lesbian cabaret star Gladys Bentley at Swingland Café in 1938.

Playwright Lorraine Hansberry was born in Chicago in 1930. A self-proclaimed lesbian married to a man, Hansberry wrote letters of support to the lesbian magazine *The Ladder* and was a member of the lesbian organization the Daughters of Bilitis. In 1959 her play *A Raisin in the Sun* premiered in Chicago before moving on to New York. Hansberry died from cancer at the height of her career at the tragically young age of 34.

WHO WAS EMMA GOLDMAN, AND WHY IS SHE BURIED IN CHICAGO?

I n 1940 the anarchist-activist Emma Goldman (once considered to be one of the most dangerous women alive) died and, in accordance with her final wishes, was buried just outside of Chicago in the Waldheim Jewish Cemetery (now Forest Home Cemetery) near the monument to the Haymarket Riot martyrs. When she was a young woman, the Haymarket Riots, which shed light internationally on workers' struggles, inspired her activist aspirations. Goldman became an outspoken advocate for gay rights and a practitioner of "free love." In her personal life she was never overtly homosexual in theory but was, by most accounts, bisexual in practice. One of our favorite anecdotes from Goldman's autobiography, *Living My Life*, tells the story about Goldman at a party, dancing and whooping it up. When a young activist approached her and told her that her behavior wasn't appropriate for a leader of the anarchist party and could hurt "the cause," Goldman wrote:

I grew furious at the impudent interference of the boy. I told him to mind his own business. I was tired of having the Cause constantly thrown into my face. I did not believe that a Cause which stood for a beautiful ideal, for anarchism, for release and freedom from conventions and prejudice, should demand the denial of life and joy. I insisted that our Cause could not expect me to become a nun and that the movement should not be turned into a cloister. If it meant that, I did not want it. I want freedom, the right to self-expression, everybody's right to beautiful, radiant things.

This quote has been boiled down to the catchy "If I can't dance, I don't want to be a part of your revolution." We agree wholeheartedly.

During the '40s, closeted and extremely, eternally influential gay poet Langston Hughes was teaching at the University of Chicago. Hansberry's play *A Raisin in the Sun* was named for a line from his poem "Harlem."

In the 1950s Chicago, like most of the rest of the Western world, reacted to the end of World War II with a pro–"family values" conservative backlash. Nonetheless, gay life carried on. Chicago's first gay magazine, *One* (the voice of the Chicago chapter of the homophile organization One, Inc.), began publication in 1950. During the '50s, two women, Tiny Davis and Ruby Lucas, operated the small nightclub Tiny and Ruby's Gay Spot (2711 S. Wentworth Ave.). Davis and Lucas were both members of the International Sweethearts of Rhythm, a multicultural all-woman orchestra that toured in the '40s. Davis, a trumpet player, was once scouted by Count Basie. Lucas played the piano. The two women, life partners for more than 40 years, were the subject of Greta Schiller and Andre Weiss's documentary *Tiny & Ruby: Hell Divin' Women*. (Rent it at Women & Children First bookstore!)

The Gold Coast Leather Bar, one of the first openly, overtly gay establishments in the United States, opened in Chicago in 1958. The bar has since closed, but owner Chuck Renslow went on to open the Chicago Eagle leather bar and the gay bathhouse Man's Country. Renslow founded the International Mr. Leather contest, which takes place annually in Chicago. He has become one of the city's most prominent activists, lobbying for gay rights statewide, as well as serving as an exemplar for the demarginalization of the leather community within the greater gay and lesbian population.

In 1961 Illinois became the first state in the nation to decriminalize sexual behavior between consenting adults in private—in essence, legalizing homosexuality. The Mattachine Society founded its Midwestern chapter in Chicago in 1965, the same year that the lesbian bar Lost & Found opened its doors. From the 1950s to the mid-60s, the civil rights movement steamrolling through the nation attracted justice-minded gays and lesbians to its legions. The movement subsequently inspired both the gay rights movement and the women's liberation movement. One of the nation's first openly gay attorneys to litigate for civil rights and gay rights causes was Chicagoan Renee Hanover. Hanover was one of the first inductees into the Chicago Gay and Lesbian Hall of Fame, when it began in 1991.

The Democratic National Convention was held in Chicago in late August 1968. Among the antiwar protesters demonstrating at the convention were openly gay writers Allen Ginsberg, William Burroughs, and Jean Genet. Almost nightly battles between protesters and well-armed local police disrupted the convention and marred the image of then-mayor Richard J. Daley. Many of these battles were caught on film, causing outrage and cries of police brutality. Eventually, seven of the protestors (known as the "Chicago 7") were convicted on charges of crossing state lines in order to incite violence.

Talkin' 'Bout a Revolution: 1970s to 2000

In 1970, in commemoration of the Stonewall Riots, which took place in New York a year earlier, Chicago's first Gay Pride Parade stepped off from Bughouse Square, in the Gold Coast neighborhood. Fewer than 100 participants marched down Clark Street to the Loop. These days the Chicgo Pride Parade attracts more that 400,00 participants and spectators annually. In 1970 a group called Chicago Gay Liberation disrupted a Chicago meeting of the American Medical Association, passing out flyers and lobbying for the removal of homosexuality as a classified sickness.

The '70s in Chicago were like the '70s everywhere—decadence and disco fever for gay men, folk music, coffeehouses, and consciousness-raising for lesbians. In the late '70s through the '80s, two openly gay DJs, Frankie Knuckles at the Warehouse and Ron Hardy at the Music Box, gave birth to a music phenomenon that revolutionized dance music and paved the way for techno and modern beat-based sound. It became known as house music.

In 1988, after contentious city council debates and an unprecedented lobbying effort by a newly unified banner of gay and lesbian organizations called Town Meeting, Chicago narrowly passed a citywide human rights ordinance that guaranteed protection against discrimination for gays and lesbians in jobs, health care, and housing and classified violent acts toward gays or lesbians as hate crimes under citywide statutes. It was a huge victory for Chicago's lesbian and gay population, demonstrating a newly burgeoning political clout.

ACT UP/Chicago formed in the late '80s in response to the government's negligent attitude toward the AIDS crisis. The group officially disbanded in 1995, after spawning Queer Nation Chicago and, subsequently, the Lesbian Avengers and the Woman's Action Coalition. A new wave of street-smart gay and lesbian activism was born.

In 1993 Cook County followed Chicago in installing a human rights ordinance that includes gays and lesbians in its protections. In 1994 Chicagoans elected their first openly gay political candidate, Circuit Court Judge Tom Chiola, followed by the election of Larry McKeon as a state representative in 1997. In following years Alderman Tom Tunney and Circuit Court Judges Nancy Katz, Sebastian Patty, Sheryl Ann Pethers, and Lori Wolfson joined Chiola and McKeon in the ranks of Chicago's openly gay and lesbian elected officials.

Today Chicago's diverse gay and lesbian population consists of several communities united by social affiliations and/or political interests.
~Photo by Mel Ferrand

Contemporary Queer Chicago

Today Chicago's diverse gay and lesbian population consists of several communities united by social affiliations and/or political interests. Queer Chicagoans are as politically active, decadent, religious, ethnically self-identified, sporty, bookish, consumeristic, sex-radical, family-valued, artistic, style-conscious, and socially aware as they choose to be, just like any other demographic. Likewise, Chicago's gay social and political groups and networks span nearly every possible area of interest. Luckily, there are many clearinghouses for information and news about Chicago's many gay-interest groups, services, and organizations, including the fine gay papers *Windy City Times, Chicago Free Press, Identity*, and *Gay Chicago Magazine*, the community-oriented bookstores Women & Children First and Unabridged Bookstore, and now, we hope, this book.

In 2002 the state of Illinois elected its first Democratic governor in about 10 million years. In 2005 Governor Rod Blagojevich signed into law the Illinois Human Rights Ordinance, making Illinois the 15th state in the nation to protect gays and lesbians from discrimination based on their sexual orientation. Chicago, the largest city in the Midwest and the third largest in the country, has long served as a Midwestern San Francisco of sorts, attracting gays from outlying small towns and rural areas who want to live openly, or at least free from overt hostility and threat of violence. Gay "ghettos" or enclaves develop and shift over time, although Chicago's gay citizens continue to span every corner of the city and have emerged as a political force in every city and statewide election.

So, put that in your pipette and smoke it, Mademoiselle Lesbienne.

GEOGRAPHICAL ORIENTATION (OR DO YOU PREFER PREFERENCE?)

Chicago is bordered on the east by the mighty Lake Michigan, and the lake is a popular reference when giving directions ("Go three blocks toward the lake"). The heart of Chicago is the Loop, so called because of the way the "L" tracks loop around its core. This section of downtown powers the economic pulse of the city, housing the Board of Trade and the Chicago Board of Options Exchange, as well as the headquarters for many Chicago financial and business institutions, such as LaSalle and Harris banks, and Quaker Oats/PepsiCo.

Chicago streets are based on a grid system, with ground zero starting at State Street and Madison Street. This makes it easy to find your way around, as everything is determined by its relative distance north, south, east, or west. For example, Belmont Avenue is 3200 north, Foster Avenue is 5200 north, Halsted Street is 800 west, and Damen Avenue is 2000 west. Chicago's diagonal streets, Clark, Lincoln, Clybourn, Milwaukee, and Elston, were all originally Native American trade routes.

From downtown, the city sprawls outward, becoming ever more residential. Skyscrapers give way to brownstones and graystones, which in turn melt into brick and frame bungalows. The city of Chicago is a crazy quilt of more than 100 diverse neighborhoods, each with its own distinct vibe and culture. Some areas seem to change block by block. Geographically, the area that constitutes Chicago proper (not counting suburbs) is immense. It consists of 606.1 square kilometers, or 234 square miles, and the population is approximately 3 million people. (Using the 10 percent statistic, that puts Chicago's gay population at about 300,000, although one could argue that this number may be higher due to the ongoing gay diaspora from small towns to urban metropolises.)

Ethnographically, Chicago is extremely diverse. We have the second largest population of Mexican people of any city in the country, as well as a proud and prominent Puerto Rican population and highly visible Korean and Eastern European populations, especially Ukrainian, Polish, and Lithuanian. North African and other Arabian people are also well represented here, as are other African and Caribbean cultures. Many ethnic communities forge their own enclaves in Chicago, in neighborhoods where English is definitely a second language, and options for interesting shopping and dining from the homeland abound. Devon Avenue is particularly striking for its array of Indian and Pakistani businesses, Pilsen for its Mexican vibe, and the Little Saigon section of Argyle Street for Vietnamese groceries and steaming bowls of the noodle soup called pho. Chinatown, Greek Town, Taylor Street (a "little Italy") . . . in Chicago you can travel the world without leaving the city boundaries. We will talk more about some specific Chicago neighborhoods in the next chapter.

THE GAYBORHOODS

Yeah, we know that there are worthy, fun, and/or interesting things to do in every corner of the city, and in this book we'll be sharing some of our favorite off-the-beaten-path thrills. At the same time, certain parts of Chicago are specifically notable for the myriad of cultural attractions they offer. Furthermore, like any social group, queers have a herding instinct, and there are certain pastures, shall we say, where they are simply more likely to gather than others. This chapter will provide a more in-depth look at the places where a gay tourist is likely to be spending the bulk of his or her time and will give a quick nod to a few other friendly hoods that are worthy destinations for dining, shopping, and culture.

Downtown Chicago

Petula Clark said it best: "When you're alone and life is making you lonely you can always go... *downtown*." Downtown Chicago is not the gayest part of the city, but whether you are staying at one of the many four-star hotels (which is likely, since about 99 percent of the city's worthy rent-a-beds are located here), catching a show in the theater district, power shopping on Michigan Avenue, or hitting a convention at McCormick Place, chances are you'll be making it downtown sooner or later.

For convenience, we've divided downtown Chicago into three distinct areas. These are River North and the Mag Mile, the Loop and Grant Park, and the South Loop and McCormick Place. Downtown may not be the epicenter of gay Chicago, but it certainly is the glittering heart of the city and is definitely worth a visit.

RIVER NORTH AND THE MAGNIFICENT MILE

River North is the aptly named area just north of where the Chicago River feeds into Lake Michigan. Encompassed within River North's loving embrace is the Magnificent Mile, the mile-long stretch of Michigan Avenue that is home to some of the most deluxe shopping, dining, and accommodations the city has to offer.

On the southernmost end of the Mag Mile, the Tribune Tower merits an up close look. Embedded in its walls are stones from famous buildings and sites from around the world, including the Taj Mahal, the Parthenon, Westminster Abbey, and many, many more, up to its most recent addition, a twisted piece of metal salvaged from the wreckage of the World Trade Center. On the northern end of the Mag Mile, the **John Hancock Center** provides breathtaking city views from the 95th-floor Signature Lounge.

Besides high-end shopping and four-star accommodations, some of the city's most expensive real estate falls within this mile-long stretch (Oprah lives here), as well as one of the city's biggest (and, we think, lamest) tourist attractions, Navy Pier.

Some gay nightlife exists in the area. The multithemed **Gentry**, the **Second Story Bar**, and the **Baton Show Lounge** reside here. You will find longer descriptions of each of these venues in our nightlife section (see Part 3).

River North is also home to a rather staid, conservative gallery scene (check out the West Loop galleries for the latest in subversive and outsider art). Many Chicago art galleries have openings on Friday nights. A great Internet resource (www.chicagogallerynews.com) lists where and when. Dress in black, murmur appreciatively, and drink wine for free until they kick you out.

FIELD EXCURSION: RIVER WEST RESTAURANT ROW

A s River North is the area of Chicago just north of the Chicago River, so River West is the area just west of it. River West was formerly (and is somewhat still to this day) home to warehouses and wholesalers, but increasingly fine dining establishments and art galleries are moving in and warehouse spaces are being converted into hipster enclaves. Randolph Street in particular is home to many theatrical fine dining options— so much so that locals have dubbed the stretch "Restaurant Row." Among the restaurants lining West Randolph are **Avec** at 615, **Blackbird** at 619, **Starfish** at 804, **Red Light** at 820, **Marché** at 833, and **Sushi Wabi** at 842.

THE LOOP AND GRANT PARK

The Chicago Loop is defined by the elevated rail tracks that wrap a steel bow around the center of cultural and commercial activity in the city.

Chicago's economic pulse beats in the Loop. And before you get the wrong idea, the Chicago Board of Trade is not a pickup joint. The Loop is also, in many ways, Chicago's cultural core. The theater district, where many big productions test their chops before moving on to Broadway, is located here, as are the **Civic Opera House** and **Symphony Center**. Across the street from Symphony Center, iconic lions guard the treasures at the **Art Institute of Chicago**.

Next door to the Art Institute, the newly unveiled **Millennium Park** gives the once glorious but more recently stagnating Loop an architectural and conceptual kick in the pants, ushering us (several years behind schedule) into the new millennium. They say it takes that long for new fashion trends to make it here, too, so it just figures.

Grant Park, with its showpiece, **Buckingham Fountain**, is all of Chicago's front yard. From spring to fall it is the almost weekly site of crowd-generating parties, like the Chicago Blues Festival, Taste of Chicago, and Chicago Jazz Festival. Lots of folks think these festivals are just grand, although there are typically a few too many drunken, obese shirtless people eating giant turkey legs with their bare hands to please persnickety Robert and Kathie (but if that's your thing, more power to ya). More to our liking is the Movies in the Park series, which often features the best of camp cinema and musicals. Add a blanket, a bucket of chicken, a bottle of burgundy, and someone to hold hands with, and you have all the makings of a beautiful Chicago evening.

There's nothing remarkably gay about nightlife in the Loop. In fact, nightlife in general doesn't really exist here after the workaday folk stagger home from one of the many generic bars and grills catering to them. So after going to the theater, head to River North or beyond for nightlife.

Fashion on State Street.
~Photo by Andy Perez

FIELD EXCURSION: GREEK TOWN

D ue west of the Loop, in the vicinity of Halsted Street and Jackson Boulevard, is Greek Town—the place to go if you like your men dark and hairy (and your women, too). For elegant, upscale Greek dining, try the grilled octopus at **Costa's**. **Pegasus** offers a spectacular view of the skyline from its rooftop deck, where they serve meze and ouzo to the accompaniment of live Greek music (especially on weekends). The corner dive **Zorba's**, open 24 hours a day, is a great place to sop up excess booze. Finally, break a curse or cast one with the icons and elixirs available at **Athenian Candle Co.**, where you can purchase such things as "Lover come back" floor wash and "Law be gone" room spray, along with column-sized church-quality gilded candles.

Costa's
340 S. Halsted St., 312/263-9700
www.costasdining.com

Pegasus
130 S. Halsted St., 312/226-3377

Zorba's
301 S. Halsted St., 312/454-0748

Athenian Candle Co.
300 S. Halsted St., 312/332-6988

THE SOUTH LOOP AND MCCORMICK PLACE

Once the gritty underbelly of downtown, the South Loop now shows signs of life with the opening of several rather flamboyant dining spots. Meanwhile, McCormick Place—the biggest convention center in the world—keeps getting bigger and bigger and bigger. Anchoring it all is the Museum Campus, home to the **Field Museum of Natural History**, **Shedd Aquarium**, and **Adler Planetarium**.

FIELD EXCURSION: CHINATOWN

Just west of the South Loop, Chicago's Chinatown offers almond cookies, rice paper candy, chopsticks, Chinese finger traps, back scratchers, and sticky buns galore. Fans of dim sum won't want to miss brunch at **Three Happiness** (209 W. Cermak Rd., 312/842-1964), the steaming roll cart dim sum emperor of the area. After brunch, shop for housewares, Hello Kitty paraphernalia, and other treats in the shops that line Wentworth Avenue and Cermak Road.

East Lakeview, or Boystown

As a neighborhood moniker, *Lakeview* is a bit of a misnomer. Sure, a narrow section of this North Side area abuts the beautiful Chicago lakefront, but viewing the lake is not the main reason why visitors and natives play and/or live in Lakeview. Lakeview is entertainment central for the city, with a dizzying array of choices in dining, clubs, theater, live music, cafés, and shops.

Halsted Street's rainbow pylon.
~Photo by Jon Peterson

Lucky for us, the gay gods above created the street known as Halsted and granted us the area from Belmont to Grace and east to Broadway to call our own. They named it Boystown and exclaimed, "Ooo, gurl, this place is going on!"

If you walk either north or south from the Bermuda Triangle on Halsted, you'll pass some rainbow pylons. You may think they look like rocket ships, or sex toys, or pieces of electrical equipment that got left behind an unfinished construction project, or you might even think they are simply fabulous. In any event, they are visible indicators that the city of Chicago felt fondly enough about its gay community to put several million dollars into marking the area as Gay Central—and how many cities like their gay hoods enough to do that?

Pylons notwithstanding, gay and lesbian life in Chicago is not quite as centered in the Boystown area as it was back in the mid-1990s. Gentrification has pushed rents higher and given us reason to move north to Andersonville and points beyond. One is just as likely to see a mom and dad pushing a stroller as a drag queen on Halsted these days, at least in the daytime. But the pleasant reality of the area is that mom and dad won't blink twice at the drag queen, unless her make-up is really bad. Despite shifting demographics, Boystown's identity as a gay commercial center is firmly entrenched, and there is not a business on the strip that does not, on some level, embrace the queerness of the hood.

The vibe in Boystown is playful and young. Indeed, one complaint leveled at the Boystown area is that it's too youth oriented and clone-ish. We call this the "Why don't the 22-year-olds want to sleep with me?" complaint. If nighttime is all about racing around from bar to bar creating a scene and looking fabulous, daytime is about running errands, getting fit, and hanging out at one of the local cafés preferred by the gays—number one on the list being **Caribou Coffee** (3300 N. Broadway St.), also affectionately known as Gay-ibou, Queer-ibou, and Cruise-ibou.

Andersonville

The history books will tell you that Andersonville is a Swedish neighborhood, and indeed, in one short stretch of Clark Street north of Foster Avenue, you can find two Swedish restaurants, a Swedish bakery, a couple of Swedish deli/food-specialty shops, and a Swedish cultural center. But for our purposes, lesbians founded Andersonville. With their sensible shoes, their calm flannel, their adopted-from-a-shelter dogs, and their herbal teas, they towed in the U-Hauls and settled in area graystones.

Once lesbians paved the streets (so their drag queen brethren could properly walk in heels) and the first restaurant opened offering arugula in the salads along with a decent wine list, property values rose, the first gay drinking establishments opened, and the Johnny-come-lately gay boys followed. Andersonville still boasts the most visible lesbian community in the city. Lezzie couples holding hands are a common sight on a sunny Saturday afternoon. The annual Dyke March, a womyn-inclusive alternative to the phallocentric antics of the Gay Pride Parade, takes place in late June. Marchers take over Clark Street, the artery of fun, food, and commerce for the area.

The vibe of Andersonville is

A great bookstore in the heart of the Queer Andersonville 'hood.
~Photo courtesy of Women & Children First

A GREAT GROUP NIGHT OUT IN ANDERSONVILLE

H ere's a fine itinerary for a Friday or Saturday night, good for a group of up to six people, gay or straight. Start off with a leisurely dinner at **Hopleaf** (p. 110). Go for the mussels. The fish sandwich is great, too, but there's nothing on the short menu that won't satisfy. You can even eat bunny rabbit if you want; it's a specialty of the Belgian cuisine. Robert was forced to eat rabbit once in Belgium, when his Belgian boyfriend's granny cooked up a special batch. Tastes like chicken, but the bones are alarmingly reminiscent of a cat's. *Anyway* . . . There's an amazing selection of European beers to accompany your meal, but go easy on it—that stuff has a kick.

You'll want to time your dinner to be done by about 10:30 P.M. so you can stroll around the corner to the **Neo-Futurarium** (p. 169) and wait in line for the Neo-Futurists' long-running late-night theater hit, *Too Much Light Makes the Baby Go Blind*. Yup—"wait in line," we said—it's all part of the *Too Much Light* ritual. The show always sells out on Friday and Saturday nights, so stop living on gay time for once in your life and be early. Chat with your date, admire the hipster art on the walls of the theater's waiting room, and anticipate the Neo-Futurists' 30-plays-in-60-minutes formula: part *Saturday Night Live*, part street theater, part confessional poetry. The socially aware and queer-friendly sketches will make you laugh and think, and if you don't like an individual play, chill—it'll be over within 120 seconds.

After the show, walk one block back over to Clark Street. If the weather is pleasant, stroll north on Clark for several blocks, just for the sheer night-strolling, window-shopping urban ambience. It'll be after midnight, and you may want to end the evening. But if you are a night owl, retrace your steps and head south of Foster a few blocks to **T's** (p. 141) for a nightcap.

T's has a pleasant outdoor seating area in the summer, a comfy couch-laden back bar area for cooler weather lounging, and a friendly staff year-round. The place is gay enough for the boys, gal enough for the girls, and mixed enough to make your straight friends utterly relaxed. Softball league dykes after the game, neighborhood straight couples grabbing a beer, tranny boys having dinner—everyone seems to call this place their own. If you find yourself hungry, you're in luck—the kitchen is open late. Speaking of late, if you are hell-bent on staying out once T's closes, you can head a few doors south.

The **Chicago Eagle** (p. 140) is open until 4 on weeknights and 5 on weekends, and you don't have to be wearing leather to get in to the front bar. This might not be the best choice for a group that includes women—the staff and patrons aren't overtly unfriendly to girls, but the bathrooms are often taken up by boys, and stalls have been known to be used as much for on-site liaisons as for the usual reasons. Still, if everyone is game and slumming it is the goal, go for it. The other late night choice is **Clark's on Clark**. The raucous and hard-drinking crowd here doesn't get going until after 2 A.M., when other area bars have closed. This is the kind of place where social strata, age, race, and preference all mix it up and converse in a boozy soup. When you are ready, cabs are plentiful on Clark Street, to get you back home or on into your dark wee-hour destinations.

HAVE A SEXY GIRL DATE IN ANDERSONVILLE

Begin the evening browsing at **Women & Children First** bookstore (p. 88), where you can be suggestive by perusing and commenting on various aspects of lesbian erotica. Then wander north and around the corner at Berwyn, and pop in to the tasteful, women-friendly sex-toy shop **Tulip** (p. 93). For dinner you can choose to dine on French fare at lesbian-owned **La Tache** (p. 110), see and be seen at the hot dyke date spot **Tomboy** (p. 109), or feed each other raw fish at **Tanoshii** (p. 109). After dinner, stroll over to **Joie de Vine** for a glass of wine and long, sultry glances, or, if it's Friday night, drop in at **Star Gaze** (p. 120) for some *muy caliente* salsa dancing.

distinctly gay village, and Clark Street is its Main Street U.S. of Gay. The pace of A-ville is slower and decidedly more domestic than Boystown (must be that lesbian influence). Nonetheless, the quantity and variety of gay-friendly and gay-specific shops and nightlife options are impressive. During the day, rainbow folks like to sip espresso at the earth-crunchy-leaning **Kopi Café** (5317 N. Clark St.), at the nearby **Taste of Heaven Cafe** (5401 N. Clark St.), or the slightly more removed **Pause Café** (1107 W. Berwyn Ave.), located just east of the Red Line Berwyn "L" stop.

Wicker Park

Wicker Park throbs with a scenester, see-and-be-seen vibe and foments creative ju-ju, along with (due to the stylish young lovelies who crawl these streets) a certain amount of self-image and fashion-sense insecurity among yours truly, your authors. While not a distinctly gay neighborhood, Wicker Park has enough outsider art, cool boutiques, funky cafés, and vibrant young restaurants to make it a popular place for young homos to live and work and a worthy destination for the queer tourist. This is a very gay-friendly hood.

The geographic crux of Wicker Park is the triangle formed between Milwaukee Avenue, Damen Avenue, and Division Street, with the park itself located smack dab in the middle. For the past several years, however, the scene has been bleeding outward, as rent prices in the triangle have skyrocketed and traffic congestion has become untenable. Today one could fairly stretch Wicker Park's artistic and funky influence as far north as Armitage Avenue, as far south as Grand Avenue, as far east as the Chicago River, and as far west as Western Avenue. These reaches have their own names and distinctive identities. They are, respectively, Bucktown, Ukrainian Village, Noble Square, and Humboldt Park.

Daytime in Wicker Park is all about alternating your shopping with draping yourself over a chair and pouting at your favorite café or bakery. Some local faves are **Earwax Café** (1561 N. Milwaukee Ave.), **Alliance Bakery** (1736 W. Division St.), **Jinx Café** (1928 W. Division St.), and **Letizia's Natural Bakery** (2144 W. Division St.). Most café and shopping options are concentrated on the main thoroughfares. You can pass a whole day shopping the triangle alone, although you'll miss out on many off-the-beaten-path treasures. Shopping here runs the gamut from crunchy new-and-used book and record shops to upstart designer fashion to pricey home décor, pleasing the gamut of queer folk, from lefty politico vegan activists to fashion queens and divas of design.

At nighttime the streets pulse with life as well-dressed hipsters dart between the many happening bars and restaurants that line the streets. The closest venue here of specific gay interest is the cabaret and piano bar **Davenport's** (p. 150), although most of the trendy restaurants and clubs will be gay-friendly enough for comfort.

Other Worthy Destinations

O kay, so now every homo and their mother knows about where to go and what to do in Chicago's most populated pink neighborhoods. However, you will truly impress your friends when you can dash off the sights and sounds of these other worthwhile city destinations.

ROSCOE VILLAGE

West of Lakeview, the charming Roscoe Village is home to a street-full of popular dining spots along with boutiques, thrift stores, and a cafe or two. We are fond of the flamboyant annual summer street fair, Retro on Roscoe, where three stages offer up great local music, including Chicago's perennially popular female Elvis impersonator Patty "Elvis" Manning, and a Neil Diamond cover band called "Love on the Rocks" that'll have you singing along to "Forever in Blue Jeans" before you know what hit you.

ROGERS PARK

The northernmost neighborhood in Chicago, Rogers Park is one of the most culturally diverse of all Chicago neighborhoods and offers plenty of worthy pursuits for both hippies and homos. Small, funky coffeehouses abound around the Loyola University campus, and a couple gay bars—**Touché** (p. 148) and **Jackhammer** (p. 147), both predominantly male—also dot the multicultural streets. Meanwhile, peaceniks of all orientations have been munching tofu for years at the decidedly crunchy **Heartland Café** (p. 102) (tie-dye welcome).

EDGEWATER

Just south of Rogers Park, in Edgewater, men troll the **Granville Anvil** (p. 146), a bar right down the street from the **Gerber/Hart Library** (p. 243), Chicago's GLBT library and archives.

UPTOWN

Uptown is the gritty urban area falling between Andersonville and Boystown. As you might guess from this locale, the gays have been moving in and helping to clean things up. Here you'll find the boy- and girl-friendly gay bars **Big Chicks** (p. 145) and **Crew** (p. 144), as well as the **Green Mill** (p. 195), a legendary jazz club.

LINCOLN SQUARE

The Germanic influence in Lincoln Square, formerly a predominantly German neighborhood, can still be felt at the annual German Day and Mayfests or year-round at such establishments as the Chicago Brauhaus. Meanwhile, everything else in the hood has been spun on its head by what has become, arguably, the single biggest new restaurant boom in the city, with the highest concentration of hot new spots lining Lincoln Avenue or Western Avenue. Head to a world music or folk concert at the **Old Town School of Folk Music** (p. 187), then step outside and simply throw a dart to decide on your dining destiny.

RAVENSWOOD

Surrounding Lincoln Square, the bucolic Ravenswood neighborhood is mostly residential, with lovely tree-lined streets and restored vintage bungalows, occasionally marked with rainbow flags. This longtime-liberal community has long had a gay-welcoming vibe.

In the Lincoln Square and Ravenswood area, gay gals and guys alike grab a queer drink at **Scot's** (p. 138).

HYDE PARK

Some miles south of the Loop is Hyde Park, anchored by the neo-Gothic campus of the University of Chicago. Racially diverse, the handsome and insular neighborhood has a huge number of cultural and academic attractions, including the world-class Museum of Science and Industry, the DuSable Museum of African American History, the archaeological riches of the Oriental Institute, and architect Frank Lloyd Wright's Robie House masterpiece. In the musty basement digs of the **Seminary Co-op Bookstore** (p. 89) you'll find the premier academic bookshop in the county, with an amazing selection of queer and gender studies works. The 57th Street Art Fair, one of the country's oldest and largest juried street fairs, takes place on the first weekend in June.

FIRST YOU HAVE TO GET HERE: TRANSPORTATION OPTIONS

Arriving in Chicago

Chicago is served by two airports as well as Amtrak train and Greyhound bus stations. O'Hare International Airport, 17 miles northwest of downtown Chicago, handles most international flights and most of the major carriers. Midway Airport, located on the city's Southwest Side, handles many of the budget carriers (e.g., ATA and Southwest). Union Station, in the southwest Loop, allows easy access to downtown for Amtrak travelers. The Chicago Greyhound bus terminal, slightly farther west of Union Station, is situated (as is the plight of bus terminals everywhere) in a slightly seedier locale.

Getting to and from O'Hare International Airport

O'Hare competes annually with Atlanta's international airport for the dubious distinction of busiest airport in the world. With four huge terminals (1, 2, 3, and 5—don't ask us where 4 is, though we'd guess it's gone the way of socks in the dryer), each having multiple concourse tentacles reaching outward, O'Hare seems mazelike. Mercifully, its pathways are well marked, making the airport fairly easy to navigate.

Chicago is the home base for United Airlines, so naturally, O'Hare is United's major hub. Terminal 1 is almost exclusively the domain of United Airlines and its "Star Alliance" partner, Lufthansa, while most other major domestic carriers arrive and depart from Terminal 2. All international arrivals land at Terminal 5, and most international carriers also depart from Terminal 5, but this can vary—be sure to check your ticket or itinerary for your departure terminal. Like pretty much every airport we've ever been to, ground transport hookups are available adjacent to the baggage claim areas for any terminal. A CTA "Train to the City" connection is located near the center of the main airport at the mouth of Terminal 2, with an airport shuttle available from all other terminals. Directions to the train appear on signage throughout the baggage claim areas.

Okay, fine. So you're at the airport and you understand all this blah blah about terminal this and that. What you're really wondering is how the hell you get outta there. Well, as with airports in any major city, O'Hare offers plenty of options for getting to the city. Transport by horse, skateboard, or rickshaw may be legitimate options, and we applaud your creativity if you choose any of these. But in the interest of serving the largest number of visiting homosexuals possible, we will focus on the more obvious alternatives. These are CTA train, taxi, shuttle, and rental car.

Getting to and from O'Hare by CTA Train

As we already stated (you were paying attention, weren't you?) CTA (that's Chicago Transit Authority, if you really need to know) trains operate directly from O'Hare to downtown Chicago, with transfer stations to other trains available once you are downtown. You can find the Blue Line O'Hare station by following the clear signage, as well as the arrows on the ground, saying, "Trains to the City."

You'll find machines that vend visitor passes at the airport train station. These one-, two-, three-, and five-day passes offer great value if you plan on making the CTA your major form of transportation once you are in the city. (They run $5, $9, $12, and $18, respectively.) Available through the CTA Web site are $20 seven-day all-you-can-ride passes. Follow the "CTA Store" link at www.transitchicago.com to order them online. There's no charge for postage, but please allow 14 days for delivery! Also, a caveat—if you lose your CTA pass, you are out of luck, so guard it carefully!

Often there will be more than one train waiting at the O'Hare station. A lighted sign indicates which one is departing next. Any train departing from O'Hare follows the same route up to and into downtown. If you are going farther than downtown, be aware that the trains split courses after the Racine stop. Once on the train, you can chart your course on the line maps posted above most train doors.

> ### NOTE
>
> **L**ook for the extrawide turnstiles if you have a lot of luggage, as maneuvering through the turnstiles with baggage can be treacherous, to say the least. Otherwise, ask a CTA employee to let you pass through a gate. For more information about how to use the CTA train, skip ahead to Chapter 5 ("Getting Around Chicago").

Taking the train to and from the airport is the cheapest way to go. It's also fast and efficient, and we strongly recommend it, especially during rush hours, which, in Chicago, seem to last from 7 A.M. until 7 P.M. Travel time to and from downtown and the airport is generally 30 to 45 minutes. Smile and wave from the window as you breeze past expressway traffic crawling along at a snail's pace, and be happy you're not in a taxi watching the meter click away all your fun money.

GETTING TO AND FROM O'HARE BY TAXI

We are CTA advocates, but there are bonuses to taking a taxi to and from airport. The number one bonus is door-to-terminal service. This is especially helpful if you have a lot of cumbersome luggage that you don't want to have to drag around all over the airport or on and off a crowded train. Taxi stands are easy to locate from airport baggage areas. Taxi queues are generally not supervised, but it is a courtesy to others to follow the queues. Then when your turn comes, you help yourself into the proper taxi. Movement is brisk and waits are usually short. A typical charge from O'Hare to the center of the city is $35 to $45.

If you are taking a taxi to the airport and you have an early flight, we recommend that you book your taxi the evening before, so it will be waiting for you when you need it. To get from downtown Chicago to O'Hare by taxi, allow 30 to 45 minutes in nonpeak hours and an hour and a half during morning and evening rush hours.

GETTING TO AND FROM O'HARE BY SHUTTLE

Continental Airport Express is the most widely used shuttle service to and from both O'Hare and Midway airports. Shuttles offer the convenience of door-to-terminal service at a cheaper rate than taxis. But because you share the shuttle with other passengers, service is usually not direct. The shuttle may stop at many other hotels or terminals before arriving at yours.

You can purchase tickets (one-way or round-trip) for shuttles from the airport to the city at one of their ticket counters, located in the baggage claim areas near doors

Chicago affection.
~Photo courtesy of Jon Peterson

1E, 2D, and 3E (and 1E in the international terminal). Fares vary depending on how many people are traveling together to the same location. The fare is typically $20 one-way or $36 round-trip for one traveler and $15 each, one-way, for two people traveling together to the same destination. You can reserve private shuttles for large groups traveling together to the same location. Please note that you can pay in advance, or you can pay the driver directly at the beginning of your trip. If you want to pay by credit card, you must do so at a ticket counter, by phone, or on the Internet. You must pay the shuttle drivers with cash.

Shuttles from O'Hare to the city do not have to be reserved in advance—just go buy your ticket at any of the Continental Airport Express ticket counters. Shuttles to O'Hare do have to be reserved in advance. You may do so at the ticket counter when you arrive in Chicago, via telephone (800/654-7871), or online (www.airportexpress.com). Shuttle trip times are similar to taxi trip times, allowing extra time for additional pickups and drop-offs.

GETTING TO AND FROM O'HARE BY RENTAL CAR

Most of the major car rental companies have kiosks available on-site in the baggage claim area. These include **Alamo** (800/462-5266), **Avis** (800/831-2847), **Budget** (800/527-0700), **Dollar** (800/800-4000), **Hertz** (800/654-3131), **National** (888/868-6203). Driving to the city from the airport is only recommended to travelers with extensive experience driving in large urban areas. Also, be aware that unmetered street parking downtown is rare and garages are prohibitively expensive. That said, the trajectory is fairly easy—just jump onto Interstate 90 heading south (watch signs for directions) and ride it gaily forward into downtown Chicago.

Getting to and from Midway Airport

T he unofficial motto of Chicago's Midway Airport could be "We fly . . . cheaply" because it is the favored airport for budget carriers and thusly a popular departure spot for rock-bottom rates to Las Vegas, the Caribbean, and other spring break destinations. The airport is much smaller than O'Hare and a piece of cake to navigate—just follow the signs to wherever you want to go. Chances are it's not far! Midway's location within the city, ten miles southwest of downtown Chicago, makes commuting to and from the airport quicker and cheaper than a last-call hookup at the Eagle.

GETTING TO AND FROM MIDWAY BY CTA TRAIN

Like CTA connections to O'Hare, taking the train to and from Midway is fast, cheap, and efficient. The CTA Orange Line operates directly between Midway and downtown Chicago, with service starting in the predawn hours and running until nearly the same. The instructions for use are the same as for O'Hare. Orange Line free transfer stations are at Washington, Library, Adams, State and Lake, and Clark and Lake.

GETTING TO AND FROM MIDWAY BY TAXI

Follow signs to taxis from the baggage claim area. Trips going to downtown cost about $25 to $30 and take 20 to 45 minutes.

GETTING TO AND FROM MIDWAY BY SHUTTLE

The Airport Express ticket counter can be found at door 3 in the lower level of the main terminal, across from baggage claim. Reservations are not required for rides to downtown, but they are required for rides from downtown. You must make payment in advance, and drivers don't take credit cards.

Make reservations by phone (800/654-7871) or online (www.airportexpress.com). For more tips and instructions for shuttle use, look under the instructions for getting to and from O'Hare.

GETTING TO AND FROM MIDWAY BY RENTAL CAR

Car rentals available at Midway include **Alamo** (800/462-5266), **Avis** (800/831-2847), **Budget** (800/527-0700), **Dollar** (800/800-4000), **Enterprise** (800/566-9249), **Hertz** (800/654-3131), **National** (888/868-6203), and **Thrifty** (800/527-7075).

If you decide to rent a car, bear in mind that Chicagoans drive like lawless fools and that parking downtown is prohibitively expensive. (By now our anticar bias should be readily apparent. Note that neither Kathie nor Robert own a car.)

Arriving and Departing on Amtrak

Union Station services the Amtrak regional and interstate train system and is also a major hub for the Metra commuter train system that transports thousands of suburbanites in and out of the financial district every Monday through Friday. The station's Great Hall, which dates back to circa 1925, was featured in that scene in *The Untouchables* where Kevin Costner is trying to keep his eye on the bad guy when that baby in a stroller gets knocked down the stairs. Remember? Anyway, arriving or departing by train at Union Station is a pretty straightforward affair. When arriving, exit the train and follow the signs up the slight ramp to baggage claim. If you've checked luggage, be warned—it takes about 5 million years for your luggage to start creeping along the conveyor belt. Once you have your bags, return to the escalators that you passed—the ones in front of the ticket counter. Go up and exit the door right in front of you. Unless we are all backward in our head as we are writing this, the taxi stand should be right there as soon as you step outside. If it is not, don't fret—just walk around the block until you find it. You could maybe take the bus or the CTA train for the rest of your trip, but hey, you just got off the damn Amtrak and you're probably five hours late, so just indulge yourself and take a taxi. And tell them to take Lake Shore Drive, no matter where you're going, because the lovely vista is sure to smooth your frazzled nerves.

If you are departing Chicago via Amtrak, and you don't have to check any bags, you can pick up your ticket at the automatic ticket machine located in front of the ticket booth. When you enter the station, you'll have to take the escalator down—follow the signs to Amtrak ticketing. Otherwise, just wait your turn in the line. The waiting room for departing passengers is a chaos of college backpackers, traveling families, the Amish, and other travelers on the cheap, as well as a pickpocket or two. If you have a long wait, you may want to pass your time instead at the bar and grill located just off the Great Hall. Kathie has begun many a journey there. There are no arrival boards there, though, so be sure to check the ones in the Great Hall from time to time to make sure you don't miss your train, as many train routes have only one departure time per day.

GETTING TO UNION STATION

Taxis to Union Station from most anywhere downtown shouldn't cost more than $10 or take longer than 15 or 20 minutes. (If you're staying in the Loop, you can cut both of those estimates in half.) The closest CTA stop is the Blue Line stop at Clinton, two blocks south of Union Station. From the North Side (e.g., Lakeview or Andersonville), the fare will be more like $25. Keep in mind that if you don't have too much luggage, Union Station is a pleasant walk from nearly anywhere in the Loop.

Check schedules and purchase tickets in advance via phone (800/USA-RAIL) or online (www.amtrak.com).

Arriving and Departing by Greyhound Bus

We don't argue that Greyhound is the cheapest way to travel within the United States, nor do we begrudge folks who want or need to save a buck. Hey, we're just happy that you're here! That said, a trip of any distance by Greyhound can be a gritty, harrowing experience. Kathie made the trip from Chicago to Minneapolis on "the dog" many times, back when she was a wee dewy youth, although she'd make sure her hepatitis vaccine was up to date before she ventured to do so again.

The station is located in a desolate spot just southwest of downtown Chicago, in the shadow of a complex cloverleaf of expressway, where Interstates 90, 290, and 94 cross paths. Don't accept rides from folks offering you one except for licensed taxi drivers in a real taxi with a light on top and a fare box. The Blue Line Clinton stop is two blocks east and one block north of the Greyhound station. Walk there from the train only during the daytime. Keep your bags with you at all times.

Reservations are not required. Boarding on Greyhound buses is strictly first come, first served. You can check schedules and purchase tickets by phone (800/231-2222) or online (www.greyhound.com). Students with a valid ID should ask for special (even cheaper) rates.

WE HAVE BEEN AROUND THE BLOCK A FEW TIMES: GETTING AROUND CHICAGO

Getting Around by Car

Okay, you cell phone queens and Danger Dykes—it's illegal to talk on a handheld cellular phone while driving in Chicago, and all passengers must wear a seat belt, so hang up and buckle up, for heaven's sake. The police department regularly sets up surprise roadblocks, where they randomly stop unsuspecting drivers and check them for violations. Kathie doesn't drive, but she routinely sees just such a roadblock in action outside her office window, and she watches it while she works. This method of catching violators is a major source of revenue for the city.

Expired parking meters are regularly ticketed, and many residential neighborhoods require residential parking permits to park on their streets. (Visitors can get temporary permits at the local alderman's office.) In the winter, be on the lookout for designated snow emergency routes. Tow trucks begin clearing these streets at the first sign of flurries. Spending your day bailing out your car from the city impound lot is an interesting cultural experience, but not recommended.

That said, Chicago's grid system makes it relatively easy to navigate a car around the city, although traffic congestion and parking shortages can be maddening beyond belief, and Chicago drivers tend to be reckless to the point of foolhardiness. If you are used to driving in L.A., New York, Paris, Madrid, or Rome, you will feel right at home behind the wheel here, but if you are used to driving in Madison or Minneapolis, driving in Chicago may put you at risk of a heart attack. In general, drive defensively. Be alert for anything. Be patient. Stay calm. Don't get your panties in a bunch, Mary! And perhaps most importantly, if you know that you are going to be drinking, leave the car at home and look for an alternative source of transportation.

Getting Around by Taxi

In central parts of the city, where there is a lot of nightlife, it's easy to hail a taxi on the street. Many hotels have taxi queues, and so do a few neighborhoods, but they are not as common as they are in other cities. In highly residential areas, it is advisable to call for a taxi. Expect the taxi to take anywhere from ten to 45 minutes to arrive.

Taxi fares are regulated by the city. At this writing, you are charged $2.25 for sitting in a taxi, which covers you for your first 1/9 of a mile, after which you are charged $1.80 per additional mile, or $2 for every six minutes of waiting time. There is a $1 charge for a second passenger, and 50¢ charge for each additional passenger after that. There are no extra charges for baggage or credit card use (although few cabs are prepared to take credit cards, so don't simply assume you can use one). Tipping is optional but strongly suggested. A couple bucks or 15 percent of the fare—whichever is more—is customary.

In terms of driving, taxi drivers are in a kamikaze league of their own. If you get the right (or, we guess, wrong) driver, taking a taxi in Chicago can be more of a thrill ride than anything they offer at Six Flags Great America. Wear your seat belt, and do not hesitate to tell a driver to slow down or to drive more carefully. Your life may depend on it (although, to their credit, we hear of very few serious accidents involving taxicabs).

Many cab drivers are gruff and terse; others are friendly and chatty to the point of being intrusive. And some Chicago cab drivers are very, very friendly. Just ask Robert.

Chicago Taxicab Phone Numbers

Checker Cab 312/243-2537
American United Cab 773/248-7600
Flash Cab (south) 312/467-1072
Flash Cab (north) 773/561-4444
Yellow Cab 800/829-4222

Getting Around by Public Transportation

The Chicago public transportation system is not particularly clean, but it is relatively efficient, and you can always count on a colorful cast of characters to make your ride interesting. Many routes run all night, while others offer limited "owl" service, and some cease operation before midnight. Unless you know what the situation is for service on

Taking a CTA Bus.
~Photo by Caldwell Linker

your closest route, don't rely on taking public transportation after midnight.

The RTA (Regional Transportation Authority) Web site (www.rtachicago.com) has great point-to-point directions for using public transportation.

CTA FARES AND FARECARDS

Y ou can pay your way on the CTA by using either a Chicago or Chicago Plus card, a transit card, or cold, hard cash. Chicago and Chicago Plus cards are renewable fare cards that offer a $2.00 bonus for every $20 deposited. They are available on the internet at *www.transitchicago.com*, or by telephone at 1-888-YOUR CTA. Chicago and Chicago Plus require an initial $5 fee for the card itself. The benefit is that it can be reloaded on the internet and replaced when lost.

To use the Chicago or Chicago Plus card, simply pass the card in front of the censor on CTA turnstiles or on the fare box on a bus. Fares using the Chicago or Chicago Plus card are $1.75 for bus or "L" train, and an additional $.25 for up to three transfers in a two-hour period.

The CTA transit card is available through vending machines at all Chicago "L" stations. Additionally, they are available in either $10 to $20 values at currency exchanges, and some Jewel/Osco and Dominick's grocery stores (at the cutomer service desk). To use the transit card, pass it through the card reader on CTA turnstiles or on the bus. Value can be added to transit cards at any transit card vending machine, but there is no $2.00 for $20 bonus, and lost cards are not replaceable.

Fares using transit cards are $2.00 on the "L," $1.75 on the bus, and an additional $.25 to transfer.

Finally, you can also pay with cold hard cash on the bus (but not on the "L," where a card of some sort is required). Cash fares are $2.00 and transfers are not available.

For a visitor who doesn't want to pay the $5 Chicago Card fee, we recommend purchasuing a transit card for however much you think you will need (bear in mind that you can add more money later if you need to, but they do not issue refunds for unused fares). Transit cards are just a lot easier to use than cash, plus you can transfer. Just keep track of it, because if you lose it you are out of luck.

TAKING THE "L"

The world's first elevated train began operation in Chicago in 1892. The Chicago "L" (short for "el") snakes out from downtown to directions north, south, and west. In general, the city is well served, although some areas must still rely on the slower, less reliable bus network.

CTA "L" lines are identified by their color and their route. You know the direction you are going if you know where the stop is relative to where you are and where the last stop on a line is. For example, say you are at the Red Line station at Chicago, and you want to go to Belmont. In one direction, the end of the line is Howard, in the other, it is 95th and Dan Ryan. Because you know (or looked on a map and discovered) that the Belmont stop is between the Chicago stop (where you are) and Howard, you know that this is the direction you want to travel.

One thing to be careful of, especially downtown: In many cases, different trains run on the same track. Make sure you are getting on the train that you want, so you don't end up running express to Evanston!

TAKING THE BUS

Chicago CTA bus routes crisscross the city via nearly all the major thruways. No matter where you are in the city, there will be a bus route traveling north and south or east and west, usually within a few blocks of you. Another convenience is that most buses stay on the same street, (for example, the Western Bus stays on Western, the Clark street bus stays on Clark, etc.) so its pretty easy to figure out how to get where you are going.

Signs at bus stops indicate the hours of service for that route. Bad weather can slow bus service immensely.

All Chicago buses are equipped with hydraulic lifts that make them wheelchair accessible. The buses can also tilt, for people who have trouble making the high first step.

Getting Around by Free Trolley

Tourist sites from Navy Pier to Union Station to the Museum Campus can be reached by a network of free downtown trolleys. Simply locate a trolley stop, wait for the trolley, and hop on. When you get to a site you want to check out, hop off again. Wash, rinse, and repeat as necessary. Not to look a gift trolley in the mouth, but waits can be long. Trolley maps are available from the concierge at most downtown hotels.

Chapter 6

COMMUNICATIONS AND CASH:
MORE BORING BUT HELPFUL PRACTICAL STUFF

Communications

TELEPHONE

The city of Chicago is served by two area codes: 312 is for the downtown area, and 773 covers pretty much everything else. If you are calling a 312 number from a 773 area, or vice versa, the prefix must be proceeded by a "1."

Public telephones on Chicago streets are virtually nonexistent. The best places to find a pay phone are hotel lobbies and public buildings, such as department stores. International phone cards, offering decent rates, are available for sale at nearly any convenience store.

INTERNET

Virtually every hotel, inn, guesthouse, or B&B in Chicago now has Wi-Fi hookup. In many cases it is free, but in some instances there's a charge, so be sure to ask about any fees before you boot up.

The same is true for many cafés. If you are not traveling with a Wi-Fi–compatible laptop, you can go online at the library or an Internet café.

The Chicago Public Library offers free computer use and Internet access at every Chicago branch. The biggest computer bank and Internet center is at **Harold Washington Library** (400 S. State St., Brown Line Library stop). Another convenient branch, in Boystown, is the **John Merlo branch** (644 W. Belmont Ave., Red Line Belmont stop).

The first Internet café in the nation, Suba, opened in Boystown in Chicago in 1995. Today you can still rent computer time at a handful of cafés citywide. Usage rates average about $5 an hour. Here are some Internet cafés that are particularly well situated for the gay traveler.

Wicker Park
Windy City Cyber Café
2246 W. North Ave., 773/384-6470
www.windycitycybercafe.com

Boystown
Screenz
2717 N. Clark St., 773/348-9300
www.screenz.com

Andersonville
Pause Café (Mac Only)
1107 W. Berwyn Ave., 773/334-3686

Screenz Andersonville
5212 N. Clark St., 773/334-8600
www.screenz.com

We gave life.
~Photo by Mel Ferrand

POST OFFICE

Need stamps? Have to send a package? Don't want to tramp all over town like some two-bit trollop? Here are the addresses of some conveniently located post office branches.

Loop

211 S. Clark St., 312/427-0016

Lakeview

1343 W. Irving Park Rd., 773/327-0345

Wicker Park

1635 W. Division St., 773/278-2069

UPS

You can also send and receive mail at UPS stores throughout the city. Branches are conveniently located, and service is much friendlier though charges are slightly higher than at the post office.

South Loop

47 W. Polk St., 312/427-7839

West Loop

27 N. Wacker Dr., 312/372-2727

Mag Mile

207 E. Ohio St., 312/664-6245

Old Town

333 W. North Ave., 312/943-6197

Boystown

3023 N. Clark St., 773/281-8988
3712 N. Broadway St., 773/975-7100

Andersonville

5315 N. Clark St., 773/728-3828

Wicker Park

1658 N. Milwaukee Ave.,773/486-5700

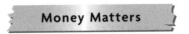

Money Matters

ATMs

Banks with ATMs are located in every neighborhood in the city. You'll also find ATMs inside major grocery stores and pharmacies, and in many neighborhood convenience stores. Using an ATM that is not affiliated with your bank will cost you. Expect a fee of anywhere from $1.50 to $2.50 per use. Be cautious at outdoor ATMs after dark.

TRAVELER'S CHECKS

Traveler's checks can be used like cash at most major Chicago retailers. Be prepared to present a photo ID.

AMERICAN EXPRESS OFFICES

Go to an American Express office for cash advances, traveler's checks, and money transfers.

55 W. Monroe St., 312/541-5440
605 N. Michigan Ave., 312/943-7840

GIRL, YOU GOTTA WATCH YOURSELF: SAFETY ISSUES

The emergency phone number for police, fire, or ambulance is 911. Chicago is a big urban center with a corresponding amount of crime (although crime rates have been dropping in recent years). Visitors don't have to travel in an armored truck, but they are strongly encouraged to keep vigilant and be aware of their surroundings. Chicago is also a cosmopolitan city, and overt homophobia or threat of homophobic violence is relatively rare. In the gayest neighborhoods, such as Boystown and Andersonville, it is not uncommon to see gay and lesbian couples holding hands or canoodling in public. The farther away you are from the homo centers, the more likely you are to confront homophobia, so have some common sense. Don't go playing same-sex kissy-face in a West Side biker bar, because we don't want to have to say we told you so. If you don't heed our advice, bear in mind that anti-gay violence (including verbal harassment) is classified as a hate crime in Illinois and carries a strict penalty. If you are a victim of an anti-gay hate crime (or any crime) while you are in Chicago, by all means, report it.

Don't leave valuables visible in your car. Smash-and-grabs are common in every neighborhood.

Muggers prey on drunks after dark, even in (maybe especially in) areas that seem the safest. Muggings in Boystown, Andersonville, and Wicker Park are not daily affairs, but they are not uncommon either. Stick to well-lit streets. Avoid strangers after dark. Stay alert and aware of your surroundings. If you feel threatened, call attention to yourself. Yell. Sing out loud. Do your best Ethel Merman. Get people to notice you. Chances are, any potential muggers will be scared away.

Chapter 8

Where to Hang Your Rainbow Boa: Gay-Friendly Accommodations

Chicago has about a bazillion and thirty hotels, and thanks to McCormick Place, North America's biggest and busiest convention center, and the subsequent constant influx of business travelers with corporate expense accounts, accommodations here are generally quite expensive. Even "discount" chain hotels can have eyebrow-arching prices. (In fact, visitors should beware if a hotel's rates are too cheap, especially if it's not a recognized name. Chances are, any hotel costing less than $60 a night is a flea-infested flophouse.)

Few hotels in big-city Chicago will bat an eye at same-sex couples or a request such as, "Where is a good gay bar for dancing?" The pricier the hotel, the more sophisticated and well trained the staff will be, but it's no secret that the hospitality industry in general is teeming with homos. So where should your gay lodging dollar be spent?

Sure, there are plenty of Marriotts, Hyatts, Hiltons, and the like in Chicago, and we figure you probably won't have difficulty finding information about any of them. Therefore we've focused on gay-friendly hotels that are more unique to Chicago—more special, too, we think. And then, with trusty ledgers in hand, we set off to actually see, with our own eyes, as many of them as we could. We think our research has paid off. What follows is, in our opinion, the cream of the crop of Chicago's gay-friendly places to lay your head. Sweet dreams!

Loop and Near South Side

Hotel Allegro
171 W. Randolph St., 312/236-0123
www.allegrochicago.com
Rates: $139–$299

Robert was already predisposed to like the Hotel Allegro, as a friend of his got married here a few years back. He checked in on a frigid January night with a paramour, intent on a one-night fight-the-winter-blahs escape. The model-handsome desk clerk quickly sized up the date-night vibe and helpfully upgraded the happy queens from a queen- to a king-sized bed, with a smile indicating this was a special "gay-knows-gay" upgrade. The room, a cheery addition to a winter's night, was more boldly and imaginatively hued than most hotel rooms.

The bath products were all Aveda (and therefore made their way into Robert's shaving kit for future savoring).

The Allegro is right in the heart of the downtown theater district, steps away from the Cadillac Palace Theatre and a quick walk from the Goodman. It's a good thing, too, because the temperature was well below zero. Robert and his date lounged too long in their room and missed out on one of the Allegro's nicer perks: a free five o'clock wine hour in the lobby, but it happens every day, so they would have worked it into the schedule if this had been a longer stay. Brunch the next morning was expensive but totally worth it. Robert enjoyed lingering over the paper and a cup of coffee in such elegant surroundings and noted yet again that the hotel staff, from the desk staff to the busboys, seemed to have been chosen as much for their beauty as for their skills.

Hotel Burnham
1 W. Washington St., 312/782-1111
www.burnhamhotel.com
Rates: $155–$230

Located in the old Reliance Building, the world's first iron and steel skeleton skyscraper (circa the Gay '90s), is an architecturally elegant hotel with posh-feeling rooms and beautiful period detail. Standard rooms and suites are colored in a blue and gold reminiscent of the French aristocracy. Assistant Manager Allan proudly points out details of this lovingly restored hotel—the marble ceilings and iron and marble staircases, for example. All rooms feature Luxe bedding and Aveda toiletries. Suites have corner views of Millennium Park and the theater district. Get free coffee and tea in the lobby in the mornings, and sip vino at a complimentary wine reception every evening at 5 P.M. There is 24-hour room service from the adjoining Robert-recommended **Atwood Café** (p. 112). The hotel also features a small workout area that is in the process of being remodeled and should be ready by the time this book has gone to press.

Hotel Burnham, like the Hotel Allegro, is part of the Kimpton hotels group, rated among the top places for gays and lesbians to work by the *Advocate* magazine. At the end of our tour of the premises, Allan shared an e-mail the hotel had recently received from Barb, a satisfied guest. With her permission, we reproduce part of it here:

> *My partner Jennie and I stayed at Hotel Burnham for the first time on June 9th to celebrate our ten year anniversary. . . . Our stay was absolutely wonderful from start to finish. . . . One person in particular made our stay especially wonderful.*
>
> *I'm not sure of his name but it may have been Alan. He was at the front desk when we checked in and was also there during the wine reception. We started talking and he found out that it was our anniversary and sent a bottle of champagne up to our room! As lesbians we have sometimes gotten*

"funny looks" when traveling together or at some bed and breakfasts or hotels. I was so impressed that the staff at the Hotel Burnham made us feel so special! Thank you for a wonderful evening!

And if you don't love the Hotel Burnham already, you may want to know that they also welcome pets.

"W" Hotel
172 W. Adams St., 312/322-1200
Rates: $181–$259

We weren't able to get in and see rooms at the mod "W" Hotel, but we do know that they offer a Pride package, which, if you request it, includes a video of *Will & Grace* or *Queer as Folk*, a complimentary cocktail, a goody-bag of lube and condoms, some "Tom of Finland"–inspired specially designed sheets, and a late checkout. We're not sure how this applies to girls (well, except for the late checkout, which Kathie adores), but there you have it. Our friends frequently mentioned the "W" when we asked where they would stay in Chicago if money were no object, and indeed, many of our friends have stayed here.

Fairmont Hotel
200 N. Columbus Dr., 312/565-8000
www.fairmont.com/chicago/
Rates: $199–$379

Life is good, when you are writing in your journal while stretched out in the tub of your 32nd-floor luxury suite in the Fairmont Hotel. While you were out to dinner and a movie, the pampering elves popped in; they stocked the ice bucket and turned down the heavenly heavy sheets. The bathroom, as big as a studio apartment, comes complete with a water closet (with a potty wall phone, so the busy executive can dial 411 while doing number 2), a shower, and the spacious tub in which you are currently recumbent. A white terrycloth robe of the appropriately luxurious thickness awaits you. If you were a drag queen, you would love the wide expanse of the make-up table. You love it anyway, actually. And the closet is big enough for anyone's drag or IML gear.

Before heading straight to your room and making a beeline for the bath, you found it difficult to bypass the lobby. It has the look of a living room belonging to a wealthy friend with impeccable taste, the sort of person who makes you feel welcome and comfortable rather than awkward and out of place even though the furnishings here are well beyond your means. But you resisted the lure of the lobby in favor of a soak in the bath, followed by a long pondering of the view. The view is a big part of the delight here—request a park or lake view, and allow yourself to be hypnotized by the evening lights of the city and the cars on Lake Shore Drive far below. You will want to stay awake a long time and ease into a state of quiet calm being. The view out the window is so splendid because of the Fairmont's near-perfect location. It's a quick walk to Navy Pier, the bustle of Michigan Avenue, or the sights of Millennium Park and a slightly longer stretch of the legs to the Art Institute or the Museum Campus. The "L" is not far away. And while situated in the thick of things, the Fairmont still manages to feel tucked away—on the Saturday night Robert stayed here, he hardly encountered another soul on his walk back to the hotel from a movie. (The Fairmont is quite close to the AMC River East 21 movie theaters.) Amenities also include on-site spa and workout facilities, a concierge on duty 24/7, and, when Heather's two mommies need a break, babysitting service. Plus pets under 20 pounds are welcome. To really treat yourself, try **Aria** (www.ariachicago.com), the acclaimed in-house restaurant. Friends have raved about its amazing fare.

Wheeler Mansion
2020 S. Calumet Ave., 312/945-2020
www.wheelermansion.com
Rates: $230–$365
Gay managed

Feel like old money at this very fancy restored pre–Chicago Fire mansion just a stone's throw away from McCormick Place. This National Historic Landmark was a home to bums before the family that now operates it carefully restored it between 1997 and 1999. Walking through today, you'll find it hard to believe that someone could have let it go to seed. Each room is individually decorated with custom-made linens and tapestries, as well as antiques imported from Europe. Televisions and stereos are inconspicuously tucked into handsome armoires, and the lovely standing showers are customized for each room (one suite features a glass-enclosed standing shower and a double Jacuzzi tub). The ceilings throughout this place, even in the bathrooms, are unbelievably high (like 15 feet!). Back bedrooms look out to a cheery courtyard. Junior and regular suites all have gas fireplaces. There is a 24-hour coffee and tea setup in an elegant dining room, where a gourmet buffet is offered every morning. The cute, friendly manager, Michael Coleman, discreetly dropped a few names of some of the bigwigs who've made the Wheeler Mansion their home away from home in Chicago. Of course, we'll never tell. . . .

The Wheeler Mansion is about a $15 cab ride from Boystown. Luckily for guests, some interesting restaurants (the flamboyant restaurant Opera, for example) and (straight) nightlife has begun trickling into this previously barren locale.

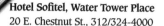

River North, Gold Coast, and Mag Mile

Hotel Sofitel, Water Tower Place
20 E. Chestnut St., 312/324-4000
www.sofitel.com
Rates: $209–$419
Highly recommended

Contrary to what one might assume, there are not many perks associated with being a gay and lesbian travel book writer, so when a query to the Hotel Sofitel about its gay-friendly policies led to an offer of a free night's stay, we were quick to scoop it up.

Kathie arrived at the hotel earlier than her girlfriend and was greeted by the French-accented V.I.P. host, who escorted her up to a top-floor room. On the elevator ride up, the host told her about an ad hoc gay group that has been throwing a big queer New Year's Eve party, called Queer Eyes Wide Shut, at the hotel for the past couple of years. Apparently the party takes over the whole hotel and is quite fun. Due to the informal nature of the party's organizational structure, we were unable to find specific details, but if you plan to be in Chicago around New Year's Eve, it might be worth sniffing around for info.

By this point Kathie had arrived at the room. The first thing she noticed was that the wall-to-wall, floor-to-ceiling window offered an outstanding view of the Hancock building and the lake beyond. The room itself wasn't huge, but it was contemporary and cheerful, with an inviting-looking featherbed and duvet. Appointed with high-end toiletries and fluffy robes, the marble bathroom, on the other hand, was huge, with a separate tub and glass-enclosed shower. Kathie wanted to take the whole bathroom home with her.

Kathie hadn't eaten, so she raided the minibar for a coke and a can of Pringles (not an FDA-approved lunch) and was just digging into this when there was a light tapping on the door. Greeting her was a complimentary tray of pastries and bottled water. Nice touch.

She was still rifling through drawers and flipping through the guest services guide when her gal pal Nikki arrived.

Then suddenly, things got all fuzzy as a mysterious vapor swept in, obscuring the scene. . . .

The Sofitel Water Tower Place is one of the newest of the Accor Group's Sofitel line and the first one to be built for the group from the ground up. Completed in 2002, the building, designed by French architect Jean-Paul Viguier, is indeed striking. Its asymmetrical, gravity-defying design recalls the front of a ship projecting outward onto the city street. Inside, the hotel is bright and airy, with bold color and artful floral displays. There is an acclaimed restaurant, Café des Architects, and a swanky lounge called Le Bar.

After returning from a dinner out, Kathie and Nikki had a drink at Le Bar later that night. The music was grooving. Kathie was happy to see that the drink menu offered Eau-de-Vie, a potent fruit-brandy seldom seen in the Midwest, whereas her girl indulged in a $30 glass of Dom Perignon (why not?). They returned to their room, which then became, once again, enveloped in a mysterious haze.

When the phone rang announcing the next morning's wake-up time, Nikki answered it, to be greeted by a heavily accented female voice, saying, "Bonjour! We have been up all night baking fresh croissants for you," or something to that effect. After a guilt-trip like that, how could we not partake?

They were fantastic! ✛

Allerton Crowne Plaza
701 N. Michigan Ave., 312/440-1500
www.ichotelsgroup.com
Rates: $169–$319

"The Allerton Crowne Plaza is pleased and delighted to accommodate a wide range of guests and clients regardless of their social, religious, or other orientations," says Allerton Director of Sales and Marketing Fredrik Houben of this Crowne Plaza location, which is housed in another historic landmark building. He could have mentioned species—the Allerton is also pet-friendly. Nice location, respectful staff, and a 24-hour lounge.

Flemish House Bed & Breakfast
68 E. Cedar St., 312/664-9981
www.chicagobandb.com
Rates: $160–$185
Gay owned

Staying at the Flemish House is like having your own charming small apartment in a swanky part of the city that your authors could only dream of being able to afford. The one-bedroom suite is, in fact, bigger than an actual apartment Kathie had in Paris. (She just wanted to drop in the fact that she once lived in Paris.) The rooms all have a Victorian feel, and each includes a small kitchenette with dishes and such. Breakfast is simply provided in each room's fridge (bagels, juice, etc.), so you can prepare it at your leisure. Those who opt out of breakfast can have $10 cut from their daily bill. Hosts Mike and Tom are genuinely nice guys.

The location, between the straight tourist pickup mecca of Rush Street and the straight tourist pickup mecca of the Oak Street Beach, guarantees that most of the clientele at the Flemish House are, well, straight. That said, 10 to 20 percent of the clientele is gay or lesbian, and guests can move about with quite a bit of autonomy. A small (but not too small) garden-level unit even has a private entrance. The house itself is on a quiet, stately graystone-lined street—an oasis amidst all the Gold Coast hullabaloo.

Old Town Chicago Bed and Breakfast
1442 N. North Park Ave., 312/440-9268
www.oldtownchicago.com
Rates: $160–$200 per room, or $650–$1,000 for the whole house, per night

Kathie was a little taken aback when we spotted more than one photo of George W. posted on the walls of the small workout room at the Old Town Chicago B&B. Maybe it was a joke? Maybe not. When coproprietor Liz (with husband Mike) Serritella caught Kathie gaping, she was quick to explain, "My husband is a big fan of Georgie W," thus triggering an instant gag reflex. After scribbling a quick, cautionary note about the place in her handy ledger, she was just about to try to politely bow out, when two of Old Town's guests returned from an outing and we were introduced. The two fellows were Old Town regulars and gayer than the Easter parade. "I remember one time when we stayed here," they recalled, "when we got taken under the wing of this redneck family from Arkansas. They loved us. We had drinks with them every night." And they reminisced about another visit, when they made acquaintance with another gay couple staying at the inn.

The rooms feel modern and are a bit masculine. Each sports an en suite shower and walk-in closet, which contains an additional foldout bed. There are numerous common rooms, including an equipped office, and a lounge area with leather sofas and a grand piano opens into a large formal dining area with a peek-through kitchen. The kitchen, fully available for guest use, is appointed with gourmet appliances, including a double-wide Sub-Zero brand fridge and freezer that may still be faintly glazed with Kathie's drool.

Breakfast is self-serve, and the Serritellas offer guests a variety of convenience food items: bread and bagels, peanut butter and cream cheese, fresh fruit, cereal, and ramen noodles.

After our tour, Kathie was invited to the Serritellas' parlor for a chat. The couple explained that they're "conservative in some ways but liberal in others." We all enjoyed a pleasant conversation, resulting in an invitation out to dinner for Kathie and her "chum." Then, as she was leaving, the Serritellas dropped the marriage question bomb on her. Kathie's feelings about gay marriage are complex and nothing that she particularly wanted to get into at that moment. She responded vaguely, "My partner and I have been together for more than five years, and I consider us to be married, for all practical purposes. I think there are certain civil rights issues being violated when an entire class of people is restricted from participating in an entitlement that is open to every other person in that society. . . ."

"Well!" Mike Serritella exclaimed. "I'm more liberal than you on that one! I think it's outrageous that gay people are denied marriage rights!" Not wanting to point out the contradiction on being a gay rights advocate and a self-proclaimed "huge fan" of George W. Bush, Kathie smiled wanly. Mike and Liz, you seem like really nice people, and we enjoyed chatting with you and mean that sincerely.

Furthermore, you run a really nice guesthouse. But "more liberal" than Kathie when it comes to gay marriage? We doubt it. Not unless you believe in abolishing marriage privilege altogether. Then, she says, we can talk.

Omni Chicago
676 N. Michigan Ave., 312/944-6664
www.omnihotels.com
Rates: $269–$379

This is where Oprah puts up all the guests on her show—those famous, those victimized, and those both famous and victimized. For information about how to have Oprah pay your hotel bill, see "Be a Daytime TV Diva!" (p. 53) about how to be a guest on the show. We're not sure where Jerry Springer puts his guests, but we're placing our bets on that Days Inn right by the Greyhound bus terminal.

The Omni Hotel is an all-suite hotel, with doors separating the sleeping area from a small sitting lounge. Each sitting lounge has a newly installed wall-mounted plasma TV. There is also a television in the sleeping area. All the rooms have been recently renovated and feature deluxe bedding, as well as a marble and granite bath. Very luxe.

Ritz-Carlton
160 E. Pearson St., 312/266-1000
www.fourseasons.com/chicagorc/
Rates: $360–$455

We were unable to arrange a visit to soak in the opulent luxury of the Ritz-Carlton, but the folks there assure us that they are very gay welcoming. Then again, they'd probably welcome a llama convention, if llamas could afford the room rates.

"W" Hotel Lakeshore
644 N. Lake Shore Dr., 312/943-9200

See notes earlier for the Loop "W" Hotel. A Pride package is offered here as well.

Boystown

Best Western Hawthorne Terrace
3434 N. Broadway St., 773/244-3434
www.hawthorneterrace.com
Rates: $139–$189

A cute, small courtyard leads up to the door of this hotel located on a stretch of North Broadway in the midst of East Lakeview's hot gay action. The small reception area, with busy patterns and a cozy fireplace, is reminiscent of a small European hotel. The rooms are generally bigger than those found at most European hotels where we've stayed, though. Each room features a coffeemaker, a fridge, and a microwave. The European-styled grocery store Treasure Island is right down the street, very convenient for getting snacks to keep in your room. The rooms also offer the usual amenities of a TV, phones, safes, and radio alarm clocks. The small bathrooms feature marble-top vanities and premium bath products. Rooms range from doubles to junior suites, and they sell out up to a year in advance for events like the Gay Pride Parade and Northalsted Market Days. The hotel has a washer and dryer for guests to use, as well as a very nice fitness center with a Jacuzzi and sauna. There are also a few ADA-compliant accessible rooms and Wi-Fi throughout. Complimentary continental breakfast includes homemade pastries and the famed cinnamon rolls from Ann Sather. We think this is a great hotel for the price, in a great location, and recommend it strongly.

Days Inn Lincoln Park North
644 W. Diversey Pkwy., 773/525-7010
www.lpndaysinn.com
Rates: $79–$170

It's a Days Inn, so what do you want? Actually, this Days Inn was recently voted the best Days Inn in all of Chicago, but that doesn't change the fact that it is still a Days Inn, with its accompanying busy patterns, brass detailing, and itchy polyester bedspreads. The location is very convenient to the Boystown action as well as public transportation, although rooms facing the busy intersection can get a little noisy. Room sizes range from regular doubles to "Business Place" rooms with a small fridge and microwave to small three-room suites with eat-in kitchens and separate sitting areas. The hotel is Wi-Fi wired. Access to the nearby Bally's health club and its indoor pool is free to all guests. Also gratis is the continental breakfast served from 6:30 to 11 A.M. daily in the breakfast room. A couple of the rooms only have showers, not tubs, at no significant reduction in price, so ask for a room with a bath if that matters to you. There are ADA-compliant accessible rooms and also a meeting room (with a coat check and a bar—unstaffed and unstocked), which can accommodate 50 people.

Neighborhood Inns of Chicago

www.cityinns.com
Rates: $109–$239
City Suites Hotel
933 W. Belmont Ave., 773/404-3400
Majestic Hotel
528 W. Brompton Ave., 773/404-3499
Willows Hotel
555 W. Surf St., 773/528-8400

Modeling themselves on the small family-run hotels of Europe, Lakeview's Neighborhood Inns of Chicago have smallish rooms in restored vintage buildings, with funky antique elevators (in the Willows and the Majestic) and cozy lobbies with antique reproduction furniture and fireplaces. Each hotel features a decorative theme: English country estate in the Majestic, French country in the Willows, and art deco in City Suites. We appreciated the vintage feel and neighborhood locations, although we found the color schemes often dreary and many examples where the stained carpeting was overdue to be replaced. If the Neighborhood Inns actually were small European hotels, we would give them two stars. Rates fluctuate and are inflated for busy times such as Northalsted Market Days (expect rate jumps for the Gay Games as well), but the hotels offer a very good value in nonpeak times, such as the middle of winter, when the fireplaces in the lobbies provide a warm respite. None of the rooms are ADA-compliant (all of the hotels were grandfathered in), nor do the inns have workout facilities on-site. Wi-Fi is available (for a fee) in all areas of the hotels. Continental breakfast in the lobby is free.

Villa Toscana
3447 N. Halsted St., 773/404-2643
www.villa-toscana.com
Rates: $99–$139
Gay owned

Shawn Smith, the buff proprietor of Villa Toscana, says he is not exaggerating when he says he oversees the premier gay bed-and-breakfast in the city. For more than ten years Villa Toscana, an 1890s Victorian-style home, has been hosting 2,000 to 3,000 guests annually in its eight rooms, in a setting Shawn feels is best described as "boutique style"—which does not mean froufrou or kitsch. "We don't have doilies or crap like that," notes Shawn. He encourages people to check out the Web site. "The online pics you see are what you get," along with free wireless Internet, an expanded continental breakfast, and the usual amenities of a quality B&B. Rates run from $109 to $139 a night for the high season (April through October) and can be higher for special events. (Prices drop a tad during the off months.) Northalsted Market Days and Gay Pride weekend are typically fully booked six months to a year in advance. In the course of the brief time Robert spent chatting with Shawn at the Villa, he had to regretfully turn away three different folks who'd phoned for rooms—so don't wait until the last minute on this one.

Shawn points out (and we totally back him up on this) that many hotels and inns say they are "steps away" from sights and nightlife. In Villa Toscana's case this is no exaggeration—you are right next door to a restaurant and smack dab in the heart of the Boystown Halsted bar strip. While the Villa is certainly known primarily as a gay B&B, Shawn points out that "very few weekends are now 100 percent gay," reflecting the changing demographics of the neighborhood. While Robert was there he met a straight woman who had stayed at the Villa many times. Some of the gay guys who book stays here bring their parents along—"there's no seedy stuff here," says Shawn. "People feel completely comfortable having their mom and dad join them." Villa Toscana is, of course, dyke-friendly. Shawn estimates that perhaps 5 percent of the clientele is lesbian, musing that the relatively low percentage may in part be because "lesbians just don't travel as much as gay men."

Andersonville/Edgewater

Ardmore House Bed and Breakfast
1248 W. Ardmore Ave., 773/728-5414
Rates: $89–$139
www.ardmorehousebb.com
Exclusively gay

We got the runaround more than once when we tried to schedule an appointment to actually see the rooms here. *Caveat emptor.* Our understanding is that they welcome women but that primarily men stay here. They have an outdoor Jacuzzi. For more info, check out their Web site or call. Hopefully, you will have more luck than we did.

Heart O' Chicago Motel
5590 N. Ridge Ave., 773/271-9181
www.heartochicago.com
Rates: $58–$70

Heart O' Chicago is a clean, cheap motor inn and not a complete dive. With its bare-bones but safe and tidy rooms, this motel is great for penny-pinchers who appreciate the close proximity to Andersonville and free parking.

In town for IML.
~Photo courtesy of Jon Peterson

Wicker Park

Wicker Park Inn Bed and Breakfast
1329 N. Wicker Park Ave., 773/486-2743
www.wickerparkinn.com
Rates: $115–$150

Besides its location on a quiet, shady street in the midst of Wicker Park café culture, shopping, and nightlife, the other huge appeal of the Wicker Park Inn rests with the fact that its owners, Laura and Mikky Wright, also own the nearby **Alliance Bakery**, which provides guests with fresh-baked pastries every morning.

Wicker Park Inn is a small guesthouse with three bedrooms falling within the $115–$150 price range. Two rooms include en suite bathrooms; the third has a private bathroom separate from the bedroom. Each room has a theme that influences its décor. The Cape Cod room is decorated in seascape colors, for example, and the Provence room has a French country feel. Rooms are not exactly posh, but the whole feel of the place is cozy. The Wrights also offer books, brochures, games, and a public fridge and microwave for use by their guests.

As a point of interest, the Wrights purchased the B&B from a gay male couple, and a lot of the gay clientele has stayed loyal to the inn.

Field Notes: Hotel Orrington
Hotel Orrington
1710 Orrington Ave., Evanston, 847/866-8700
www.hotelorrington.com
Rates: $150–$259

Evanston (home of Northwestern University), a suburb just to the north of Chicago, is close enough to be considered an extension of the big city to the south. What Evanston shares with Chicago is an urbane sensibility and cultural curiosity. What differs is the intimate, village-type feel of downtown Evanston. In short, staying in Evanston offers Chicago visitors all the excitement of big-city life but from an environment of calm and charm. Best of all, a Purple Line express train offers quick access to the city center, as well as a stop in Boystown (at Belmont). At Howard Street you can transfer to the Red Line, which has stops in Andersonville (Berwyn stop), Boystown (Belmont stop), River North (Chicago stop), and the Loop (Washington stop).

The Hotel Orrington is, perhaps, the premier hotel of downtown Evanston. The vintage art deco hotel recently underwent a $32 million renovation. Because Kathie is committed to doing the best research possible for this book, in service to you, dear reader—even if it involves staying in luxury hotels and dining at super fancy restaurants—when she was offered a free night's stay, and dinner to boot, at the newly refurbished Hotel Orrington, she knew that it was her responsibility to you to accept.

The first thing that impressed Kathie when she and gal pal Nikki entered their room was the sheer size of it. You could park a car in the middle. A large car. Pulling back a curtain revealed a walk-in closet the size of a New York condo. There was another small closet, too, wherein hung some nice fluffy robes. Looking deep, cozy, and inviting with its down duvet, the feather bed was turned down, covered in multihued Hershey's Kisses, and adorned by what appeared to be 400 pillows piled up on top.

The bathroom was of vintage quality with a not-so-very-deep bathtub, but it featured a wide assortment of Aveda bath products, which is Kathie's personal favorite product line. (To anyone from Aveda reading this: Feel free to send her complimentary products in exchange for this endorsement.) Other nice touches included a shaving kit and toothbrush with toothpaste, floss, and mouthwash. After marveling over the bathroom amenities, the gals drew their collective attention over to the minibar, which had the widest assortment of offerings available for sale of any minibar they had previously seen. These included playing cards, a disposable camera, a glass bear filled with gummis, marzipan, two kinds of Pringles, both cashews and pistachios, an assortment of beers and mixers, wine, and a half-sized bottle of Veuve Clicquot champagne. There was also an "intimacy kit" that included condoms, lube, and Kathie forgets what else.

The gals had 8 P.M. dinner reservations at the hotel's upscale restaurant, Narra. (The hotel also has a casual restaurant, the Global Café, and a funky lounge.) Once they were seated, the floor manager, Douglas, greeted them and availed himself to them for the duration of the meal. Based on his recommendation, both Kathie and Nikki chose the chef's tasting menu, which was a good value at $50 and even better at $75 with paired wines. Narra specializes in grilled and roasted meats served with the diner's choice of several different dipping sauces, served on customized plates. Even though both got the tasting menu, each dish was different and Kathie and Nikki enjoyed sampling everything, along with the paired wines. Service was exceptional—cordial, efficient, and in no way stuffy. The whole experience, from the minute they sat down at their table until the time they finally rolled out of the restaurant for a postdinner stroll around downtown Evanston, Kathie and Nikki were treated like princesses. Big lesbo princesses.

The next morning they splurged on a room service breakfast that arrived table and all. Having made arrangements the night before for a late checkout, Kathie and Nikki spent the rest of the morning lollygagging around and just relaxing. Only 20 minutes away from home on the Northwest Side of the city, these princesses felt like they were on a real vacation. ✦

STAYING IN CHICAGO DURING THE GAY GAMES 2006

T housands of hotel rooms in Chicago have been set aside for attendees to the 2006 Gay Games. The following hotels are offering special rates for Gay Games attendees. For discounted rates, book the hotels online at http://www.gaygameschicago.org/chicago/hotels.php.

Best Western
Fairmont
Hilton*
Holiday Inn Mart Plaza
Hotel Allegro
Omni East
Palmer House Hilton*
*A Gay Games "hub" hotel (whatever that means).

Some folks wear something fancy just for a casual summer stroll.
~Photo by Robert McDonald

Part 2

THE SUN ALSO RISES: DAYTIME DIVERSIONS IN CHICAGO

Ahhh, daytime. That mythical time between dawn and dusk. Your authors believe that daytime is gay-time. That's because daytime in Chicago offers myriad diversions for the queer tourist. In this section, we cover the three "S's" of gay-time in Chicago: Sightseeing (from the mainstream to far from it), Sports and recreation (including lakefront leisure and where to work out), and, finally, Shopping (the real gay sport). Forget nighttime pursuits. Chicago offers so many worthwhile ways to occupy your daytime hours. It is well worth setting your alarm clock so you don't miss out.

BE A DAYTIME TV DIVA!

Have you overcome adversity? Do you have a heartwarming story to share with the world? Or did you have gay sex with your sister's husband, or your husband's sister? Moreover, do you have a compelling urge to air your dirty laundry on national TV? If you're sitting there thinking, "Why, yes, I do have a story to tell! What next?" then Chicago is the city for you! Chicago is, after all, the home to both *The Oprah Winfrey Show* and *The Jerry Springer Show*. There's plenty of dirty laundry flapping in the breeze in the Windy City.

To be a guest on the *Oprah Winfrey Show*, first go to her Web site (www.oprah.com) and follow the "Be on the Show" link to get a list of possible show topics. Pick the one that suits you, and fill out the appropriate form. At the time of this writing, topics included "Living a Secret Life?" "Are you a mean mom?" "Ever done something *crazy* for love?" "Attention, Bon Jovi fans!" and, more in sync with our readers, "When did you first realize you were gay?" and "Do you want to 'come out' on the *Oprah* show?" ("Grandma, you may want to tune in to *Oprah* next Tuesday. . . .") If you don't want to be an actual guest on the show but would like to be in the studio audience, you can book reservations by telephone. The show only tapes from autumn through spring, so if you're passing through town in July, you are out of luck. Reservation lines for the fall season (taping begins in September) open up on August 15. Call 312/591-9222 to reserve tickets. Occasionally you can score last minute via Oprah's Web site, so check it out if you didn't plan ahead. Concierges in fine hotels may also have ticket connections.

As for Jerry, contact the show (at 800/96-JERRY) to pitch story ideas. For tickets, call 312/321-5365, go online at www.jerryspringertv.com, or submit a request by snail mail (maximum of four tickets per request):

Jerry Springer
454 N. Columbus Dr., 2nd Floor
Chicago, IL 60611
The *Jerry Springer Show* tapes from September through April, Monday to Wednesday only.

Chapter 9

LET US SHOW YOU WHAT WE GOT:
OUR PICKS FOR CHICAGO SIGHTSEEING

There are a million books that can probably do a better job than we can of guiding you through the kazillion mainstream sights in Chicago, and the truth is, we really don't think this book is necessarily where you want to look for that kind of general information. But people do ask us, "Robert, Kathie, I am coming to Chicago. What are the things that I really shouldn't miss?" So, in case this is the only guide to Chicago you are using (and we thank you for your vote of confidence) and because, like everything else in the world, we have opinions on this subject and feel compelled to put in our two cents, the following is a quick look at what we think are some of the best, don't-miss sights of our city.

Major Downtown Sights

The Art Institute of Chicago
111 S. Michigan Ave., 312/443-3600
www.artic.edu
Hours: Mon.–Wed., Fri. 10:30 A.M.–4:30 P.M.
Thurs. 10:30 A.M.–8 P.M.
Sat.–Sun. 10 A.M.–5 P.M.
Admission: $12 "suggested" donation, $7 for students and seniors
Free Thurs. evenings, 5 P.M.–8 P.M.

Grant Wood's *American Gothic*. René Magritte's choo-choo train coming out of the fireplace. Edward Hopper's creepy, lonely *Nighthawks*. Gustave Caillebotte's *Rainy Day in Paris*. Georges Seurat's *La Grande Jatte*. Mark Rothko's *Lipstick Lesbian Shopping for Labrys Pendant*. Okay, okay, Kathie made up that last one. In any case, the collection of nineteenth- and twentieth-century painting at the Art Institute of Chicago features way more iconic art than you could shake a stick at, were you at all inclined to stick shaking. And on top of that, the museum houses the largest collection of Impressionist art outside of Paris.

Truly one of the treasures of the city, the Art Institute of Chicago is a must-see. Everybody should have it on their itinerary, if at all possible. Your faithful authors have both been there on numerous occasions, but we decided on an outing together to reacquaint ourselves with its wonders, and to explore potential queer echoes and fancies and framings—in short, to give the place our own queer eye once-over. It is difficult, not to mention exhausting, to do the whole of the museum in a single day. An all-encompassing attempt is likely to result in frayed tempers, sore feet, and the inability to look at anything artier than reality TV for days after. We recommend several shorter visits, if that's an option. If not, choose the sections and sights that interest you most and take it from there.

The place to begin, of course, is the front steps on Michigan Avenue, with the famous lions flanking them. As long as the weather is fine, this is the perfect spot to arrange to meet friends and watch the constant pageant of street performers, geeky art students, society matrons, and dashing foreign visitors milling about the building.

On our visit, we briefly poked our noses into the lower level, down the stairs just past the front entrance. This is where the most prominent restrooms are. Yes, we started with the place to pee, as Robert generally has to get that task accomplished before he can relax and focus on the art. The photography galleries also happen to be downstairs, and the ever-changing selection is always worth seeing. Also downstairs is an area specially made for kids, as well as the miniature rooms, dioramas of teeny-tiny to-die-for interior design from the past—an essential stop if you were the type who played with Barbies.

The first floor, just past the entryway, features ancient art from Africa and the Americas, as well as the Chinese, Japanese, and Korean galleries. Determined to take in as much art as we could, we zipped through Africa and the Americas. Two sculptures in the Latin American collection (room 124) gave us pause. The *Figure of a Seated Chieftain* drew Robert's attention. The sitting Chieftain is tattooed and pierced, but the rough trade look is disrupted by the sad fact of his tiny endowment, which may explain his woebegone expression. Across from the Chieftain is the statue *Dancing Female Figure*, a naked woman appearing to have a lamp on her head. Upon spotting her, Kathie announced, "Hey, I think I was at that party!"

Across the hall, we stopped off in the Japanese art galleries. In room 107, Toshusai Sharaku's color woodblock prints of drag actors from the late 1700s sported the charmingly La Cage Aux Folles–style title as *The Actor Iwai Hanshiro IV Disguised as Otoma, a Country Girl.*

We hastened on to more paintings before fatigue set in. We plunged into the Middle Ages, where, typically, there were a lot of boring religious pictures. Things started to pick up at the onset of the Renaissance. Joos Van Cleve's *The Infants Christ and John the Baptist Embracing* (room 209) depicts two Gerber babies smooching each other on the lips. It's not child porn, but given Pee-Wee Herman's recent legal woes, we don't recommend downloading the image on your computer.

Luca Giordano's *Abduction of the Sabine Women* in room 213 shows the perils of patriarchy in action. Another painting, of Diana and Actaeon, tells the story of Actaeon crashing Diana's all-girl bathing party, after which Diana, in her fury, turned him into a stag. Good thing he stayed clear of the Michigan Womyn's Music Fest. Bartolomeo Manfredi's painting *Cupid Chastised*, with Mars about to lash the pale bare bottom of an adolescent cupid, provides artful fodder for fetishist fantasies.

"I'd kill for abs like that," Robert thought to himself, while viewing Francisco de Zurbarian's stunning, larger-than-life *Crucifixion*, which dominates room 215.

The Albert Munger Gallery (room 218) was notable for the fact that a young woman wearing a baseball cap hit on Kathie here. Kathie would like to point out that she was gazing at *Tiepolo's Tasso Cycle* when this alleged hitting-on occurred. It's clear to Kathie that the two women in this painting, purportedly about the attempted seduction of a snoozing crusader, only have eyes for each other.

This might be the place to mention that, in the middle of a Friday afternoon, we saw gays and lesbians of all varieties throughout the museum. If one is so inclined, meeting and/or pick-up potential does indeed exist in these hallowed halls.

"Hot-cha-cha," exclaimed Kathie as we entered room 222. "Now we're talking." Besides presenting images of woman reading (by Lawrence), woman thinking (by Gérome), and woman reclining (Lefebvre's sexy Odalisque), room 222 is also home to a lovely painting of two women bathing, by the Rococo painter Bougeaureau.

In room 225, Henry Fantin-Latour's startlingly realistic Still-Life: *Corner of a Table* (1873) offers a simple table with pears, rhododendrons, and a glass of red wine, reminding us that cocktail time was near. If you had any doubts about the origins for the set design of the Nicole Kidman–Ewan McGregor musical extravaganza, Toulouse-Lautrec's 1895 *At the Moulin Rouge* will lay them to rest. Toulouse-Lautrec, of course, is also known for his numerous paintings of lesbians and lesbian cafés, although, unfortunately, none of those paintings reside at the Art Institute.

If you did not know American poet and artist Marsden Hartley was a big homo, you would pick up on that by the unmistakable pre-Tom of Finland vibe in his 1940 *Madawaska-Acadian Light-Heavy*, a portrait of a hairy-chested young man in a black jock-strap, in room 248. Well, hel-lo, Dali! Salvador Dali's *Anthropomorphic Tower* is

🎨 *The Art Institiute of Chicago.*
~Photo by Sebastian Pinon

not as well known as his melting watches. Let's see . . . big thick pinkish tower, round scrotal huts underneath, plume of white "smoke" coming out of the tip—yup, it's an erection all right. No esoteric symbolism here. Bruce Nauman's *Second Poem Piece* is a steel panel on the floor with the words "You. May. Not. Want. To. Screw. Here." If you do, resist the impulse. Guards are everywhere.

By the time we reached the modern era, with Andy Warhol's imposing *Mao*, where blue eye shadow and careless lipstick tart the Chinese dictator up a bit, we were getting a tad punch-drunk—or art-drunk, as it were. "Is it just me," Robert asked Kathie, "or in the wavy cream and black squiggles with flashes of color of Jackson Pollock's *The Key* do you see a huge gay orgy starring Ed Harris as Pollock?" "Get away from me, you freak," said Kathie. It was time to call it a day.

Of course, there's much more to the Art Institute than just paintings and Japanese drag queens. There's decorative arts stuff, suits of armor, a paperweight collection, and Greek statues, and we had intended to take it all in, but at this point we said, "Ah, screw it," because the fact is, 99.9 percent of visitors to the Art Institute are interested in the painting collection, and nothing but the painting collection, and while there are many other things to see here, the paintings are what you really must not miss. ✦

Museum of Contemporary Art
220 E. Chicago Ave., 312/280-2660
www.mcachicago.org
Hours: Tues. 10 A.M.–8 P.M.
Wed.–Sun. 10 A.M.–5 P.M.
Closed Mondays
Admission: $10, $6 for students and seniors
Free on Tuesdays 5–8 P.M.

Chicago's beautiful contemporary art museum includes work by artists such as Barbara Krueger, Jenny Holzer, Cindy Sherman, and Claes Oldenberg, to name a few. Among the gay artists represented are Jasper Johns, Andy Warhol, David Wojnarowicz, and influential lesbian painter Hollis Resnick, a Chicagoan who succumbed to breast cancer in 2001. The museum offers free tours of the collection or special exhibits (which are always eye-opening and thought provoking). Gather just to the left of the ticket booth for the tour, which is given regularly on Tuesdays at 1 and 6 P.M., Wednesdays through Fridays at 1 P.M., and Saturdays and Sundays on the hour from 11 A.M. to 3 P.M. There's a Wolfgang Puck restaurant on-site with sit-down service and a to-go counter that whips up a lovely cappuccino.

MUSEUM CAMPUS

Anchoring the South Loop, the Museum Campus consists of the Shedd Aquarium, where you'll see more fish than at the Dinah Shore Golf Classic (Kathie apologizes—she couldn't resist); the Field Museum of Natural History, home to a really big dinosaur (no, not that old queen you saw hunched over her Gin Ricky at Little Jim's last night, although the two may have more in common than you know—research is currently under way to determine whether Sue, the world's biggest *T. rex* skeleton, may actually be a *boy named Sue*); and, rounding out this trio of world-class museums, the Adler Planetarium. Check the Web sites for special summer night concerts at the Shedd and stargazing nights at the Adler. The Roosevelt stop on the Red Line train is the closest "L" stop to the Museum Campus. Simply go through the underpass, and there you are.

Shedd Aquarium

1200 S. Lake Shore Dr., 312/939-2438
www.sheddaquarium.org
Hours: Weekdays from Memorial Day to Labor Day, all weekends 9 A.M.–6 P.M.
    Weekdays from Labor Day to Memorial Day 9 A.M.–5 P.M.
Admission: $16–$23 (varies depending on ticket type)

Adler Planetarium

1300 S. Lake Shore Dr., 312/922-7826
www.adlerplanetarium.org
Hours: Mon.–Fri. 9:30 A.M.–4:30 P.M.
    Sat.–Sun. 9 A.M.–4:30 P.M.
Admission: $13–$20

Field Museum of Natural History

1400 S. Lake Shore Dr., 312/922-9410
www.fieldmuseum.org
Hours: Mon.–Sun. 9 A.M.–5 P.M.
Admission: $9 (kids), $19 (adults)

Buckingham Fountain

Grant Park, between Jackson Boulevard
and Balbo Avenue

It's a spurter, all right! Buckingham
Fountain is to Chicago what the Eiffel
Tower is to Paris, and, in fact, the
fountains at Versailles inspired its design.
Try to check it out sometime on the hour

*One of two 50-foot glass block towers
that comprise Jaume Plensa's Crown
Fountain in Millennium Park.*
~Photo by Sebastian Pinon

from 10 A.M. to 11 P.M. daily, April through October, when the center fountain shoots
150 feet into the sky. As the sun sets, and into the night, this display is accompanied
by lights and music. It's as thrillingly gaudy as Zsa Zsa Gabor on a trapeze.

Millennium Park

Michigan Avenue, between Randolph Street and Monroe Street
www.millenniumpark.org

There's something faintly homoerotic about Jaume Plensa's Crown Fountain, two
gi-normous glass brick panels facing each other, each one displaying a different hyper
close-up of a face (often both of the same gender), alternately smiling at each other or
looking serious, until each one puckers their lips and . . . Well, we don't want to spoil
the fun or the surprise. We also love *Cloud Gate*, Anish Kapoor's giant sculpture,
affectionately known as "The Bean," and architect Frank Gehry's stunning Jay Pritzker
Pavilion, with its immense stainless steel ribbons unfurling into the sky. Never has
such an assortment of wonders been jammed together in such a cramped space.

Chicago Skyscrapers

We're famous for them. Here are a few ways to get a good look.

Chicago Architecture Foundation
224 S. Michigan Ave., 312/922-3432
www.architecture.org

The Chicago Architecture Foundation is the launching ground for nearly every imaginable type of architectural tour, from general surveys to special interests. Several tours depart daily. Check the foundation's Web site for schedules and registration information.

Riverboat Tours

River tours of Chicago's architectural sights launch several times daily, April through November, from the docks at 400 N. Michigan Avenue. Reservations are not necessary. Tickets for Wendella cruises cost $19 for adults and $10 for kids. Be sure to watch out for tour buses passing by on the bridges overhead. The driver for the Dave Matthews band once infamously decided to dump the bus's septic tank into the river, showering lame-o pseudo rock-star turds on a tour boat passing below. We are not making this up. Anyway, for more information about Wendella tours, go to www.wendellaboats.com. The Chicago Architecture Foundation also offers river tours, departing from Michigan Avenue and Wacker Drive (look for the blue awning). Tickets are $25 on weekends and holidays, $23 on weekdays. Reservations are recommended. Go to the foundation's Web site (posted in the preceding) for more details.

Hancock Center
875 N. Michigan Ave.
www.johnhancockcenterchicago.com
The Signature Room at the 95th
312/787-9596
www.signatureroom.com

Forget Sears Tower. For our money, the best sky-high perspective on the city is at the Hancock Center. Eschew the observation deck and head right to the 95th-floor Signature Room lounge, where for the same money you can partake of a fancy cocktail while enjoying the view. As an added perk for girls, the women's bathrooms feature the same stunning view. Kathie has long suppressed an urge to leave the stall door open and share her private business with the twinkling city below.

CITY PASS VS. GO CARD

Two tourist passes are available that can offer substantial savings on admission fees for diehard sightseers. The **City Pass** (www.citypass.com/city/chicago) offers admission to the Field Museum of Natural History, Hancock Observatory, Shedd Aquarium, Adler Planetarium, Art Institute of Chicago, and Museum of Science and Industry and can be used over a period of nine days. It costs $49.50 for adults ($39 for kids) and is available for sale at any of the participating attractions.

The **Go Card** includes admission to all the same attractions plus several more sights, including Sears Tower and Frank Lloyd Wright's Robie House, as well as architectural and other organized tours (more than 25 sights and activities in all). Go Cards can be purchased for use over one, two, three, five, or seven days, with prices ranging from $49 for a single day to $149 for seven days. The card is activated upon its first use. You can purchase cards online at www.gochicagocard.com or at locations throughout the downtown area, including the shop at the **Chicago Cultural Center** (78 E. Washington St.) and the **City of Chicago store** (163 E. Pearson St.).

Gay Sights

And now for some things you *won't* find in Baedeker's . . .

VISIT THE FORMER HOMES OF CHICAGO'S ILLUSTRIOUS HOMOSEXUALS

The City of Chicago Department of Cultural Affairs publishes a brochure called *Chicago Tribute: Markers of Distinction*, with a map of the historic plaque marked "homes of prominent Chicagoans of the past," amongst whom are several personages of gay and lesbian interest, including the following:

Margaret Anderson

The founder of the *Little Review* lived at 837 W. Ainslie Street.

L. Frank Baum

There'd be no Dorothy without him. The creator of *The Wizard of Oz* once lived at 1667 N. Humboldt Boulevard.

Bessie Coleman

A role model for independent women everywhere, aviator Bessie Coleman was the first black woman licensed to fly. In Chicago she dwelt at 4101 S. King Drive. She probably wasn't gay but we still think she was a worthy role model.

Lorraine Hansberry
The playwright and former Daughter of Bilitis once lived at 5936 S. King Drive.

Pearl M. Hart
One of the namesakes of the Gerber/Hart Library, Pearl Hart was a legal advocate for oppressed people including women, immigrants, and the gays. Her life partner was the lesbian novelist Valerie Taylor. Hart lived at 2821 N. Pine Grove Avenue.

Women of Hull House
Jane Addams and all her gaggle of gal pals resided at Hull House, 800 S. Halsted Street. The Hull House museum is open to the public.

Lorado Taft
The gay sculptor once lived at 1001 E. 60th Street. See his depressing public work *The Fountain of Time* near his former home at the Washington Park Lagoon.

Ida B. Wells-Barnett
Ms. Wells most certainly was not a homosexual, but we think there is much to admire about this former newspaperwoman who was an outspoken advocate for the rights of the oppressed. Pay tribute to her at her former home at 3624 S. King Drive.

Copies of the *Chicago Tribune* brochure are available at the **Cultural Center** (78 E. Washington St.) and the **Gerber/Hart Library** (1127 W. Granville Ave.).

Or Visit The Current Home Of A Non-Chicagoan Who Was Not Necessarily Gay But Was Definitely Still Cool— Oh, And Also . . . She Is Dead

Emma Goldman's Grave
Anarchist leader and advocate of free love, Goldman is buried near the monument to the Haymarket Riots martyrs at the Waldheim Old Jewish/Forest Home Cemetery, at 863 Des Plaines Avenue in Forest Park. Goldman, who was born in Russia, was radicalized by the Haymarket Riots and expressed a desire to be buried at this site. At the time of her death in 1940, Goldman had been kicked out of the United States for her radical activities, and special permission had to be acquired to move her body here from Toronto.

Formerly a Native American burial ground, the historic cemetery opened to the dead public in 1873. To get there, take the Blue Line train to the Forest Park stop (the end of the line), and walk about a half-mile south on Des Plaines Avenue to the cemetery.

OTHER INTERESTING GAY SITES

The Pride Pylons on North Halsted Street

Halsted Street, between Belmont Avenue and Grace Street

These somewhat phallic rainbow markers designate North Halsted as the city's "official" gay neighborhood.

Gerber/Hart Library and Archives

1127 W. Granville Ave., 773/381-8030
(Red Line Granville stop)
www.gerberhart.org

Gerber/Hart Library, one of the nation's only exclusively GLBT libraries and archives, was founded in 1981 and moved to its current 5,000 square foot space in 1998. The library has a gallery that regularly features the work of local artists. A lending library is available to members.

Leather Archives and Museum

6418 N. Greenview Ave., 773/761-9200
www.leatherarchives.org
Hours: Thurs.-Fri. 12-8 P.M., Sat.-Sun. 12-5 P.M.,
Getting There: #22 Clark bus, #36 Broadway bus. Cabs common. Street parking.

On a warm spring day, we joined forces for an excursion to the Leather Archives—the nation's only museum of leather sex, B&D, and related kinks. Although the Archives has been around in some form since 1991, neither of us had seen the collection, and now that the Archives has its own home (with the mortgage paid off, free and clear—we should all be so lucky) on the city's Far North Side, we thought it was time to enter this temple to kink and community. Getting in requires becoming a member of the Archives, currently a fee of $5 for 30 days. We paid and began our tour entering the Etienne Auditorium, a stately and comfortable room that would work well for a variety of lectures or programs. All the chairs are, of course, upholstered with leather, and most of the murals in the room are the work of Dom Orejudos, also known as Etienne. You may think you haven't seen an Etienne image before, but once you see his work labeled as such, you'll realize how much one individual's art has contributed to gay culture's archetype of the perfect leather man, and you'll also realize there are some cheap Etienne knock-offs out there in the world. Accept no substitutes.

Kathie pointed out that when you travel and zip through one or more major museums in a day, you lose track—"Was that Munich or Berlin where we saw the Rodin statue, honey? And wait, where was that little Matisse you liked so well?" But you *will* remember what museum you were in when you saw the sculpture of one youth being doubly penetrated by two other statues. And we bet you will recall the where and when of your first sight of the painting *Last Supper in a Gay Leather Bar with Judas Giving*

Christ the Finger, by Steven Brown. The man had chutzpa, we tell you. While it's obviously designed to be provocative, more than a cursory glance at the work will tell you that it owes at least as much to that painting of the dogs sitting around playing poker as it does to da Vinci.

The quiet, lovely library contains leather and bondage how-to guides, art books, video guides, fiction, and extensive back issues of leather and fetish magazines. One of the exhibits that impressed us the most in the main gallery was the "Timeline of Leather History." It's available online, but seeing it all spread out is the prime way to view it, we think. Joan of Arc and Ben Franklin, neo-leatherfolk. Who knew?

One of Robert's favorite main gallery sightings was the Etienne-designed ad for "Bedside Wipe-ups." It reads, "Love, the most delectable of all feasts, deserves the finest napkin." It made Robert think of a dandy in a white shirt, cummerbund, and gold cuf-flinks, delicately wiping his mouth, or something.

Like any museum, the Leather Archives has a gift shop, so don't forget that Aunt Fran asked you to pick up something nice for her on your trip to the Windy City. You have your choice of pins, T-shirts, photos, prints, paddles, whips, handcuffs, chains, restraints, coats, and vests, among other souvenirs.

Neither of us is particularly into leather and all the surrounding accoutrements, but we have no objection to expanding our horizons, and we greatly enjoyed our visit to the Archives. By focusing on something specific in the GLBT community, the Archives brings some light to all of our shared histories. ✦

The Leather Museum and Archives.
~Photo by Kathie Bergquist

Chapter 10

ARE YOU A PITCHER OR A CATCHER?
QUEER SPORTS AND RECREATION

Chicago is well documented as a city of sports fans, and we have several professional sports teams to prove it. Your authors, however, are not particularly sporty, although Kathie did once belong to a lesbian softball team and tromps gracelessly around a tennis court from time to time. But there are many athletic gay folk in the Chicago area and, by extension, many ways to support the habit or hobby of sport. Whether you are athletic yourself,or simply like to watch other folks working up a sweat, the following section looks at all things sporty in the city, from organized league play and tournaments to lakefront leisure and gay-friendly gyms and spas. Spas? Yeah, that sounds more like it. . . .

Touchdown.
~Photo by Jeremy Lawson
Photography/Gay Games Chicago

Organized Sports in Chicago

When considering Chicago's organized queer sports culture, we consulted with someone far more qualified than we are to address the subject. Mike Sarna is a veteran of Chicago's gay sports leagues. At 39 (you'd never guess it) he has been playing on Chicago teams since 1989. His sports include volleyball, softball, tennis, and, more recently, badminton, in a Chicago league that he essentially spearheaded. "My partner says he's a sports widow," Sarna jokes, explaining that he plays sports nearly every night of the week. "Instead of going out to bars with my friends, I get to go out and play with them. A bunch of my best friends—we've been playing together on the same teams for years."

Chicago has two gay sports leagues: the Chicago Metropolitan Sports Association (CMSA) and the Windy City Athletic Association (WCAA). Collectively, the leagues organize a spectrum of sports, including basketball, flag football, darts, bowling, volleyball, badminton, tennis, and softball. As for what they might offer someone just passing through, who doesn't have the leisure to commit to a whole season of play, Sarna points out that Chicago's queer sports leagues host a handful of tournaments that anyone can enjoy, as a participant or a spectator. Among these are the Chitown Classic Tennis Tournament, the Second City Tennis Classic (part of the GLTA tennis tour), the Senior Cup softball tournament, the Queen of the Beach and Summerfest beach volleyball tournaments, and the Sam Cody basketball tournament. For more information about any of these tournaments, check out the CMSA and WCAA Web sites, www.chicagomsa.com and www.wcaa.net, respectively.

For lesbians and gays who like to run, jog, walk, stroll, trounce, mince, and meander, Frontrunners/Frontwalkers meets twice a week—Saturdays at 9 A.M. and Tuesdays at 6:30 P.M.—for a lakefront two-mile walk or a three- to five-mile run, rain or shine. Afterward they often grab something to eat. If it's your first time attending (everyone is welcome), you are advised to introduce yourself, and the team will do the best they can to make you feel at home. Meet at the Totem Pole in Waveland Park, at Addison Street and the lake.

If your participation in sports is wholly as a spectator, Chicago still has plenty of options. Summer is softball season. Pack a cooler and go catch the games all day at Waveland Park. Saturday the guys play, and Sunday it's all about the ladies (see the sidebar on this). In the fall, cheer your favorite queer during flag football games at Warren Park, located on Western Avenue, between Devon Avenue and Pratt Boulevard. As with softball, the boys play on Saturdays, and on Sunday, it's the women's leagues getting their faces smashed in the mud.

If pro sports are more your thing, every year sometime in July, *Chicago Free Press* helps organize "Out at the Ballpark," an unofficial gay day at Wrigley Field. Keep your eyes on their Web site (www.chicagofreepress.com) for details.

Working Out

Most hotels of three-star quality or higher offer workout facilities to their guests. If your hotel doesn't, or if you're staying with your aunt Madge or in some other arrangement that interrupts your workout routine, all is not lost. A few Chicago gyms offer short-term or day-by-day access to their gear. Here's the skinny on some of the more gay-ly situated spots where you can work out if you are just passing through.

BOYSTOWN

Chicago Sweatshop
3215 N. Broadway St., 773/871-2789
www.chicagosweatshop.com
   The Chicago Sweatshop offers a day pass for $12.

Quads Gym
3727 N. Broadway St., 773/404-PUMP
www.quadsgym.com
   Quads, a gym with an emphasis on weight training, offers daily passes for
$11, weekly passes for $40, monthly passes for $75, and ten-visit passes for $80.

ANDERSONVILLE/EDGEWATER

Cheetah Gym
5248 N. Clark St., 773/728-7777

Cheetah Gym
5838 N. Broadway St., 773/728-6600

WICKER PARK

Cheetah Gym
1934 W. North Ave., 773/394-5900
   Cheetah is a gay-owned gym especially popular with the gays but welcoming
to Chicagoans of every orientation. The facilities are spacious, clean, and well
appointed. All Cheetah Gyms offer short-term access: daily for $15, weekly for
$49, monthly for $119, and a ten-visit punch pass between $119 and $139. All
three branches can be reached via the same Web site: www.cheetahgym.com.

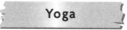

Yoga

We can recommend these two convenient yoga centers, both offering a
variety of classes at every level, with drop-in rates for short-term visitors.

Yoga Circle
401 W. Ontario St., 312/915-0750
www.yogacircle.com
Drop-in rate: $16 per class

Global Yoga
1823 W. North Ave., 773/489-1510
www.globalyogacenter.com
Drop-in rate: $13 per class

Spas

A fter a day of sightseeing or a night of overindulgence, what better way to renew yourself than a day at the spa? Here are a couple of very gay-friendly choices.

GAY GAMES, JULY 15–22, 2006

M ore than 12,000 athletes and athletic supporters (chuckle chuckle!) are anticipated to descend on Chicago for the seventh quad-rennial gay sports and cultural festival, taking place in Chicago from July 15 until July 22, 2006. Events are planned citywide, from the opening ceremony at Soldier Field (home of the Chicago Bears—the football team, that is), to the closing ceremonies at Wrigley Field, with "sports villages" located at the campuses of the University of Chicago in Hyde Park, the University of Illinois on the Near West Side, to the Northwestern campus in north suburban Evanston, and spanning the North Chicago lakefront. Competitive sports run through the alphabet from badminton, basketball, beach volley-ball, bowling, cycling, dance, darts, and diving, spanning all the way through to tennis, track and field, triathlon, volleyball, water polo, and wrestling. Big-name entertain-ment is promised, along with loads of arts and cultural events and parties. A worthy excursion even for those of us whose best sports include glass tipping, channel surfing, or mind games. Plus, hello? 12,000 queer athletes! Can anyone say "yum"? Tickets, a complete schedule, and registration information are available at www.gaygameschicago.org.

Spacio Spa
2706 N. Halsted St., 773/244-6500
www.spaciospa.com

Spacio, a gay-owned spa, offers a mind-boggling array of facials, massages, wraps, manicures, pedicures, and so forth. Spa packages range from day-long to a few hours, and several treatment options appeal specifically to men (facials and such—get your mind out of the gutter). We have both had massages by masseur Owen, who works at Spacio, and we advocate that everyone have him knead away their overworked muscles.

Thousand Waves Spa
1212 W. Belmont Ave., 773/549-0700
www.thousandwavesspa.com

Thousand Waves started as a women-only spa and Seido Karate classroom. The classroom's gone co-ed and moved up the street, allowing the spa facilities to expand into the whole space. Facilities include a Jacuzzi, a dry sauna, a eucalyptus steam bath, and an exhilarating cold plunge shower. Massages and herbal wraps are available by appointment. For true restorative and detoxifying indulgence, splurge on a $125 combo package that includes use of the facilities, an herbal wrap, and a massage. Finish off with a cup of herbal tea or a nap in the relaxation room, and feel miles away from cell phones, faxes, e-mails, and regrettable beer-goggled pick-ups. Cost of a regular spa visit without massage or wrap is $20 for three hours. Cost of the urban escape: priceless.

Play bald.
~Photo by Jeremy Lawson
Photography/Gay Games Chicago

Lesbian Softball at Waveland Park

Every summer Sunday, from the time the season begins in late April until it ends in late July (play-offs trickle into August), the softball diamonds at Waveland Park (Waveland and the lake—look for the totem pole) are taken over by lesbian softball leagues. Games start at 9 A.M. and run until about 3:30 or 4 in the afternoon. The only exception is Gay Pride Sunday, when all the leagues take a day off.

For the less athletic, a Sunday afternoon is a great time to pack a picnic and go check out the action as a spectator. Lesbians with varying degrees of athletic prowess come by to show off their dogs, their kids, and their latest conquests (or to scout out new ones). The park borders the lake, making for a lovely detour from the action on the field. Public bathrooms are available, and a concession stand serves overpriced soft drinks and weenies. As an aside, we feel we must mention that drinking alcohol is prohibited in all Chicago parks (except in designated restaurants), and violators may face a fine (although it's more likely that they will be asked to dump out the offending contraband). We would never want to seem as though we are condoning lawlessness. This being said, plenty of folks do bring coolers along that we suspect may harbor something stronger than lemonade. Discretion is the key.

Lesbian softball has its own culture and rituals. Heck, there's a whole book about it, written by fellow Chicagoan Yvonne Zipter, called *Diamonds Are a Dyke's Best Friend* (Firebrand Books). Robert's friend Renee tells of her ambivalence about playing with a new team until the captain announced that everyone had to go to her van to "smoke up" to encourage bonding. And Kathie, who is decidedly not the sporty type, once belonged to a team called "the Tarts," composed of equally nonsporty types, including Kasia, a purple-haired high femme Wiccan who played in long skirts; Audrey, a skinny asthmatic who wore cowboy boots and chain-smoked in the left field; a set of twin sisters who were both strippers; a motley array of barflies; and a rock star drummer, Laura "Pow-Pow" Masura, who once stripped down to her bra and panties in the outfield to distract the batter. It worked. The Tarts were cheered on by a hirsute assortment of pompom–shaking bears, radical faeries, and Goths. Their rallying cheer was the opening bar of the Black Sabbath song "Iron Man."

But that was all a long time ago, and Kathie wanted to be sure that the rituals hadn't changed. So, packing up a blanket, some sandwiches, and her best gal, Nikki, she decided to see for herself.

The weather was perfect—80 degrees and sunny—on the mid-June afternoon when Kathie and her permanent love slave went to check out the action. At the park, they were happy to run into the gals from the rockin' Chicago all-chick band **Stewed Tomatoes** (www.stewedtomatoes.com), whose drummer, Katie J., plays shortstop on "Team Fun." Katie's T-shirt for the game was adorned with metallic tape spelling out "Fuck Bush," which became a kind of verb as the game progressed. "Fuck Bush into the outfield, Katie!" someone yelled, as she went up to bat.

There are a number of gals who take their softball very seriously and approach it with an admirable degree of athleticism. League play is actually sorted into three divisions, with division A being the most competitive and division C being purely recreational. Team Fun, like the Tarts, was solidly division C.

The Tarts softball team.
~Photo by Kathie Bergquist

"Who wants a Jäger bomb?" Katie J.'s bandmate, Martie, asked from behind Kathie. "Tits in the dirt, Katie!" someone else shouted.

"Cheers to queers," ban mate Lisa announced, before tipping her Jäger bomb bottoms-up. "Good morning!"

Kathie is heartened to report that nothing has changed. ✦

The Lakefront

The 3,600-acre Chicago lakefront greenway is truly one of Chicago's recreational glories. Dotted with tennis courts, play lots for the kiddies, softball diamonds, and two golf courses (Waveland and Jackson Park) and boasting an eighteen-mile bicycle path, Chicago's lakefront is where everyone in the city gathers to picnic, rollerblade, sunbathe, or hook up (and none of these activities are mutually exclusive).

BEACHES

Chicago's beaches are generally named or referred to by the street point where they intersect with Lake Michigan. **Oak Street Beach** (at Oak Street and the lake) is a yuppie-breeding ground. **North Avenue Beach** is a yuppie-breeding ground *and* a beach volleyball mecca. To reserve a net, call 312/742-3224. The **Belmont Rocks**, while not a beach per se, is a sunbathing spot adjacent to Belmont Harbor, particularly popular with gay folk (it's basically an extension of Boystown). Note that swimming at the rocks is forbidden due to the rocky shoreline (hence the nickname).

The city's unofficial gay beach is **Hollywood Beach** (5800 N. Lake Shore Dr.), officially called the Kathy Osterman Beach. Boys and girls alike hang out here in varying degrees of buff and tan, specifically on the south end of the beach (the north end is more family oriented). There are volleyball nets, lifeguards on duty, and public restrooms and outdoor showers at the beach house. The restrooms (no surprise there) and the parking lot are particularly action oriented.

It seems appropriate to insert some words about the lakefront and the law. The entire Chicago lakefront is considered to be part of the public park system, and like all city parks, it closes at 11 P.M. If you're in the park after that time, you may be subject to police interrogation. Furthermore, police do enact stings against indecency and solicitation in the parks, and at Hollywood Beach in particular, especially at times when public outcry (remember that "family-oriented" side of the beach?) prods them to do so. Violators are subject to fines, court dates, and, in worst-case scenarios (involving underage parties), being listed, forever, on the Illinois sex-offenders public access Web site.

The parks are not particularly unsafe after dark, but neither are they particularly safe. This is the big city, after all, and the parks after 11 P.M. are dark and isolated. Be smart.

Furthermore, drinking alcohol in city parks is forbidden. Violators may be subject to a fine. If you choose to break the law (which we do not advocate), please, for Pete's sake, for your sake, and for our sake, do so carefully, responsibly, and discreetly!

WHO THE HECK WAS KATHY OSTERMAN, AND WHY IS A BEACH NAMED AFTER HER?

K athy Osterman was a civic activist and eventually alderman in the Edgewater neighborhood, where this beach is found, before she headed the Mayor's Office of Special Events. As an alderman, she was a major figure in the contentious city hall fight to pass a human rights ordinance guaranteeing equal rights to gays and lesbians in the city of Chicago. As head of the Mayor's Office of Special Events, she opened channels of communication between the mayor and the political branch of Chicago's gay community. Osterman succumbed to cancer in 1992. The following year she was inducted posthumously into the Chicago Gay and Lesbian Hall of Fame as a "friend of the community."

CYCLING AND BLADING THE LAKESHORE

On a Saturday afternoon in the summertime, the lakefront bicycle path is a traffic jam of bikers, rollerbladers, stroller pushers, dog walkers, and the greatly feared rollerblading, stroller-pushing dog walkers. By comparison, weekdays in the late morning and early afternoon are bastions of scenic tranquillity.

Bikes and blades can be rented at beaches throughout the city, with prices arranged hourly (typical rates start at about $8.75 per hour and go up to $15 for a two-seater bike), in blocks of four hours, or daily. At Millennium Park, the **Millennium Park Bike Station** (239 E. Randolph St., 888/Bikeway, www.chicagobikestation.com) offers bike rentals, indoor bicycle parking, lockers, showers, maps, and guided tours. **Bike and Roll** (866/Rentabike, www.bikeandroll.com) rents bikes and in-line skates at Millennium Park, Navy Pier, North Avenue Beach, and Foster Avenue Beach.

The Chicago Park District can provide maps and a helpful guidebook for the lakefront. Call the district at 312/742-PLAY.

PICNICS IN THE PARK

Hot dogs, burgers, chips, and the like are served at food kiosks along the lakefront. For something special, try one of these places.

From Streeterville or the Mag Mile, **Fox & Obel** (401 E. Illinois St., 312/410-7301) can fix you up with whatever you need for a picnic in Grant Park, in Millennium Park, or at Oak Street Beach. The local gourmet emporium includes excellent cheeses, fancy cured meats, a modest wine department, and imported caviar, if that's your thing.

For Lakeview and Boystown picnics, head gaily forward to the gay-owned and -operated artisan cheese and wine shop **Pastoral** (2945 N. Broadway St., 773/472-4781), where they offer truly delish ready-made sandwiches (Serrano ham and Manchego sandwich with quince paste, for example, or a juicy, extra-tasty Caprese sandwich) and picnics to go.

In Andersonville, you can pick up a sandwich, a drink, and chips at **Wikstrom's** (5247 N. Clark St., 773/275-6100, www.wikstromsgourmet.com), a Swedish deli. Kathie loves their limpa bread and liver sausage. Or opt for a Mediterranean picnic with freshly made spinach pie, baba ghanoush, and still-hot pita bread at the **Middle Eastern Bakery** (1512 W. Foster Ave., 773/561-2224).

Shopping—the Real Gay Sport!

Okay, we confess that we hate shopping—loathe it, in fact. And chagrined though we may be to admit it, approximately 95 percent of our shopping takes place at Marshalls, T.J. Maxx, the Gap Outlet, or the Village Thrift.

All the same, we know that for many—nay, most—homosexuals, shopping is far from a loathsome experience. Fortunately for you, and our curmudgeonly approach aside, Chicago offers a bounty of fab shopping opportunities, from the deluxe designers lining Michigan Avenue and Oak Street, to gay-specific tchotchkes the likes of which you'll find at Gaymart, to hippie crystal and new age shops, awesome indie book and record stores, and some of the best vintage and thrift shopping to be found. The options are truly too wide and diverse to offer up here in their entirety, but we are happy to put in our two cents about the most worthy gay shopper's destinations. So warm up those platinum cards, ladies and gents. On your marks, get set, shop!

Those shops marked with a 🛍 are très très gay.

Michigan Avenue and Oak Street Shopping

Dubbed the Magnificent Mile, the stretch of Michigan Avenue from the north bank of the Chicago River up to and just beyond Chicago Avenue, is a fashion queen's platinum card paradise. All of the big-name, big-dollar shops are located on or directly adjacent to this strip: **Nordstrom, Giorgio Armani, Ermenegildo Zegna** (for hand-tailored suits), **Fratelli Rossetti** (for Italian leather), **Jil Sander** (for designer day and evening wear), **Bloomingdale's, Barney's, Neiman Marcus, Nicole Miller, Tiffany & Co., Gucci, Van Cleef and Arpels, Chanel, Hermes** . . . the list goes on. One of the most recent additions to this embarrassment of riches is the first North American outpost of the European department store **H&M**, which offers European style at reasonably afforable prices.

Ermenegildo Zegna 645 N. Michigan Ave., 312/587-9660
Neiman Marcus 737 N. Michigan Ave., 312/642-5900
Giorgio Armani 800 N. Michigan Ave., 312/751-2244
H&M 840 N. Michigan Ave., 312/640-0060
Gucci 900 N. Michigan Ave., 312/664-5504
Bloomingdale's 900 N. Michigan Ave., 312/440-4460
Fratelli Rossetti 909 N. Michigan Ave., 312/337-5496
Nordstrom 55 E. Grand Ave., 312/414-1515
Hermes 110 E. Oak St., 312/787-8175
Jil Sander 48 E. Oak St., 312/335-0006
Barney's New York 25 E. Oak St., 312/587-1700

Clothes

I s there a gay fashion aesthetic? Shows like *Queer Eye* and terms like *metrosexual* seem to imply one. We like to think our diversity can't be so easily categorized. In any case, some shops in Chicago do cater specifically to gay men (and grrl-bois). As for the girlies, well, Kathie laments, outside of the Gap and J. Crew, we are left to fend for ourselves.

MEN'S CLOTHING STORES

Because every gay is crazy about a sharp dressed man.

Bad Boys 📷
Boystown: 3352 N. Halsted St., 773/549-7701

Perhaps the longest established of the clothing boutiques marketing to the gays, Bad Boys is located on the Halsted strip next to Roscoe's. They carry jeans and T-shirts, club wear and such, and they also sell lube. Kathie was actually surprised by how slutty/trashy many of the clothes were, so if that's your thing, boy toy, then this is your shop.

Universal Gear 📷
Boystown: 3153 N. Broadway St., 773/296-1090

Universal Gear carries the Diesel line, along with other club wear, a large selection of swimwear from trunks to speedos, and lots of shorts, button-up shirts, and T-shirts that would look just as lovely on a handsome butch gal as on a stylish guy.

Market Days wares.
~Photo by Jon Peterson

Duomo Men's Designer Resale
Boystown: 2906 N. Broadway St., 773/325-2325

Buy gently used Prada and Armani at a fraction of new prices. The selection includes suits, shoes, and accessories. To help perpetuate a longstanding inside joke between Kathie and her friend Owen, ask the guy behind the counter, "How you doin'?"

His Stuff 📷

Andersonville: 5314 N. Clark St., 773/989-9111
www.hisstuffchicago.com

Gay-owned, gay-operated, with gay air to breathe, His Stuff offers a small, carefully chosen selection of casual wear and accessories from around the world. The "enhancing" effects of the Baskit brand underwear they carry, frankly, make us giggle. Robert appreciates the friendly, personalized service (the owners are most often on-site), without the aura of hard sell or false cheer. These guys care about fashion, and it shows. Robert likes the shirt selection especially—they always stock dress shirts that manage to be contemporary and stylish without feeling like fads that you won't want to be seen in a year from now. Our buddy Ianni, shopper extraordinaire, recommends their sleek and sexy swimwear.

WOMEN'S CLOTHING STORES

Okay, we already made the crack about the Gap and J. Crew! Here are a couple other options for the ladies.

Presence

Andersonville: 5216 N. Clark St., 773/989-4420

The store for earth mama femmes with a sense of style. Cute sundresses, funky accessories like hats, scarves, bags, and sandals, and big girl sizes, too. Also, you can buy your hippie skirt and sarong here for Michigan Womyn's Music Fest. Kathie did.

Belmont Army Surplus

Lakeview: 857 W. Belmont Ave., 773/525-5064

This may seem like a weird choice, but face it, butch dykes look hot in tank tops and cut-off-at-the-knee army fatigue pants, not to mention the WAC boots. The first floor hosts two boutiques: one with trendy shoe styles and the other featuring women's club and streetwear—Paul Frank, Diesel, Emily the Strange, etc. The second floor is where you find the military cast-offs. Oh, also on the second floor are bandanas in every color imaginable for those who are hanky-code inclined. The store is slated to move a half-block east from this address in Spring 2006.

CLOTHING STORES FOR BOTH WOMEN AND MEN

Where boys and girls can shop together.

99th Floor

Boystown: 3406 N. Halsted St., 773/348-7781

There's something comfortingly familiar about the fact that nothing has changed about this store in the 15 years since I started coming here, says Kathie. Lots of leather, vinyl, and plaid, with platform KISS boots and loads of zippers, buckles, and straps. Fashions fall somewhere between punk and Goth, firmly circa the late 1980s USA, via 1970s England.

The Alley
Lakeview: 3228 N. Clark St., 773/883-1800

The "Alternative Complex" includes this store, along with a naughty lingerie store, a resale shop, a smoke shop, a silver jewelry boutique, and a plaster gargoyle shop. The Alley represents a rite of passage for Chicago youth—all the trappings of adolescent rebellion are sold here: big shoes, black strappy clothes, metal and punk T-shirts, clunky stainless jewelry, biker jackets, and Special Effects hair dye in neon colors. They even do piercings and tattoos on-site.

Gap Factory Outlet
Logan Square: 2778 N. Milwaukee Ave., 773/252-0594

Who doesn't eventually shop at the Gap? Here you can find last season's discontinued jeans, khakis, polos, etc., at outlet store prices. Airport lose your luggage? This is the place to restock.

Shoes

Hey, you gotta have shoes! Actually, one of two things Kathie enjoys shopping for is new shoes. The other is wine. When you think about it, what more do you need? (Robert has a sudden vision of Kathie nude, save for her Italian leather boots, sipping well-aged Bordeaux.)

Hanig's Slipper Box
Boystown: 2754 N. Clark St., 773/248-1977

Hanig's, a Lakeview staple, has a nice selection of men's and women's shoes in contemporary styles. The store is conveniently located across from the Century Shopping Center.

Alamo Shoes
Andersonville: 5321 N. Clark St., 773/784-8936

We're sure gay men shop here, but Alamo is hands-down the most lesbian shoe shop in town. It's not the staff. They are, in general, your usual professional, commissioned shoe hawkers. It's the selection (and the Andersonville location) that appeals to our Sapphic sisters. Alamo carries a wide variety of those fashionable, comfortable shoes and sandals that women who prefer to have sex with other women seem drawn to. That is, Clarks, Mephisto, Timberland, Earth Shoes, and certain ubiquitous brands we shouldn't have to name (clue: rhymes with Mirkinclocks). The store features a lot of expensive European designs that are as comfortable as they are stylish—and we assure you that we are not being facetious. Quality comes with a high price tag, but it's worth it. The shoes here were built to last. On a recent visit, we overheard a shoe vendor tell a customer, "People, they come here for comfort, but you, you're young, so you want to look cute, too." And that pretty much says it all.

And, oh yeah, Alamo is a great place for chicks to cruise each other on a Saturday afternoon.

DSW Shoe Warehouse
Boystown: 3131 N. Clark St., 773/975-7182

This is what shoe shopping is all about: rows and rows of discontinued designs from top names, all at value prices, which usually means one-stop shopping. Plus you help yourself, so you don't have to worry about some sweaty shoe salesman pawing all over you.

John Fluevog
Wicker Park: 1539–41 N. Milwaukee Ave., 773/772-1983

We adore these funky European shoe styles and wish we could afford them.

Accessories and Jewelry

Y̶ou know—to give you that "finished" look.

Spare Parts
Boystown: 2947 N. Broadway St., 773/525-4242

This shop carries all kinds of nice upscale bags, jewelry, candles, scarves— lots of stuff you didn't know you needed until you saw it here. Really great selection of stylish messenger bags, man-purses, sacks, and backpacks. Try on the hats just for fun.

Jan Dee Jeweler
Lincoln Park: 1425 W. Diversey Pkwy., 773/871-2222

Jan Dee is a Chicago gay and lesbian institution for custom-made fine jewelry. Come here to order unique commitment rings and other special-occasion (or just for a splurge) jewelry.

Squint II
Boystown: 3178 N. Broadway St., 773/935-3798

Here you'll find lots of silver jewelry with semiprecious stones. The person working behind the counter the day we asked said they usually do have some gay- and lesbian-specific designs in stock, despite the fact that they didn't at that time. The main reason to come here is the great selection of top-name designer sunglasses, including Dior, Dolce & Gabbana, Armani, Versace, and Calvin Klein.

Vintage and Thrift Shopping

Whether it's upscale resale, funky vintage finds, or junk-store treasures, Chicago offers a bit of resold everything for the thrift-minded shopper.

VINTAGE SHOPPING

The difference between "vintage" and "thrift"? About forty bucks.

Beatnix
Boystown: 3400 N. Halsted St.,
773/281-6933

This très gay store is Chicago's drag queen headquarters. They vend all the necessary accoutrements: wigs, theatrical make-up, large-sized pumps, and gaudy jewelry and accessories. Kings don't get left behind, either. Beatnix also sells faux facial hair for paste-on moustaches and beards. For the rest of us, there is a decent selection of vintage clothes—more men's than women's— and shoes. Kathie was mesmerized by a pair of platforms with water and plastic goldfish in the heel. Beatnix is a popular shop for Halloween costumes or for that one extra touch to funkify any hipster outfit.

Thrifting.
~Photo by Caldwell Linker

Recycle
Wicker Park: 1474 N. Milwaukee Ave., 773/645-1900

This co-ed shop features both trendy resale and truly vintage clothing and accessories, although the prices are a little steep by our measure: $40 for a used Lacoste polo? Come on.

Land of the Lost
Boystown: 614 W. Belmont Ave., 773/529-4966

This tiny, step-down shop is great for vintage jackets, funky T-shirts, polyester blouses, and goofy collectibles attesting to the adage that one person's trash is another person's treasure. Land of the Lost carried original Fonz and Dukes of Hazzard T-shirts before they started to be reproduced for trendoid shops like Urban Outfitters.

Ragstock
Boystown: 812 W. Belmont Ave., 2nd Floor, 773/868-9263
Wicker Park: 1433 N. Milwaukee Ave., 773/486-1783

As a teenager, Kathie worked at the original Ragstock Warehouse Store in Minneapolis, and the job is not filed away in her cabinet of happy memories. But don't let that keep you from the racks and racks of vintage here, along with kimonos, army pants, lots of new irregulars, and these frilly lime green tuxedo shirts with matching polyester pants that Kathie begrudgingly admits are pretty dang spiffy.

Hollywood Mirror
Boystown: 812 W. Belmont Ave., 773/404-4510
Here you'll find a bonanza of vintage wear at reasonable prices, along with lots of kitschy gifts: Bettie Page alarm clocks, Smurf stickers, plastic kewpie doll face masks, and lots of things featuring Magic 8 Balls, dice, and skulls. Hollywood Mirror is also notable for their wacky window displays.

THRIFT SHOPPING
If you are a hard-core thrift shopper, then you know that thrift shopping does not consist of flipping through racks of clean, well-arranged, previously used fashions. Thrifting means digging through pile after pile of torn, dirty, stained crap, looking for those elusive deals in clothes, furniture, vinyl, books, or collectibles. Lucky for you, Chicago has a huge network of super gritty thrift stores with rock-bottom prices. On a recent outing at the Village Thrift, Kathie found a good-condition BCBG fitted suit jacket that once cost someone between 100 and 200 smackers. She acquired it for a mere buck-fifty. Different chains of stores (Salvation Army, the Ark) benefit different causes, while others are strictly for profit (Village Thrift, Unique Thrift). In some cases, the best values can require a trek to otherwise unexplored outskirts of the city. One thing that all of Chicago's thrift chains have in common is row after jam-packed, narrow, filthy, cluttered row of out-of-fashion dreck, with a secret treasure or two hidden within. Here are some of the more convenient locations for your thrifty pleasure.

Unique Thrift
Uptown: 4445 N. Sheridan Rd., 773/275-8623
Avondale: 3748 N. Elston Ave., 773/279-0850
Thrifty hint: Check out half-priced Mondays!

The Ark
Wicker Park: 1302 N. Milwaukee Ave., 773/862-5011
West Lakeview: 3345 N. Lincoln Ave., 773/248-1117
Thrifty hint: More furniture and housewares than most.

Salvation Army
Wicker Park: 1515 N. Milwaukee Ave., 773/489-5194
Bucktown: 2270 N. Clybourn Ave., 773/477-1300
Andersonville: 5556 N. Clark St., 773/728-8079
Thrifty hint: Andersonville location has better-than-average selection of women's clothes.

Village Discount Outlet
1-866-Like-VDO
www.vdoil.com
Andersonville: 4898 N. Clark St.
Logan Square: 2032 N. Milwaukee Ave.
Roscoe Village: 2043 W. Roscoe St.
Albany Park: 3301 W. Lawrence Ave.
Thrifty hint: After shopping at the Albany Park location, have lunch at one of the many great, inexpensive Middle Eastern restaurants lining Kedzie Avenue.

BROWN ELEPHANT

Boystown: 3651 N. Halsted St., 773/549-5943

Andersonville: 5404 N. Clark St., 773/271-9382

Wicker Park: 1459 N. Milwaukee Ave., 773/252-8801

When Howard Brown Health Center (HBHC) established the first Brown Elephant resale store in 1982, it was the only retail shop in the country with the specific goal to raise money for HIV/AIDS research and treatment. Since the opening of the Boystown shop on North Halsted, the Elephants have expanded to new stores in Andersonville and Wicker Park—basically all the city's gayest hoods.

The selection consists of furniture (usually of the tattered variety—but at least the prices are low), clothes, books and music, lots of knickknacks, and such. In a nutshell, it's the same selection you'd find at the Salvation Army or Village Thrift, with a slightly gayer feel. Because HBHC is a gay health center, more than the usual share of donors are of the homosexual variety. This is apparent in the book and music selections—think Katherine V. Forrest and RuPaul—and in more subtle ways throughout the store. A recent perusal of the "art" offerings uncovered a framed photo from the original Stonewall site, along with a large Victorian-era reproduction portrait of a young woman in a vintage oval frame that now adorns the sacred space above Kathie's bed. At $25 it was an absolute steal.

Household Decoration and Gifts

Places where you can pick up that certain special vase to die for.

Equinox 🏠
Boystown: 3401 N. Broadway St., 773/281-9150
Hostess gifts, vases, lamps, cards, campy books, and fancy holiday ornaments—all are jammed onto shelves, giving us a bull-in-a-china-shop complex. Gay-hued merchandise, reasonably priced.

Porte Rouge
Wicker Park: 1911 W. Division St., 773/269-2800

Visit France in Wicker Park with this great housewares store specializing in all things Français. Tabletop items, cookware, coffee, tea, soaps, antiques—one-stop gift shopping for the homophile Francophile in your life. Or for Kathie.

Surrender
Andersonville: 5225 N. Clark St., 773/784-4455

Here you'll find lots of last-minute hostess gifty stuff, including fancy toiletries, scented candles, glassware and housewares, and some pet items. The selection of upscale goods seems to be based on the caprice of the store's buyers.

Cards and Paper Goods

These are the places to shop for your gay cards and gift wrap!

Paper Trail
Andersonville: 5309 N. Clark St., 773/275-2191

This shop features a great selection of blank and humorous cards, along with stationery, scented candles, and cute gift items, many with a decidedly gay bent (for example, gay car air freshener). It is the source for sushi-decorated bandages. And Paper Trail has the best window displays on this stretch of Clark Street in Andersonville.

He Who Eats Mud 🏳️‍🌈
Boystown: 3247 N. Broadway St., 773/525-0616

This campy card and gift shop has remained steadfastly un-air-conditioned for many a year, and we hate to tell the owner, but leaving the door open on a humid August afternoon is not helping. That gripe aside, this is the place to pick up that souvenir T-shirt proclaiming yourself a "fuck buddy kind of guy" or that you "heart" lesbians. There are a few serious and tasteful greeting cards and many more that are humorous and less tasteful. The shop also has really cool wrapping paper, and if you happen to be here the day after Christmas, go in and stock up on super fancy holiday wrap for the next year—a steal at half-price.

Collectibles, Kitsch, Toys, and Ephemera

And now for some irresistible goodies for the queer kid in all of us.

Uncle Fun 🎬
Roscoe Village: 1338 W. Belmont Ave., 773/477-8223
www.unclefunchicago.com

Ted Frankel (a.k.a. Uncle Fun) loves the things he stocks in his hard-to-describe shop. The fun and love includes bobble-headed dolls, toys of all sorts (especially old-fashioned non-electronic kinds), plastic collectible figurines from long-gone television shows (think Fonz dolls) and Burger King kid meal giveaways, snow globes, little nuns, army men, dinosaurs. . . . The list is endless. A wealth of ephemera, junk, and delights are tucked away in the shop. Open the drawer of a cabinet and you might find it full of plastic ants or rubber balls painted to look like eyes. You might find bride and groom cake toppers or cartoon flip books. Uncle Fun's love of the silly is infectious, and we defy you to remain here five minutes without getting in the mood to buy a knickknack—an Elvis clock, perhaps, or Marilyn Monroe dish towels, or a wind-up Godzilla—for someone on your gift list. Robert has been known to do almost *all* his Christmas shopping here in one fell swoop. We also recommend it for a hard-to-buy-for birthday guy or gal—no one *needs* Martian salt and pepper shakers, but who can resist them? Oh, and Ted is family, too, just so you know. The Web site is cheery as well.

Gay Mart 🎬
Boystown: 3459 N. Halsted St., 773/929-4272

Forget blue-light specials. At Gay Mart you can find everything you need to . . . Okay, maybe you don't *need* anything at this goofy gift store and emporium of all things gay. After all, whose shopping list reads: milk, toilet bowl cleaner, Tom of Finland doll, eggs? In addition to kitschy dolls and toys, Gay Mart is also one-stop shopping for rainbow-covered everything—stickers, feather boas, rainbow steering wheel covers, and the ubiquitous flag, of course. Be glad this store exists. Where else can you pick up the board game Gayopoly, a dancing hula clock, Pride Suds soap, a Wonder Woman cookie jar, and a "weenie baby" (a cute and cuddly teddy bear with a disturbingly enormous endowment) all in one place?

Music

Following are some of our favorite local record and CD emporiums.

Borderline Music 🎬
Boystown: 3333 N. Broadway St., 773/975-9533
www.borderlinemusic.com

A music store named after a Madonna song? How gay is *that*? Pretty darn gay, as it turns out. Blond cutie proprietor Scott first laid his blue eyes on the Material Girl in concert in 1987 after scoring tenth-row seats to her "Who's That Girl" tour. And he met her in person in 1997 while he was living in L.A. and they were both at "a very unknown Kabbalah meeting, months before it hit the news and she had to stop attending classes." But Scott's abiding Madonna love really goes back to 1984: "I remember being at my aunt's house watching a new music channel, MTV, and seeing the video for 'Borderline' as it *premiered*. It was definitely love at first sight—I went out and bought the cassette and vinyl the next day! Hence the record store's name." Scott's store, while a shrine to Madonna, does not skimp on the other gay faves. The walls are covered with signed posters from the likes of Cher,

♫ *Borderline Music.*
~Photo by Robert McDonald

Britney, Kylie, Bette, and other one-name identifiable divas, and the store features both domestic and hard-to-find imports of dance, techno, and pop music, as well as DVDs. There are great finds in the used section, and Scott and his staff are happy to recommend their favorite new arrivals. Some of Scott's favorite local DJs include Greg Drescher and Ralphi Rosario (look for them at **Hydrate**), as well as house music godfather Frankie Knuckles. Outside the realm of dance music, he recommends listening to Chicago-based performer Amy Armstrong: "An amazing voice and extremely funny too. You will want to see her again and again. We are proud to carry her CD." (We second this thought and direct you to www.amythediva.com for Ms. Armstrong's busy schedule.) In addition, Scott raves about the trippy-soul stylings of the group P-1 (www.p-1music.com), calling them "Everything but the Girl Meets Dee-lite." Scott also told us we had to mention the downtown drag club **Baton**: "This is a must for any visitor," and if you check out our theater section, you'll see that we did mention it. We'd like to add that Borderline Music is a must for a gay dance music fan. A large-screen TV plays the hottest music videos while you shop, and to top it off, as Scott says, "what would a dance record store be without a disco ball?"

Gramaphone Records
Boystown: 2843 N. Clark St., 773/472-3683

Gramaphone is Chicago's DJ headquarters and the number one source for house, jungle, techno, trance, acid jazz, or whatever other category of dance music or electronica that floats your boat. The vinyl's so fresh it's still sizzling. Gay DJ Doug Brandt (check out his schedule at www.djdougbrandt.com) says he swears by this place: "*Always* support the local stores first! And *pay* for your downloaded music from respectable sources."

Reckless Records
Boystown: 3161 N. Broadway St., 773/404-5080
Wicker Park: 1532 N. Milwaukee Ave., 773/235-3727

As the name suggests, you can still find vinyl, both new and used, at the Chicago branches of this London-based record store. They even carry 45s, which is great for small bands hankering for nostalgia and a great way for listeners to discover upstart talent. Of course, they have used and new CDs and DVDs and even some cassettes and VHS videos. Reckless also offers listening stations featuring artists you may not have heard of but the staff thinks you should. They pepper their displays with staff-typed recommendations, which will often entice you to purchase one or two more CDs than you'd set out for. Robert buys most of his music here—he often is able to find review copies that the reviewers sold to the store, thus getting the current CD he was after at a third of the usual cost. Reckless also carries zines, hosts a bunch of interesting in-store performances, and basically represents everything worthwhile about independent music stores. Staff members aren't as unapproachable as they may seem—crack that tousle-headed indie band ennui and you'll find they are passionate about music and friendly to boot.

Tower Records
Loop: 214 S. Wabash Ave., 312/663-0660
Lincoln Park: 2301 N. Clark St., 773/477-5994

We are reticent to steer you to big chain stores that you can find in any city in the U.S. Nonetheless, if you can't find the CD or hip imported magazine that you're looking for at Tower, it's probably not all that great anyway.

Books

We have a special affinity for Chicago's awesome bookstore and literary scene. There are enough quirky independent shops to satisfy any interest (many stores have comprehensive selections of gay literature), as well as several conveniently located chains for an emergency lit fix.

Unabridged Bookstore
Boystown: 3251 N. Broadway St., 773/883-9119

Well, let's just say up front that we have both been employed here. But that should not make you take what we say about Unabridged with a grain of salt because, no lie, it carries the best selection of gay books and magazines in the city.

(See **Women & Children First** for the best selection of lesbian titles.) Owner Ed Devereux has been in business for more than 25 years, and his store vision remains much the same as it did when he began: a comfortable, casual general bookstore where the gay titles are as important as anything else in the store. The small staff all work full-time, and they tend to stick around—one guy has been here for 20 years—so they know the stock and, best of all, they actually read. Index cards with handwritten staff recommendations are a hallmark of the store, and many customers swear by them. The gay section includes areas devoted to fiction, mystery, erotica, sex, gay photography, travel, transgender issues, religion, HIV, and lesbian fiction and nonfiction, among others, while the store also has a *great* general travel section. Other strengths include general fiction, home design, calendars, history, current events, and film. The store boasts an award-winning children's section. As a matter of fact, although known as a "gay" bookstore, Unabridged sells at least as many kids books per week as they do copies of *Mandate* or *Inches*. Oh yeah—magazines. All the usual suspects, like *People* and the *New Yorker*, are here, as are a host of home design periodicals and, yes indeed, those male nude pictorials, from *Playgirl* to *Bound and Gagged*. Unabridged carries the gay

Browsing at Unabridged Books.
~Photo by Robert McDonald

weeklies from Washington, D.C., San Francisco, and New York, as well as monthly gay mags, both special interest titles and Australian and Brit counterparts to *Out* and the *Advocate*. The store hosts a free monthly book discussion group on the third Tuesday of the month. Anyone who wants to chat about literature is welcome. The group tends to be 90 percent gay men, but a few women often join the talk, and there are always new folks showing up, so you won't be the only fresh meat, er, new face, we meant to say. Unabridged also offers a free story hour for kids ages two to four on Tuesday mornings at the elementary school across the street. Right by the front door you can pick up all the free gay Chicago papers, load up on flyers and pamphlets from gay organizations, and check out the bulletin board for plays, concerts, and community events. And about that staff . . . You will not find a friendlier, more helpful, and (no need for false modesty here) *sexier* group of folks anywhere.

Women & Children First 🏳️

Andersonville: 5233 N. Clark St., 773/769-9299
www.womenandchildrenfirst.com

Women & Children First may be the nation's largest feminist bookstore. Besides offering lesbian and feminist books, they have a great children's book section, a large section of women's music (everything from old-school womyn's music to Ani DiFranco to world music and then some), and DVD and video rentals (*Desert Hearts* to *The L Word*). Moreover, they carry jewelry, posters, and cards. Is it obvious that we love this store? Maintaining an active program schedule, Women & Children First has hosted everyone who is anyone in feminist thought, including Adrienne Rich, Robin Morgan, Margaret Atwood, Alice Walker, Hillary Rodham Clinton . . . the list goes on. Check out their Web site for the latest schedule (you can also order books, videos, and music there). The store—with its giant bulletin board that literally overflows with postings for apartments for rent, healing circles, and mortgage refinance offers, as well as a Michigan Womyn's Music Festival ride-share board—functions as a lesbian and feminist community center and information clearinghouse. Owners Ann Christophersen and Linda Bubon are truly pillars of Chicago's women's community. In a time when feminist bookstores are becoming a dying breed, in 2004 Women & Children First celebrated a quarter-century of existence. Kathie worked here during five very formative years of her young adulthood. Based on that experience, she would like to add that Women & Children First is a *great* place to cruise and meet chicks.

Quimby's

Wicker Park: 1854 W. North Ave., 773/342-0910

Quimby's used to be called "Quimby's Queer Store," but the queer store moniker fell by the wayside. Actually, Quimby's was never a queer store in terms of the "We're here, we're queer, get used to it" attitude but rather in the "My, isn't that unusual?" usage of the word. In any case, Quimby's specializes in alternative and counterculture books, zines, and comics. You can find edgy small press and dark-minded maestros here—your William Burroughs, John Fante, and R. Crumb, Lydia Lunch, Kathy Acker, and Eileen Myles—along with a handful of those "We're here, we're queer" titles.

Myopic Books

Wicker Park: 1564 N. Milwaukee Ave., 773/862-4882

Everything a used bookstore should be. Stacks of books. Labyrinthine aisles. Tottering shelves. A lazy shop cat. Stern admonishments: No cell phones! Check your bags! Put books back where you got them—or else we'll raise the price! Coffee is for sale from behind the counter. And a small gay studies section is located on the second floor, next to a larger cookbook section.

Barbara's Bookstore
UIC: 1218 S. Halsted St., 312/413-2665
Oak Park: 1100 Lake St., Oak Park, 708/848-9140
www.barbarasbookstore.com
This Chicago-based independent chain has been around for more than 40 years! The Oak Park branch (yes, it's in the suburbs) is the most gay-adoring.

Barnes & Noble
Boystown: 659 W. Diversey Pkwy., 773/871-9004

Borders
Boystown: 2817 N. Clark St., 773/935-3909
The Boystown branches of these monolith chain stores have demonstrated their marketing savvy by featuring prominent selections of gay titles and magazines.

Seminary Co-op Bookstore
Hyde Park: 5757 S. University Ave., 773/752-4381, 800/777-1456
www.semcoop.com
If you are an academic in the humanities, or merely a talented amateur, this is your bookstore. Often cited as the best academic bookstore in the country, the co-op is tucked away in the basement of gothic Chicago Theological Seminary, just across from the main campus of the University of Chicago. Don't let the name scare you off. While the bookstore does indeed possess a comprehensive religion section, its name derives from its location only. If you can sniff out any theological leanings here, they are decidedly to the left. The underground labyrinth of 100,000 university press and mainstream titles makes for a compulsively browsable, if slightly claustrophobic, experience. Strengths here include fiction, poetry, anthropology, sociology, economics, history, and religion, and the co-op also carries fine sections in queer and gender studies. If you are looking for books in these fields, and the titles are from a small or an academic press, here's the store in the city most likely to have them. As the name indicates, this is a co-operative. For $30 you can buy three shares and become a lifetime member, entitling you to a 10 percent discount on all purchases. The Co-op has another Hyde Park location, **57th Street Books** (1301 E. 57th St., 773/684-1300), with more general interest titles and a children's section, and also, just north of downtown, a small, beautifully appointed bookshop (with a great card and blank book selection) nestled inside the **Newberry Library** (60 W. Walton St., 312/255-3520). Seminary Co-op sponsors an active free lecture and reading series, leaning toward the academic and specialized. Check out their Web site for a schedule. Queer theorists and gender studies scholars are not uncommon on the docket.

Afrocentric Bookstore
Loop: 333 S. State St., 312/939-1956
This bookstore features books and special events documenting and celebrating African-American life.

Transitions Bookplace
Near Northwest: 1000 W. North Ave., 312/951-7323
www.transitionsbookplace.com

Transitions started life as a store specializing in 12-step and recovery titles, and while that's still one of their strengths, they have expanded their mission to include all areas of spirituality and metaphysics. Books are the main focus, but the store also stocks CDs, DVDs, magazines, jewelry, and gift items. Their ongoing series of author events and workshops is perhaps the busiest in the city. While Transitions does not have a lot of queer-specific programming, the recovery and alternative spirituality community tends to be both accepting and embracing, so don't let shyness prevent you from learning about positive energy flow, tarot, personal improvement, spiritual guidance, Buddhism, angels, the power of now, the meaning of dreams, and a lot more.

International Magazines and Newspapers

For those international travelers who want to keep up with the local news . . .

Europa Books
Old Town/River North: 832 N. State St., 312/335-9677

Here you'll find a good selection of books, magazines, and newspapers from France, Germany, Italy, and Spain.

Tower Records
Lincoln Park: 2301 N. Clark St., 773/477-5994

See listing under record stores (p. 86).

New Age and Wiccan Shops

For radical faeries and other witchy queers . . .

Alchemy Arts
Andersonville: 1203 W. Bryn Mawr Ave., 800/WITCHES

Come here for everything you need for do-it-yourself spell casting: oils, herbs, roots, cauldrons, and chalices. Alchemy Arts also carries books on Wicca and the Craft.

Two Doors South
Lakeview: 3230 N. Clark St., 773/404-7072

This trippy-hippie new age shop specializes in beads, candles, runes, pewter statues of dragons, crystals, incense up the wazoo (ouch! not literally, we hope!), sarongs, and toe rings.

Stuff to Eat and Drink

These carryout food and wine shops are good for gifts, picnics, and spontaneous meals and on-the-spot snacks.

Pastoral
Boystown: 2945 N. Broadway St., 773/472-4781

This gay-owned gourmet take-out shop, with a knowledgeable and friendly staff, carries a tasty selection of cheese, olives, charcuterie, and wine. They also offer tasty prepared sandwiches and picnics to go.

Fox & Obel
Streeterville/Mag Mile: 401 E. Illinois St., 312/410-7301

This upscale gourmet grocery is pricey, but a food snob (like Kathie) will have a field day strolling through the deli aisles.

Whole Foods
West Lakeview: 3300 N. Ashland Ave., 773/244-4200
Near Northwest: 1000 W. North Ave., 312/587-0648
River North: 30 W. Huron St., 312/932-9600

Everyone's favorite earth-friendly crunchy food corporation offers lots of veggie and vegan options with a good deli perfect for packing a picnic.

Kafka Wines
Boystown: 3325 N. Halsted St., 773/975-9463
www.kafkawine.com

No, it's not a shop run by a huge cockroach. Someone else will have to open that. In fact, this bright corner shop is owned by two pleasant gay guys. You'll find a selection of wines from around the world, chosen for taste and affordability—most of the bottles go for under $15. Robert was directed the other day to a white Côtes du Rhône he's been extremely happy with. Luckily for him, the guys here can track one's purchases, so next time Robert walks in the door, there's no fumbling for, now, what was the name of that vineyard? The computer will cough up the answer. The Kafka boys also stock bubbly and some select beers and liqueurs. Plus they have a snazzy Web site and a monthly series of around-the-world wine tastings to boot!

Windy City Sweets
Boystown: 3308 N. Broadway St., 773/477-6100

Our favorite local fudge packers! What we're referring to, of course, is the fact that Windy City Sweets makes their own tasty, ultrarich fudge right on the premises. What were *you* thinking? Wall-to-wall candy, sweets, and treats. In the summertime, Windy City Sweets does a brisk business in ice cream. Their good selection of low-fat and fat-free options appeals to Boystown gym queens.

In Fine Spirits
Andersonville: 5418 N. Clark St., 773/506-9463
www.infinespirits.com

We've recently discovered this immaculate, spiffy little wine shop, and we're pleased to report that the homo-friendly, straight owners are knowledgeable about their wines and happy to make recommendations. Best of all, their prices are wonderfully low. Bottles are arranged by type and then price, making it easy to pick out a bottle for under $10 or $20. Their classy packaging means you can go directly from here to the party without needing to stop for a fancy wine bag. They offer an eclectic liquor selection and a modest but hand-picked array of specialty beers and microbrews. Every other Saturday afternoon they host a free wine tasting—a surefire way to give luster to your Andersonville excursion.

Wikstrom's
Andersonville: 5247 N. Clark St., 773/275-6100

This Swedish deli is a cornerstone of the Andersonville neighborhood. They make tasty sandwiches to go, and on Fridays they feature fantastic fried fish. Among the imported items you can find here are salmon in a tube and an array of sweets that include licorice pipes and (of course) Swedish fish.

Middle Eastern Bakery
Andersonville: 1512 W. Foster Ave., 773/561-2224

Far more than just a bakery, this shop carries a variety of inexpensive stuffed pies, such as spinach, eggplant, mushroom, and chicken. Also great hummus (try the spicy) and baba ghanoush are made on the premises. Homemade pita bread hits the shelves still piping hot. Round off your Middle Eastern feast with some imported kalamata olives and feta cheese.

Shopping for Grown-Ups

Here's where to find those souvenirs you won't want to show Aunt Doris.

ADULT TOYS
Because you're never too old to play . . .

Pleasure Chest
Boystown: 3155 N. Broadway St., 773/525-7151

The Pleasure Chest is the granddaddy of Chicago sex toy stores. Along with the usual novelty gifts, they carry all the sexy basics—vibes, dildos, and lube, as well as leather slings and harnesses. You can also buy "incense burners" (a.k.a. weed pipes) and rolling papers here.

Cupid's Treasure
Boystown: 3519 N. Halsted St.
773/348-3884

Along with penis enlargers, dildos, butt plugs, and lube, Cupid's carries T-shirts, stickers, and gag gifts. On a recent visit, Kathie noted a T-shirt proclaiming, "I slept with Marcia Brady," a penis tiara, a pink pocket rocket ("It was cute!"), two racks of plus-sized sexy lingerie, and an assortment of pasties. Now, what's in your shopping cart?

Doggy style.
~Photo by Caldwell Linker

Batteries Not Included
Boystown: 3420 N. Halsted St., 773/935-9900

While they still carry a small number of sex toys, Batteries Not Included seems to have carved out a niche for itself as the bachelorette party headquarters. Lots of gag gifts for the soon-to-be betrothed.

Early to Bed
Andersonville: 5232 N. Sheridan Rd., 773/271-1219
www.early2bed.com

Early to Bed describes itself as "woman oriented, boy-friendly." This feminist-minded sex toy store also functions as a sex-positive community center, hosting regular sex workshops and other events. Signs near the impressive vibrator selection coax shoppers to "pick up and turn on" all the toys, and the staff is happy to direct horny earth-huggers to their vegan-friendly products. They also carry "packing dildos" (Mr. Softees) for the tranny boy and drag king set. Kathie gives Early to Bed a double thumbs-up and says, "Girls, this shop is definitely worth going out of your way for!"

Tulip
Andersonville: 1480 W. Berwyn Ave., 773/275-6110

This small, tasteful store just off of the Clark Street drag feels like an art gallery of naughty fun. Who knew dildos and vibes were so colorful and sculptural? Tulip produces a line of body products: body oil, body butter, body milk, body honey . . . all you need is body flour and body eggs, and you have a body cake. Like Early to Bed, Tulip is refreshingly free of gag gifts.

FETISH WEAR

So you can look the part . . .

Leather

Chicago hosts a decent selection of leather community–oriented, gay-friendly leather shops. The following are oriented more toward males than females, though of the lot, Leather Sport probably has the most gear for gals.

Leather Sport
Boystown: 3503 N. Halsted St., 773/868-0914
Leather wear for her or him, as well as toys, videos, cum towels . . . You know, the essentials.

Caliber Leathers
Rogers Park: 1614 W. Devon Ave., 773/262-2838
This leather shop, located right down the street from the **Leather Archives and Museum**, is very in tune with the gay male leather community.

Eagle Leathers
Andersonville: 5005 N. Clark St., 773/728-7228
www.eagleleatherschicago.com
Affiliated with (and next door to) the Chicago Eagle leather bar, Eagle Leathers also offers tattooing and piercing services (see p. 140).

Mephisto Leathers
Boystown: 3922 N. Broadway St., 773/549-0900
Rogers Park: 6410 N. Clark St., 773/262-9938
Another leather fetish shop closely affiliated with Chicago's gay leather community.

Early to Bed.
~Photo by Caldwell Linker

Other Fetish Merchandise

Haberdashery, shoes, lingerie, and such.

Black Market Chicago
River West: 1105 W. Chicago Ave., 312/421-9690
"Chicago's fetish emporium since 1995" offers one-stop shopping for canes, crops, whips, and floggers.

Tabou Taboo
Lakeview: 854 W. Belmont Ave., 773/723-3739
This sexy lingerie shop carries lots of kinky femme costumes.

Alcala's Western Wear
Ukrainian Village: 1733 W. Chicago Ave., 312/226-0152
www.alcalas.com
Hey, cowboy! Alcala's shelves boast 5,000 cowboy hats and 10,000 styles of boots, along with belt buckles, clothes, bolo ties—basically everything an urban cowboy needs. There's free boot cleaning for the life of your boots when you buy them here. You can also get free hat shaping and fitting for all of their cowboy hats.

Skyscraper Heels
Roscoe Village: 2202 W. Belmont Ave., 773/477-8495
www.skyscraperheels.com
Skyscraper Heels specializes in, you guessed it, sky-high heels. This shop, which is very trans-friendly but open to anyone who wants to walk tall, features footwear—including ankle-, knee-, and thigh-high boots—in sizes 5 to 17 with heels ranging from two to eight inches in height. They also carry a line of pricey but sublime English corsets.

Tattoos and Body Piercing

Robert doesn't have any tattoos, but he keeps threatening to get one. Kathie has two, but the tattoo artist who did her first one has since retired, and she got her second one in San Francisco. Therefore, we don't have any personal recommendations regarding where to get inked in Chicago. All the same, pretty much every tattoo artist in the world is gay-friendly. It comes with the territory. After all, historically, it's always been the subversive types who have gotten tattoos, right? Tattoo artistry was built up from the margins of society to the place it now holds in the mainstream, and tattoo artists are well aware of that.

The following tattoo parlors are well regarded by the locals. Each one, in response to a telephone inquiry, also pronounced themselves "gay-friendly." All of the following venues also have someone on-site who does body piercing.

Eagle Tattoo
Andersonville: 5005 N. Clark St., 773/728-7228
This is the only tattoo parlor in the city that is 100 percent gay owned and operated. The person on the phone said that they don't inquire as to the sexual orientations of their tattoo artists and piercers, but that probably about 99 percent of their business is gay.

Tattoo Factory
Uptown: 4408 N. Broadway St., 773/989-4077
At the time of this writing, Tattoo Factory had two openly gay artists on staff: a dude named Sol and a chick named Jay. Possibly it is the other way around.

Jade Dragon
Far Western Boondocks: 5331 W. Belmont Ave., 773/736-6960
Jade Dragon definitely goes out of its way to market to the gay and lesbian community. Maybe you'll want to go out of your way to be inked by one of their many artists!

Here are some other shops with fewer gay connections but that claim to be gay-friendly, at least, and are conveniently located.

Chicago Tattooing and Piercing Co. Inc.
Lakeview: 1017 W. Belmont Ave., 773/528-6969, www.chicagotattoo.com

Tatu Tattoo
Wicker Park: 1754 W. North Ave., 773/772-8288

Tomato Tattoo
Ukrainian Village: 1855 W. Chicago Ave., 312/226-6660

Shopping with a Naked Guy
As we have noted, we're not the most enthusiastic shoppers in the world, so we figured we'd talk to some folks who do indeed enjoy doing the deed. And who better to discuss an appreciation of shopping, especially clothes shopping, than a \person who spends a substantial part of his professional life completely nude? Actor and singer John Cardone stripped down and sang his heart out in the popular long-running show *Naked Boys Singing* at the Bailiwick Repertory Theatre every Friday and Saturday night for more than three years. (Check out Chapter 14, on Chicago theater, for more information on Bailiwick, or go to their Web site, www.bailiwick.org.)

We figured we'd start with the basics by asking John if, when clothed, he is a boxers guy or a briefs dude, but it turns out he prefers to go commando. "I swear I'm clean!" he adds. When he does don undies? "I like 2xist and Jockey shorts. I haven't been a boxer short guy since high school, and being the oldest Naked Boy in the cast, that was in the late '70s." Let's just pause for a moment to give kudos to Bailiwick for including some sexy over-30 gents in the gratuitous nudity.

When John shops for clothes, he admits to a **"Gap** addiction." (Someone write to us and let us know where and when the 12-step program meets.) But he adds, "When I'm feeling more grown up I like **His Stuff** on Clark in Andersonville, when I'm feeling rich I love **Barney's** on Oak Street, when I'm feeling cheap and European I like **H&M** downtown." And who at some point in their life does not feel cheap and European or want to feel a cheap European? For thrift stores, John emphasizes, "I *love* **Beatnix** on Halsted in Boystown. They have the coolest stuff."

We asked John to imagine that a fairy waved a magic wand (now, now—minds out of the gutter) and gave him a $5,000 line of credit at a downtown Chicago store, the only catch being that he had to spend all the money on clothes, and all at one place. "First of all," he wisely said, "I would want Clinton Kelly and Stacy London from TLC's *What Not to Wear* to accompany that $5,000 line of credit. I would love to have a second opinion from some hip New York make-over divas! But if I were left on my own, I would probably go to **Barney's** or **Armani's** on Oak and get something tailor-made for my body and really nice that would be a classic and not go out of style, like a fine suit and some great expensive shoes. Could I take a $1,000 and go to **Dolce & Gabbana's** just for fun?" Sure, John, our fairies honor all reasonable requests.

Our fashion consultant, John Cardone, shows off his Pride Parade style.
~Photo courtesy of John Cardone

As far as body lotions, scrubs, and skin-care products go, John confesses, "I order most of the fancy stuff online because some great stuff is made in California, but for my shaving, sunblock, facial scrub, and under-eye cream needs, Target works out just fine." And for watches, baubles, and accessories, he says, "I've found great Kenneth Cole watches at **Universal Gear** on Broadway. **Beatnix** has great faux sunglasses, and **Two Doors South** has some great chokers, necklaces, and ankle bracelets."

Since John was born and raised in Los Angeles, we wondered if he felt that Midwestern men have a fashion sense or style distinct from that found on the coasts. "Well," said John, "are we talking Midwest *gay* men or Midwest men in general? Midwest gay men with any vanity or style keep their eyes open and usually stay with the trends. Midwest men in general I see as a strictly khaki and polo shirt crowd. Now in Los Angeles, men, women, and dogs all dress like they are celebrities whether they are or not. I think the constant 70 degree weather, and the fact that there are so many people desperate to just be noticed, bumps up the fashion IQ. I find it refreshing that in the Midwest people seem to judge you more on your self rather than who you are wearing." At this Kathie and Robert glanced at their clothing choices for the day and breathed a sigh of relief—they weren't wearing anybody.

"I personally *love* fashion," says John. "I guess you could say that you can take the boy out of L.A., but not L.A. out of the boy! I love to shop, and if you look carefully, Chicago has some great stores and great finds. I especially love to hit Marshalls or T.J. Maxx and spend hours finding discarded, marked-down, last-season gems. I've found some great Steve Madden shoes, some amazing Abercrombie and Fitch jeans, some triple five/Calvin Klein dress shirts, a $1,500 Nicole Miller classic three-button gray pinstripe suit for $500, and other great steals. I think you really have to be committed to have a nice wardrobe, and if you are on a budget, then you have to be creative and patient." When the fairies do wave those magic wands for us, John, we'll be as patient as all get-out—and we'll be calling to let you lead our shopping spree. ✦

Part 3

I Love the Nightlife:
The Best of Queer Chicago After Dark

O kay, you are in town for a conference, you are visiting that crazy Aunt Doris, you just moved here from small-town South Dakota (or big-town elsewhere), you have only one evening, or you have the rest of your life—whatever your situation, at some point the responsibilities and pleasures of the day will be done, and you'll want to explore the smorgasbord that is Chicago after dark. We are tickled pink to have assembled our primo picks for the best of Chicago's food, drink, entertainment, and after-hours options, from the well-known hot spots to the (shhhh—don't spread it around) unspoiled nooks and undiscovered dark joys. Please note: Many "nocturnal" activities may also be accomplished in the full light of day.

Speaking of smorgasbords, you have to eat, right? If you are more interested in dining in a room where the staff, the décor, the patrons, the very air itself is gayer than a Broadway chorus boy's delighted exhalation, we have some splendid options for you. We also have highlighted vegetarian eateries and let you in on our fave places in and near the gay neighborhoods. We end our recommendations with some fine dining choices and a plea to take us with you when you go. (Hey, we work in the arts—it's not caviar and lobster every night.)

Chicago has more drinking establishments than you can shake an empty beer bottle at: neighborhood dives, scenester salons, bars where you can take Aunt Doris for a fruity cabernet (or a fruity cabaret), and clubs where Aunt Doris would faint dead away. The Halsted strip alone has multiple options in terms of climate, clientele, and all-around vibe. With several fluid ounces of modesty, we admit to more than a passing

~Photo by Jon Peterson

knowledge of the city's watering holes, and we promise to give you the true lowdown on everything from high-energy danceterias to low-key, pint-of-ale pubs.

Beyond the bars, we offer up splendid choices from Chicago's happening nighttime, with the best in theater, live music, movies, and more, always focusing first on the queer stuff, because hey, that's our way.

Finally, we come (pun intended) to the realm of sex. Call us crazy, but humans, we have found, may want to know where they can go in a city to find possibilities for getting themselves a little sumthin' sumthin'. Or to find someone special—we're not *that* cynical. From bathhouses to late-night bars, from online resources to specific locations where boys go to meet boys and girls go to meet girls, we offer a heated array of chase, mate, and date potentialities.

LOOKING GOOD ENOUGH TO EAT: DINING OUT IN CHICAGO

Ah, food, glorious food! Eating out is one of the great pleasures in life—to us, at least—and Chicago is a town with the best of everything, from hotdog stands to fine dining. As Gertrude Stein wrote regarding her visit to the city in the 1930s, "On the whole we did eat well, some places much better than others but on the whole we did eat well and well."

We have to rein ourselves in, because we'd like to tell you about every eating well experience we've ever had here. Maybe in the next book. In this one, we'll offer up options for the vegetarians among you, give you a heads-up on the way-gay places, present our greatest hits list of personal dining recommendations (the places we take our friends and families), and deliver our wish list of places we wish we could afford to go to more often. (Feeling generous? Have a hefty expense account? When in town, just let us know!) We'll end with that not-to-be-overlooked meal, *brunch*, and tell you where we like to go to get it. We have, for the most part, stuck to the tried and true and forgone the trendy. Today's hot new dining spot can become yesterday's tired zone of blah with alarming speed. For the most up-to-date info, the newest of the new chefs, and the hippest of the hip eateries, we suggest looking at a current issue of *Chicago* magazine or *Time Out Chicago*. To find out where the general populace enjoys eating, look at the most current *Zagat Chicago* dining guide or check out the reviews and listings in our beloved free weekly *Chicago Reader* (www.chicagoreader.com). Kathie, in addition to her many other charms and talents, writes restaurant reviews for them.

Vegging Out in Chicago

It used to be that when you asked for vegetarian options in a Chicago restaurant, the waiter would point to the chicken on the menu. These days, thankfully, most restaurants are a little more veggie savvy and serve up at least a pasta dish or two without meat. With stalwarts like the **Chicago Diner** and the **Heartland Café** leading the way, Chicago's vegetarian eateries are finally starting to come into their own, offering a diversity in prices and flavors more on par with the Chicago dining scene in general and, as a result, being looked at as legitimate dining options instead of just some lefty-radical cults (despite the fact that several local veg operations seem to be, in fact, run by lefty-radical cults). For old-school veggie fare, along with the tie-dye and folk music, head up to the

Heartland Café (7000 N. Glenwood Ave., 773/465-8005). The Fartland, oops, the *Heartland* (Kathie giggles with adolescent glee) isn't all veg—they offer buffalo burgers of all things—but they do serve a decent selection of veggie burgers, chili, burritos, and the like, along with a few macro plates. There's also a bar with a good beer selection, plus a nice screened-in patio and a hippie store that sells eco-friendly goods and liberal propaganda.

Right in the thick of the Halsted strip, the **Chicago Diner** (3411 N. Halsted St., 773/935-6696) has been serving up exclusively veggie eats since 1983. The restaurant is smoke free and features a long menu of veggie offerings, including vegan desserts. Robert thinks they do the simple things best—go for the chili with a side of their delicious cornbread.

Earwax (1561 N. Milwaukee Ave., 773/772-4019) is a Wicker Park café and video store that offers veggie grub along with high-quality caffeinated beverages. The bright funky space is a hipster haven in a hipster hood. Food specialties include a homemade black bean burger and Kathie's favorite, the seitan Reuben. Robert loves the sweet potato and black bean quesadilla. Others rave about their breakfast, which is served all day.

Only open for breakfast and lunch, **Victory's Banner** (2100 W. Roscoe St., 773/665-0227) is a vegetarian restaurant run by the soft-spoken, reverent followers of Sri Chinmoy. Sari-clad servers dish out wholesome and impeccably prepared nosh to the throngs—the place is especially busy during weekend brunch time. If it happens to be your birthday, the Banner's special version of the birthday song concludes with the line "We love your soul."

Alice and Friends Vegetarian Café (5812 N. Broadway St., 773/275-8797) serves pan-Asian cuisine with a specialty of meat substitutes (unchicken, unbeef, etc.). While Robert didn't find the unchicken very chickenlike, it was still mighty tasty, and the unbeef was roundly applauded by his vegetarian date. Alice is also influenced by a guru—a motivational video of Supreme Master Ching Hai plays quietly in the background while you dine. One of the supreme master's slogans is, "So be a hero, be a vegetarian!" Robert knows folks who swear by the tasty fare offered here, as well as the generous portions at reasonable prices. Many vegan options are offered. Alcohol is strictly forbidden.

Vegans travel out of their way for the Zen Buddhist–inspired Korean fare at **Amitabul** (6207 N. Milwaukee Ave., 773/774-0276), where

Bright lights, big coffee.
~Photo by Caldwell Linker

everything served is a plant from land or sea, and they use no meat or dairy at all and very little oil.

Any vegetarian knows that many ethnic restaurants not specifically vegetarian nonetheless offer a lot of meat-free choices. Foremost among these are the cuisines of Asia (both east and west) and the Middle East. **Andies**, in the heart of Andersonville (5253 N. Clark St., 773/784-8616), has terrific baba ghanoush and falafel, along with more creative veggie fare, like a lentil and portabella sauté served over rice and a spicy Moroccan eggplant stew. For Thai food, two of our favorites are **Joy's Noodle and Rice**, located in the heart of Boystown (3257 N. Broadway St., 773/327-8330) with their cute gay Thai staff, and the more off-the-queer path **Opart Thai House** (4658 N. Western Ave., 773/989-8517), where the food comes in four degrees of heat: mild, medium, hot, and very hot. Kathie loves spicy food but can only tolerate Opart's medium level of hotness, so be warned! Another worthy Thai option, in close proximity to the lesbian bar Lost & Found, is **Dharma Garden** (3109 W. Irving Park Rd., 773/588-9140), where meat options are limited to fish and seafood.

Even farther off the lavender brick road, Devon Avenue in West Rogers Park is lined with Indian restaurants for more than a city mile surrounding the intersection at Western Avenue. Most Indian restaurants offer a reasonable amount of vegetarian fare. Three in particular on this strip are exclusively vegetarian. These are the northern Indian **Arya Bhavan** (2508 W. Devon Ave., 773/274-5800) and two southern Indian places, **Mysore** (2548 W. Devon Ave., 773/338-8160) and **Udupi Palace** (2543 W. Devon Ave., 773/338-2152). Of the three, the northern Indian offerings at Arya Bhavan will be the most familiar to many diners. For example, they offer saag paneer (spinach with homemade cheese) and lentil *dals*. In general, northern Indian cuisine uses more dairy and is not as spicy as its southern counterpart. Indian buffets are offered in many of the restaurants on Devon. The buffet at Arya Bhavan stands head and shoulders above most—everything is fresh, and the selection always includes some surprises. It's also a good value: $6.99 during lunchtime Monday through Friday and $10 on weekends for all you can eat.

Fans of either Mysore or Udupi Palace like to argue the relative merits of their preferred restaurant over the shortcomings of the other. Their spicy cuisines hail from southern climes. Offerings include *idly* (steamed rice and lentil patties), *uthappam* (Indian-styled pancakes served with beans and veggies), and *dosai* (giant rice crepes served with several varieties of chutney for dipping). Wash any or all of it down with a mango lassi (a sweet yogurt drink that helps you beat the heat). To get to this stretch of Devon if you are not traveling by car, take the Brown Line train to Western, where you can transfer to the #49B North Western bus, which will take you north to Devon (about a mile and a half).

Finally, for a vegetarian splurge, try **Green Zebra** (1460 W. Chicago Ave., 773/243-7100), Shaun McClain's mostly vegetarian (they serve some fish and poultry) trendy and upscale restaurant, or go for the vegetarian tasting menu at

Charlie Trotter's (816 W. Armitage Ave., 773/248-6228) or **Arun's** (4156 N. Kedzie Ave., 773/539-1909), two of Chicago's most acclaimed eating emporiums, where the tab can run you upwards of $100 per person, not counting drinks.

The Boystown Standards

The Lakeview/Boystown area has something for everyone. Whatever cuisine or price range you want is a short walk or cab ride away. Here are some Boystown restaurants where lesbigay clientele are not only accepted, they are expected.

Kit Kat Lounge and Supper Club
3700 N. Halsted St., 773/525-1111
www.kitkatchicago.com

Drag with your dinner? This is the spot. Female impersonators perform in the restaurant while you are dining, and it's possible that your server might be a girl with something extra packed under her skirt. Our friends are divided on this spot: some *love* the camp glam, some find the sight of a drag goddess lip-synching to Marlene Dietrich right next to their table during the appetizer too distracting. It's the gay version of a mariachi band playing tableside. In the summer the Kits boast outdoor seating. We say it's a swank place for a martini at least, if you don't want to commit to a complete dining experience. The menu leans to supper-club fare: steaks, shrimp, and pasta.

Las Mananitas
3523 N. Halsted St., 773/528-2109

It has to be the margaritas that keep the gay crowds coming back here—the margaritas and the central Halsted location—because it sure isn't the food, which is overpriced and unimaginative (basically consisting of all the different ways to dress up rice and beans). But the crowd here is way, way gay. On weekend nights you can expect a brief wait for a table as the boys and girls start off with Mexican fare before heading out to the bars. We don't want to diss the place. We've had fun here, they are used to big groups, service is quick—but let's face it, you won't be remembering the food. And if you have more than one of the powerhouse drinks, you might not remember much of anything. For better and cheaper Mexican fare right in the hood, we'd steer you to **El Mariachi** (3420 N. Broadway St., 773/549-7020). There won't be quite the crowds of queers—in fact, the teeny space can't fit more than 20 or so people of any persuasion—but the place is still entirely gay-friendly.

Joy's Noodle and Rice
3257 N. Broadway St., 773/327-8330

If Thai food is your thing, you'll want to check out Joy's Noodle, which is about the gayest Thai restaurant you will ever see. Always busy because of the budget prices and quick service (by a mostly GLBT staff), this is a Boystown standard. Some locals cop to eating here at least once a week. We wonder how many gay first dates have taken place at Joy's. Too many to count, probably. We find the food always adequate but not amazing. In other words, by all means go here before a movie or to grab a pleasant lunch, but it's not the spot to celebrate a special occasion. For even better Thai food (and no more expensive), we steer folks to the North Side, to **Opart Thai House** (4658 N. Western Ave., 773/989-8517) near Lincoln Square and **Yes Thai** (5211 N. Damen Ave., 773/878-3487) up Andersonville way.

X/O
3441 N. Halsted St., 773/348-9696
www.xochicago.com
    Ed Devereux, the owner of Unabridged Books, lives practically across the street from this new queer hot eatery and dining spot, and he loves it, especially the secluded outdoor seating area, which he calls "the best place to enjoy a cocktail outside in the entire city." When we went, the crowd was leaning to the homo, with a group of power lesbians in Prada and several gay boy dates around us. The atmosphere is Japanese garden meets Frank Lloyd Wright, with simple lines and subdued color. The service was top-notch, the extra-handsome waiter attentive, the wines excellent. The menu is a sort of Asian fusion, with small-plate, tapas-style servings, perfect for sharing. We each ordered two dishes (the rock shrimp salad and the crabcakes were the most memorable) and two glasses of wine. Our bill, with tip, came to about $100. We highly recommend X/O for a date night or small gathering of friends who want to treat themselves to something snazzy.

Arco de Cuchilleros
3445 N. Halsted St., 773/296-6046
    The food is indeed as much of a lure as the location at the way-gay friendly Arco de Cuchilleros, Robert's favorite spot for Spanish tapas dining in the city. It's not as fancy and trendy as many more recently opened small-plate hot spots, but the sangria is good, the margaritas swell, and the tapas menu generally just divine, with the garlic potato salad and the shrimp cooked in oil and garlic among the must-haves. We've both been here on numerous dates and never had a disappointing meal.

Angelina's Ristorante
3561 N. Broadway St., 773/935-5933
www.angelinaristorante.com
    Another good date spot is this Italian eatery. The darkish, candlelit interior lends itself to romance or an intimate conversation between friends. There's outdoor seating here. Avoid it. Chicago has gone outdoor seating *crazy*, and every restaurant and pub these days seems to need streetside tables. Now this is a fine trend, and we are all for dining under the stars. Location is key, however. If, as is the case at Angelina's, your streetside tables are right next to a bus stop, at a busy and unremarkable urban corner, just a bit of slow city traffic means you are dining under the bus exhaust.

Enjoy Angelina's pasta and traditional Italian dishes (Robert fondly recalls a pork loin special) and fine wines in the comfort of the great indoors. Service is casual and super friendly, and the environment—well, it's just *cute*, pipes in Kathie.

Mark's Chop Suey
3343 N. Halsted St., 773/281-9090
Mark's is known more for their takeout and delivery than their dining room. All the better for those who want to dine in at this small cute space located right on the Halsted strip, as there is seldom a wait. Mark's does better-than-average standard Americanized Chinese fare. Their egg rolls are really, really good. Ditto the spicy eggplant and the moo-shu dishes.

Cornelia's Roosterant
748 N. Cornelia Ave., 773/248-8333
www.ilovecornelias.com
Neither of us had been to this Boystown standard before we started researching this guide, and we are happy to have discovered the charms of this quirky hunting-lodge-meets-cabaret-lounge and add it to our favorite places list. There's popular outdoor seating, steps away from Halsted but far enough that the quiet side-street atmosphere is intact. Robert and his friend Sebastian chose to eat inside, and they admired the deer antlers, the movie star photos, and the funky ambience of it all. Sebastian said, "The only things missing are the romantic shimmering candles that wink at you while you dine." Instead of candles, the flirty waiter winked. The food? The pork tenderloin was a tad undercooked to Robert's taste, but Sebastian's halibut was "delicious." And the watermelon gelato they shared for dessert? Perfection! Their bill for a bottle of wine, an appetizer, the entrées, and the gelato came to about $85. Cornelia's has recently added live entertainment. The night Robert was there, chanteuse Kathryn Payne basically read his mind and played every one of his favorite standards, from "I'm Always Chasing Rainbows" to "Dream a Little Dream of Me."

Pingpong
3322 N. Broadway St., 773/281-7575
With Korean-influenced Asian food and a stark white interior (wear black and you'll look good), this *tiny* restaurant often has crowds gathered outside waiting for a table—it quickly became one of *the* places to see and be seen for local Boystown studs. Outdoor seating in the summer doubles the size, but expect a wait. And they don't do reservations. Pingpong is BYOB, but the owners, recognizing the need, opened **Valhalla Wine Shop** (3317 N. Broadway St., 773/296-6800) directly across the street. If the wait is too long, you can try **Joy's Noodle**, just a half block up the street on the other side of Broadway.

Firefly

3335 N. Halsted St., 773/525-2505

The bright orange décor of Firefly is perfect for helping chase away winter blues. The bistro-style menu includes plenty of French favorites, and the full bar and competent wine list make this an appealing place for an aperitif or nightcap even if you don't do the full meal. Robert has had several very satisfying date/dining experiences here.

La Creperie

2845 N. Clark St., 773/528-9050
www.lacreperieusa.com

We hesitate to mention this slightly off-the-Halsted-beaten-path charmer, because we still want to get a table, but if French fare is your thang, you won't want to miss La Creperie. It is one of our favorite dining places *ever*. It's got a dilapidated Euro charm, a reasonably good wine list, an outdoor garden seating area, and an inexpensive menu. Everything's good but not fancy or haute cuisine by any standard. The specialty of the house is a wide selection of basic, well-executed crepe dishes: crepes with cheese, or crepes with coq au vin, or crepes with seafood . . . you get the picture. Save room for the truly exceptional dessert crepes. On Thursday nights a trumpet-and-accordion combo of live music graces the place. Seating a large party is not their strong suit here, but if you are on a date or with a small group of friends, we can't recommend this charming venue enough. Special shout-out to the back outdoor patio for dates in nice weather.

HB: A Hearty Boys Spot

3404 N. Halsted St., 773/661-0299
www.heartyboys.com

The gay owned HB is right in the heart of Boystown, with owners who recently won a chance to have their own show on the Food Network. We may have visited on an off night, but our meals didn't *quite* live up to the lucious descriptions on the menu. We have heard glowing reports from others, however. Local gossips say you have to look like a super model to work here. Even if you don't think the food is all that, the servers provide yummy eye-candy.

Pepper Lounge

3441 N. Sheffield Ave., 773/665-7377
www.pepperlounge.com

A perennial favorite for its late-night kitchen and swanky vibe. The elbow-to-elbow seating arrangements don't exactly make for an intimate setting. Instead diners feel like they are guests at a boozy dinner party—until they get the bill, that is.

Nookies Tree
3334 N. Halsted St., 773/248-9888

This is the third Nookies (one, two, *tree*, get it?), and this branch has been feeding the pre- and postbar crowd on Halsted for as long as the street has been the center of gay Chicago nightlife. The food—typical diner fare: omelets, sandwiches, burgers, and so forth—is served up quickly and with a dash of style. You aren't going to leave here with memories of gastronomic delights, but if you are looking for a nice quick meal, you won't leave disappointed. And you won't leave broke. Open until midnight on weeknights, Nookies is open 24 hours on Friday and Saturday, so you and the hot babe you met at **Roscoe's** or **Chix Mix** can get acquainted over a meal before dining on each other.

Ann Sather
Boystown: 929 W. Belmont Ave., 773/348-2378
Boystown: 3411 N. Broadway St., 773/305-0034 (breakfast, brunch only)
Andersonville: 5207 N. Clark St., 773/271-6677 (breakfast, brunch only)

Ann Sather is owned by openly gay Chicago Alderman Tom Tunney, who bought the flagship restaurant on Belmont (just east of the "L" stop) from the original Ann. Tunney has since opened several cafés. The restaurant and cafés are best known for their Swedish specialties, including pancakes, Swedish meatballs, and the ever-popular cinnamon rolls. Robert's mom calls this place "Ann Slathers," because of the way they slather icing on the rolls.

Melrose Restaurant
3233 N. Broadway St., 773/327-2060

That the Smellrose serves very large portions of blandly average fare at prices kinda high for a diner doesn't deter the throngs of brunchers who come here with their night-before trade for weekend brunch. The restaurant does possess a nice floral deck. The food itself tries its hand at ambitious diner fare, albeit in a rather ill-conceived fashion, in our minds. (For example, the grilled cheese is a double-decker—that is, it's made with three pieces of bread—what's with that?!) They're open 24 hours, and Melrose's bowl of cabbage soup and basket of rolls is a known curative for drunkenness. Once, many years back, as she was staggering home from the **Closet** up the street, Kathie ran into—literally—Liza Minnelli here. No, not some drag queen Liza, the real deal! She was just leaving with her entourage as Kathie was passing by. Go figure.

Stella's Diner
3042 N. Broadway St., 773/472-9040

Everything that the **Melrose** does wrong, Stella's does right. Their diner fare is traditional and well executed with no real pretensions at being high falutin'. And the veteran waitstaff tease and rib the regulars by name.

Andersonville/Uptown Eateries

Just like Boystown, there are not really any dining spots in this neighborhood where queer folks are going to feel at all awkward or unwelcome. And again like Boystown, there are a heck of a lot more options than we have put to paper here. What we do offer are the homo-spots where there are generally more gay diners than you can count even if you use your toes.

Charlie's Ale House
5308 N. Clark St., 773/751-0140
www.charliesalehouse.com
   This crowd-pleasing joint has been serving the masses ever since it opened. Someone in our circle nicknamed it "the gay Bennigan's," for the clientele and fare. While the all-American comfort-food menu—steaks, chicken, meatloaf, mac and cheese—is similar to that national chain, the food is a high notch better and the service is efficient and friendly. Robert nominates this spot as the parent-pleasing place in Andersonville, if your parents are like his, reluctant to try anything outside the realm of the tried and true.

Tomboy
5402 N. Clark St., 773/907-0636
www.tomboyrestaurant.com
   Tomboy has been the perennial date place in Andersonville ever since lesbian restaurateur Jody Andre opened it about ten years ago. Andre has since sold the joint (check out her other ventures: **South** at 5900 N. Broadway St., 773/989-7666, and the **Speakeasy Supperclub** at 1401 W. Devon Ave., 773/338-0600), but the homo-friendly vibe lives on. Better yet, the formerly BYOB place now has a liquor license. The menu still features Tomboy's own spin on classic American supper club meets new American hip cuisine.

Tanoshii
5547 N. Clark St., 773/878-6886
   If you're brave and you love your fish raw, sit at the bar and have Sushi Mike give you the treatment. Tell him you want a Sushi Mike special, and be prepared to be surprised and delighted at the creative array of made-up-on-the-spot sushi and sashimi dishes he will keep putting in front of you until you throw in your napkin and say "unkle-san." Be on the lookout for unusual ingredients such as fruit, smoked fish, and Italian and French seasonings. A fun place for a date, if not particularly intimate. Regular, more traditional sushi options (and cooked food) are available on the menu. BYOB.

La Tache

1475 W. Balmoral Ave., 773/334-7168

This lesbian-owned French spot—with its low-key, pleasant ambience and a friendly, unsnobby staff—is a great place for a date or an intimate gathering of friends. Snobby Francophile Kathie attests to the authenticity of a kitchen that mixes traditional and contemporary preparations à la Français. Vive La Tache!

Andies

5253 N. Clark St., 773/784-8616

www.andiesres.com

Way before the lesbians moved in and made Andersonville safe for gay men, Andies pleased carnivores and vegetarians alike with its well-executed Mediterranean cuisine. Since then the place has undergone a major facelift (long gone is the cheesy mural that featured the wine glass, dice, and sexy lady eyes), doubled in size, and upscaled its menu. We still like to stick to the basics here— tasty soup, shawerma, and baba ghanoush.

Reza's

5255 N. Clark St., 773/561-1898

www.rezasrestaurant.com

People are split over whether Reza's or neighbor Andies offers the best Middle Eastern fare on this strip, despite the fact that, technically, Reza's is a Persian restaurant and Andies bills itself as Mediterranean. For her part, Kathie prefers Andies, whereas gal pal Nikki hangs her hat at Reza's. Nikki loves the lentil soup and the generous portions of bread, hummus, feta, etc. Kathie says there's just too much damn rice. Try them both and you decide. You'll be well fed in either case.

Jin Ju

5203 N. Clark St., 773/334-6377

Robert's upstairs neighbors, both chefs, declare this to be their favorite local restaurant. The media has raved about Jin Ju's hip Korean menu, innovative cocktails made with a Korean liquor distilled from sweet potatoes, the warmth of the surroundings, and the friendliness of the staff. Great queer date spot.

Hopleaf

5148 N. Clark St., 773/334-9851

www.hopleaf.com

This neighborhood tavern serves up Belgian fare, including the best mussels we have had outside of Europe, and pomme frites served with garlic mayo that are about the most wonderful things you will ever put in your mouth. Plus they have an impressive selection of Euro beers. You won't find Bud on the menu, so delve into the many microbrews from both home and abroad.

Francesca's Bryn Mawr
1039 W. Bryn Mawr Ave., 773/506-9261
www.miafrancesca.com
The **Mia Francesca** location in Boystown (3311 N. Clark St., 773/281-3310) is a victim of its own popularity—the Roman and Tuscan food has been bringing in the droves since 1992, with no sign of its popularity waning. It's hard to get a table there, and the quarters are close when you do. Mia Francesca's more spacious sister restaurant was adopted by the gays as one of the first upscale dining places to hit this part of Uptown, and while both spots are entirely gay-friendly, we find the Bryn Mawr location to be the most queer in terms of clientele. Maybe it's the proximity to Hollywood Beach. A snazzy, celebratory spot for pastas, pizza, risottos, and more, plus generously heaped salads.

Off the Rainbow Road: Restaurants We Love

Here's a selection of restaurants away from the gayborhoods that we know and love from around the city. While not as uber-homo as other spots we've mentioned, no one is going to blink twice at GLBT patrons, either. Unless that wasn't a blink, it was a wink—the hottie at the next table is flirting with you. . . .

Italian Village
Loop: 71 W. Monroe St., 312/332-7005
www.italianvillage-chicago.com
The Italian Village complex actually consists of three different restaurants in three floors. On the basement level, **La Cantina's** theme is casual seafood, although one would be well advised to stick to the basic, classic dishes here. The first floor, **Vivere**, has fine dining pretensions in an overstated room, and on the third level, the **Village** offers casual, old-school traditional Italian in a tacky yet adorable room replicating an old Italian village. Themes aside, what Italian Village really has going for it is an incomparable wine list—the thing has the heft of a phone book—featuring hundreds and hundreds of wines. And they're well situated for dinner before a show in the theater district or at Orchestra Hall. The kitchen is open late, in case you'd rather have a bite *after* your show.

Kamehachi
Old Town: 1400 N. Wells St., 312/664-3663
www.kamehachi.com
This sushi spot is a perennial favorite with the locals for its fresh sushi served in a pleasant atmosphere. The second floor features private tatami rooms with their own stereo systems and televisions, as well as a small bar.

Bistro Campagne

Lincoln Square: 4518 N. Lincoln Ave., 773/271-6100
www.bistrocampagne.com

This lovely traditional French restaurant features mostly organic foodstuffs, including some organic wines. Lots of gays come here on dates or small group outings. In nice weather, the private patio recalls a French country garden. Kathie strongly recommends Bistro Campagne. It is one of her favorite restaurants in the city—nay, in the world!

Café Matou

Logan Square: 1846 N. Milwaukee Ave., 773/384-8911
www.cafematou.com

Attention, crazy cat lesbians: *matou* is French for "tomcat," and Café Matou features an appropriately catty theme. Yet another great Chicago French restaurant, Café Matou is off the beaten path so you don't usually have to fight for a table. They regularly feature Tuesday theme nights with elaborate tasting menus that book up quickly. Conversely, midweek they offer a three-course menu for a mere $22, making it a good value for an excellent nosh. Did we mention that the staff here is really friendly, knowledgeable, and *très charmant*? And that there's a subtle cat motif? *Miam*!

Las Palmas

Wicker Park: 1835 W. North Ave., 773/289-4991

Las Palmas offers much more than your standard margarita joint fare. Appetizers and entrées here are creative and excellently prepared, and the margaritas are nothing to sneeze at either. Have your guacamole prepared tableside to your specifications! This restaurant is a great place for a fun date or group outing. An occasional strolling guitar player adds to the ambience, and they have a better-than-average assortment of vegetarian dishes, along with the steak and seafood.

Café Bernard

Lincoln Park: 2100 N. Halsted St., 773/871-2100
www.cafebernard.com

That Café Bernard is a little frayed around the edges only adds to the Paris bistro feel, which is further underscored by the Piaf and Paris Combo soundtrack and classic cuisine bourgeois. Foie gras, steak au poivre, and crème brûlée are regular features of the menu. There is also a very good wine list. We are drooling as we type this.

Atwood Café

Downtown: 1 W. Washington St. (inside the Burnham Hotel), 312/368-1900
www.atwoodcafe.com

Part of the attraction of this downtown eatery is its splendid space, surely one of the most beautiful dining rooms in all of Chicago. You'll feel as though you are in the solarium of a kind but tasteful millionaire. The other attraction is, of course, the food. Robert and a date each ordered two starters and treated the whole meal like a tapas dining experience—not a bad idea, but this made them miss out on the delicious main courses.

Frontera Grill and Topolobampo
River North: 445 N. Clark St., 312/661-1434
www.fronterakitchens.com/restaurants/
   A few years back we had the good fortune of dining in Frontera Grill's special event room with writer Ruth Reichl, who was then the chief food critic for the *New York Times.* Our party enjoyed Frontera's usual fine service, when suddenly the whole atmosphere changed—obviously word had gotten out about which Random House author was in the house, and platters of delectables that had not been part of our original menu began appearing, "compliments of the chef," the chef in this case being owner and media personality Rick Bayless, who has done a great deal to convince Americans that Mexican food can be part of their fine dining experience. Bayless himself soon appeared to chat with Ms. Reichl, and our meal escalated from Frontera Grill's usual good food to something truly extraordinary—like the fare you get in the fancy room of sister spot Topolobampo. Frontera does not take reservations—expect a wait, and have one of their exceptional margaritas. For Topolobampo, you *need* a reservation. They recommend some weeks in advance. Robert's Topo experience with a pheasant dish in mole sauce remains one of his best taste memories ever.

Brasserie Jo
River North: 59 W. Hubbard St., 312/595-0800
www.brasseriejo.com
   Delicious French bistro fare in an upscale environment. A recent harried trip here (Robert and his friends had theater tickets and were running late) was calmed by the waitstaff's clear-headed professionalism and swift service. Oh, and the food was great!

Pizza D.O.C.
Lincoln Square: 2251 W. Lawrence Ave., 773/784-8777
www.pizza-doc.com
   We both love the rustic wood-fired pizzas here, but don't ignore the other Italian options, from the perfect calamari to the pasta and meat dishes. A special shout-out to the friendly waitstaff and the best martinis around. A great date spot.

WE WISH!

Brief descriptions of notable Chicago restaurants that we can't afford:

Alinea

Lincoln Park: 1723 N. Halsted St., 312/867-0110

www.alinea-restaurant.com

Chef Grant Achatz, one of Chicago's new pioneers of the kitchen, applies scientific principles to reengineer fine dining. And if that sounds confusing, we'll just add that the food here (and indeed, the whole experience) is "conceptual."

Arun's

Albany Park: 4156 N. Kedzie Ave., 773/539-1909

www.arunsthai.com

Not your neighborhood Pad Thai joint but rather a prix-fixe upscale Thai restaurant offering exquisite food preparations and presentations. When the owner found out that we were writing a gay guide to the city, Arun himself sent us a note to say that not only is the restaurant gay-friendly, in fact they adore their gay patrons and staff. But he didn't offer us a free meal, natch.

Charlie Trotter's

Lincoln Park: 816 W. Armitage Ave., 773/248-6228

www.charlietrotters.com

Charlie Trotter is the forefather of Chicago's innovative cuisine revolution. Book well in advance and bring your platinum card—prices for the prix-fixe only menus start at $115.

Everest

South Loop: One Financial Place, 440 S. LaSalle St., 40th Floor, 312/663-8920

www.leye.com

Fancy, Alsatian French cuisine with a great view and a cute-as-a-button local celebrity sommelier, Alpana Singh.

Japonais

River North: 600 W. Chicago Ave., 312/822-9600

www.japonaischicago.com

Upscale Franco-Japanese fusion in a sleek room.

Moto

River West: 945 W. Fulton St., 312/491-0058

www.motorestaurant.com

Another "food as science project" high-concept, high-priced eatery.

Tizi Melloul

Old Town: 531 N. Wells St., 312/670-4338

www.tizimelloul.com

Posh Moroccan date place, recommended by some of our friends who are of the homosexual persuasion.

Tru

River North/Mag Mile: 676 N. St. Clair St., 312/202-0001

www.trurestaurant.com

   Over-the-top food with exquisite presentations.

Vermillion

River North/Mag Mile: 10 W. Hubbard St., 312/527-4060

   Indian-Latin fusion in a warm, sophisticated setting.

Brunch Spots

Brunch is nearly a sacrament with the gays. The straights, too, for that matter. Many if not all of the fine hotels downtown offer competent brunching, and here are some other brunch options in the city that we recommend.

Lincoln Restaurant

West Lakeview: 4008 N. Lincoln Ave., 773/248-1820

   We have to mention this spot because where else will you find omelets named after Civil War generals?

Lula Café

Logan Square: 2537 N. Kedzie Blvd., 773/489-9554

www.lulacafe.com

   A lesbian couple of our acquaintance begged us not to list this Logan Square brunch spot, for fear it will become more popular than it already is, but they do say, off the record, that it is way gay-friendly.

M. Henry

Andersonville/Uptown: 5707 N. Clark St., 773/561-1600

   Robert's fave brunch spot ever! Gay owned, this newish restaurant is so fixated on brunch that they really don't do anything else. You'll find plenty of vegan and vegetarian options, but carnivores can chow here, too. Everything is good, but order the breakfast bread pudding if it's being offered—you'll be glad you did. Very gay crowd.

North Coast

Boystown: 3613 N. Broadway St., 773/549-7606

   Unremarkable but entirely competent breakfast fare. You'll have a lot of queers dining with you here.

Café times.
~Photo by Caldwell Linker

Orange

Boystown: 3231 N. Clark St., 773/549-4400

Don't linger too long in bed or you'll miss your chance to eat here—they close at 3 P.M. (And they don't take reservations.) Orange is known for their "frushi," fresh fruit served up like sushi, as well as "flights" of pancakes, so you don't have to limit yourself to one yummy variety.

Svea

Andersonville: 5236 N. Clark St., 773/275-7738

Svea serves up inexpensive Swedish fare—pancakes with lingonberries, Swedish meatballs, and sausage. Look for the picture of the owner shaking hands with the king of Sweden. Robert loves this tiny charmer. He eats here at least once a week.

Tweet

Uptown: 5020 N. Sheridan Rd., 773/728-5576
www.tweet.biz

Proprietress Michelle Fire, the owner of gay bar Big Chicks (right next door), often plays hostess to the hordes of hungry queer folk who frequent Tweet. Not to worry, straights are welcome, too—in fact, this bright, art-bedecked spot is a fine place to bring the straight relatives. Brunch is maybe a dollar or so more expensive than you'd pay for similar items elsewhere, but the quality of the ingredients shines through—no bland or sour fruit in the fresh fruit cups, and the eggs are all from happy Amish chickens. Tweet got its start as a brunch place but has branched out—try their $20 prix-fixe dinner menu. Check out the Web site for cost-cutting coupons.

Wishbone Loop

West Loop (near Oprah's studio!): 1001 W. Washington St., 312/850-2663
West Lakeview: 3300 N. Lincoln Ave., 773/549-2663
www.wishbonechicago.com

We have to agree to disagree here. Robert loves both Wishbones, with their

Southern-influenced fare, and considers their corn muffins an actual food group and the Bloody Marys a new kind of lovely water. Kathie says she's never been very happy here. You'll have to try it and take sides in this, one of our very few ongoing disputes.

Heartland Café
Rogers Park: 7000 N. Glenwood Ave., 773/465-0005
www.heartlandcafe.com
"Where's a great brunch opportunity in the city?" we asked performance poet Cin Salach. She said, "I'm a hippie at heart. Give me the Heartland Café any weekend." The Heartland is also good for hearty hippie fare in the evening. And the attached small bar is rather charming.

Salt and Pepper Diner
Lakeview: 3537 N. Clark St., 773/883-9800
Lakeview: 2575 N. Lincoln Ave., 773/525-8788
Real diner food served in a setting complete with vinyl-covered booth seats, cranky line cooks, and harried waitresses who call you "hon." Robert used to get a milkshake with breakfast, his own personal hangover cure. The Clark Street location has a booze license, for hair-of-the-dog situations.

Golden Nugget
Seven locations around the city, but the one closest to Boystown is at 2720 N. Clark St., 773/929-0724, and the one closest to Andersonville is at 4747 N. Ravenswood, the corner of Lawrence and Ravenswood, 773/769-6700. Real, no-nonsense, cheap, filling diner fare. Open 24 hours.

 Chapter 13

HOW ABOUT A COCKTAIL, DARLING? GLBT BARS IN CHICAGO

The bars in Boystown used to be pretty much the only game in town, other than a few outlying North and South Side pubs. But as the GLBT population has moved farther north, many of the city's queer inhabitants never make it south to the Halsted strip, preferring to do their drinking and socializing closer to home, in the Uptown, Andersonville, Ravenswood, and Rogers Park neighborhoods. The Halsted strip and its satellites in the area of Lakeview known as Boystown continue to thrive, however, and on the strip you can find pretty much whatever kind of bar experience you are looking for, from boozy dive to bass beat dance club, from the sophisticated martini to the ice-cold bottle of beer grasped in a leather daddy's big rough hand. There aren't a lot of strictly lesbian bars in Chicago, so we'll start by letting the ladies know where the lezzies can be found, then give everyone the lowdown on the bars in Boystown and nearby, and after that dart up Andersonville way to tell you about the many options there. We'll also offer our take on drinking establishments located farther north, downtown, and in the western and southern reaches of the city. While there are gay drinkeries outside the city limits, we tipped back enough glasses just tackling the ones within Chicago proper—check the free gay weeklies for the haps on suburban and Northern Indiana booze joints and nightclubs. We end with a selection of drinking establishments that are (shockingly enough) *not* gay. As the saying goes, we *are* everywhere.

Where the Girls Are

The women's nightlife scene in Chicago is ever shifting. In addition to the brick-and-mortar lesbian venues (and there seem to be fewer of these than ever), women's special club nights rise up and fade away with assuring consistency. In addition, there are various "men's" or "mixed" bars that gain favor with women who lick other women, but, like everything else on the scene, these venues are always changing. At the time of this writing, the following are the most likely places in town to see and meet other lesbians, but bear in mind that some of the winds do change direction. For an up-to-date resource, check out the **Dyke Diva** message boards (www.dykediva.com). What follows is a quick run-down of the women's nightlife scene in Chicago. For more in-depth information, flip to the neighborhood-by-neighborhood bar listings.

Circuit

One Friday a month, the ladies of Chix Mix (who also bring us the annual Black Bra party in February) host Fast Forward, a femme-friendly night of mingling, flirting, and booty-shaking. Among the monthly-changing themes are the Uniform Party and Traffic Jam (where red, yellow, and green indicate your availability status). With great music, a state-of-the-art sound and light show and super hot dancers, Chix Mix has been going strong for five years; keep your fingers crossed that it lasts at least another five more. Check out their website for their latest schedule and promotions: www.chixmixproductions.com.

Star Gaze

Boys are welcome at this primarily lesbian bar, one of the few left in the city. Weekends feature DJs and dancing, but any evening is a good time to catch a pool game or a barside chat.
(p. 142)

The Closet

This lesbian bar seems to attract as many guys as girls. No matter, it's still a fun place for girls to watch videos and mingle with friends or strangers.
(p. 133)

Chix Mix: Where the girls are.
~Photo by Emilio Alexandrov

Joie de Vine

This great get-to-know-you-better lesbian-owned wine bar is a great place for a more elegant night out.
(p. 143)

Lost & Found
(p. 151)

T's Restaurant and Bar

This mixed neighborhood bar, very popular with Andersonville lesbians, is a great place to grab a brew and a bite with pals.
(p. 141)

Atmosphere

Whether for dancing or just hanging out, this Andersonville mixed bar makes a genuine effort to court favor with females.
(p. 142)

Spin

Spin is one of the most truly mixed of the mixed bars. Must be the ubiquitous pool table.
(p. 123)

WOMEN HAVE BEEN CARVING OUT THEIR OWN SPACES IN THESE PRIMARILY MALE ENCLAVES

Scot's (p. 138)

Crew (p. 144)

Hydrate (p. 127)

Cocktail (p. 126)

A Chix Mix dancer, chained to the beat.
~Photo by Emilio Alexandrov

Boystown Bars

Getting There: Don't drive your car to Boystown. Street parking is hard to come by; most of the side streets close to Halsted are zoned for residents only after 6 P.M. If you do not have a resident sticker or guest pass displayed in the window of your car and you park in a resident-only zone, you will get a ticket, plain and simple. If you are staying with local friends, your hosts can get you a guest pass from their alderman's office. You will get a ticket if you park at a metered spot and let the meter run out. And meters most places now run until 9 P.M., start at 9 A.M. the next day, *and* must be fed on Sundays. If we still haven't dissuaded you from bringing the car, we will admit that there are a couple of small pay lots available on Halsted, and **Sidetrack** offers a valet service directly in front of the bar. But if you take CTA, the Red Line will drop you only a few blocks from your destination. The Belmont or Addison stops are your departure points, depending on if you are going to bars on the north or south end of the Halsted strip. The Brown and Purple Lines also stop at Belmont. From downtown, the #22 and #36 buses on Dearborn or the #141, #151, and #147 buses on Michigan Avenue will all put you only a few blocks from Halsted. And we have never met a cab driver who didn't know how to get to Halsted and Roscoe—it's a very common request.

The good news about cabbing it is that when you are ready to leave, cabs are as abundant as the sequins on a drag queen's frock. Robert was informed by a cab driver recently, "I like you gays, you know? No trouble, very polite, and you tip good, too." Robert then felt unable to sully the reputation of all gays everywhere by tipping poorly. Clever cab driver!

So, on to our tour. Please note Halsted's pride pylons when you are strolling the street. These rainbow rocket-shaped edifices, while joked about by the locals as giant sex toys, were put up by the city of Chicago at great expense to celebrate and specifically mark our main gay neighborhood. We will begin the tour at the southern point of the Halsted strip, at Belmont, and proceed north.

Lucky Horseshoe
3169 N. Halsted St., 773/404-3169
The Vibe: Tuck another dollar in the dancer's jockstrap.
The Crowd: The kind of guys who like tucking dollars in the dancer's jockstrap.
The Space: Two bar areas, each with its own stage.
When to Go: The dancers are there every night.

Closet beers.
~Photo by Sebastian Pinon

You can't really call the entertainers here "strippers," since that would imply they were completely clothed in the first place. But if you are a guy who appreciates the wearing and disrobing of itty-bitty, teeny-weeny short shorts and skin-tight sleeveless shirts, you will like the view here. This Halsted standard has cleaned itself up a tad since our first visits, lo these many years gone by. Back then, the floor was suspiciously sticky, the room was dark, the dancers looked a few years too young to be plying their chosen trade, and we wanted to make them eat a sandwich. These days the boys look more nourished, and their high school days seem firmly behind them. Think *Freshmen* magazine. You may occasionally find (as we did) a bachelorette party in progress, complete with the bride-to-be dressed in one of those T-shirts with Lifesaver candies sewn on so that strangers can suck them off (the T-shirt), but it's mainly a man joint. Our friend Neil said, with obvious disappointment, that he found the Horseshoe "not nearly as seedy as I'd expected. The lighting fixtures are rather elegant, as I recall."

Spin

800 W. Belmont (at Halsted St.), 773/327-7711
www.spin-nightclub.com
The Vibe: "I'm comin' out, so you better get the party started."
The Crowd: Men, but lots of women, too, baby dykes and twinks, generally in their 20s.
The Space: Large front bar with video screen and pool tables, back bar and roomy dance area.
When to Go: Wednesdays for dollar-drink night, Friday nights for the shower contest and dancing.

One of our many claims to fame is that we know a former winner of the fabled Spin shower contest, an event where boys and girls right off the street doff their clothes in favor of a white terry cloth towel and damply gyrate, trying to keep the towel covering the legally must-be-covered bits, all for glory and a cash prize. The girl participants have to put on duct tape pasties to cover their nipples and keep things legal. Let's just all say "Ouch" once together. Boy participants are allowed to parade their nips all over the damn place, but everyone has to keep the downstairs goodies covered with the towel. Anyway, Kathie was dating a very nice girl named Janice (hi, Janice!) and Janice's best friend, visiting from another town, was a young man so hunk-adorable and muscle-rific that he won handily. All this is neither here nor there but just a lead-in to say that Spin, more than any other Halsted bar, is a homo habitat for guys and gals. There's some kind of drink special every night, but far and away the most popular is Spin's "What the Fuck" Wednesdays, with all well drinks and tap beer only one little dollar. The slight catch is a $5 cover charge to get in. A roster of primo DJs and rotating music styles on different nights keep things hopping and bopping on the dance floor.

Gentry on Halsted

3320 N. Halsted St., 773/348-1053
www.gentryofchicago.com
The Vibe: "Life is a cabaret, old chum."
The Crowd: People who know the lyrics to Stephen Sondheim songs. Men, women welcome.
The Space: Intimate, swank space dominated by the piano and whoever is singing at it. Dartboard and pinball area in back if you want to escape the live music.
When to Go: Tuesday nights for open mic, live performances all other nights.

A chilly Monday night in April is not the best time to go to Gentry on Halsted. (It has a sister bar, Gentry on State, downtown.) We learned this firsthand when we stopped in, to find only six other people there. And two of those were the singer and piano player. The inauspicious start to our visit was dimmed even more by our beverages: a pallid glass of white wine from a bottle opened long before and a martini with a miserly amount of gin and too much vermouth. But any place can have an off night. Movie star–handsome performer Paul Marinaro sings just swell, while veteran accompanist John Paluch has the most calming aura of any piano player we've ever met. You have to love a spot that, without a cover charge, provides live vocal entertainment every night of the week and avoids the plague of TV screens thrown up onto every vertical surface that infects just about every other gay bar in the city. If you aspire to stardom yourself, step up to the microphone on Tuesdays and show off your velvet-throated prowess. (No, singing, we mean.) Gentry on Halsted is a great spot to bring your mum and Aunt Agnes when they want to hit the bar with your friends, drink an old-fashioned, and "see just what it is that you boys do at these places." The bartenders will flirt, Aunt Agnes will hum along to "Moon River," and Mum will realize that not every gay nightspot is redolent of Crisco and the cries of the paddled. You can take her to the **Cellblock** for that.

Sidetrack

3349 N. Halsted St., 773/477-9189
www.sidetrackchicago.com
The Vibe: If none of the boys please you, there's always TV.
The Crowd: Mostly 20- to 30-something men. Women welcome.
The Space: Many bars in one!
When to Go: Sunday evenings and Monday nights for show tunes, Thursday nights for comedy.

Robert will always have a wet spot in his heart for Sidetrack, the first gay bar he ever set foot inside. The way this monolithic Chicago staple adds another room or storefront every couple of years, it's going to need its own zip code before long. Within all that space, Sidetrack offers a lot of options, including a beautiful atrium with a strict nonsmoking policy, an understated lounge area, a popular outdoor upper deck, and three other rooms, each with its own bars. Sidetrack is a video bar; you are never far from a television screen. Our favorite option from their weekly menu of video themes is the Sunday evening and Monday night show tune extravaganza, where in the main room you can join the crowd in belting out songs to accompany the stars of screen, stage, and TV. Another treat is Thursday's comedy night, with an amazing array of clips from sitcoms, stand-up, films, and commercials, most of them with a queer tinge. The perfect antidote to the winter blahs. Or summer ones, for that matter.

We have heard complaints that the Sidetrack crowd is unfriendly. Our theory, from observation and our own experience, is that Sidetrack is a bar where locals go (often in groups) to meet up with friends, and they are not looking to make new acquaintances. The solo reveler may well find that many of the patrons are chatting among themselves and ignoring others. But that's what all the video screens are for. That being said, we have been here in our own big chatty groups and experienced delightful cross-pollination with other big chatty groups.

Clean, fully staffed, and not tolerant of obnoxious drunks or tomfoolery,

Sidetrack is often a place that the gays bring their straight friends to. A recent *Chicago* magazine article cited it as a place for straight girls to go for a fun "girls night out." The age of the crowd varies—Friday and Saturday bring in a 21-to-35 stand-and-pose crowd, while show tunes and cocktail hour attract some older gents. The gay and lesbian community of Illinois has few better advocates and allies than the owners of Sidetrack—their financial and personal support for gay politicians, AIDS organizations, and those who promote gay rights has been unwavering.

Roscoe's Tavern
3356 N. Halsted St., 773/281-3355
www.roscoes.com
The Vibe: "Young man! Young young, young man! Has anyone ever told you that you look like a young prince out of the Arabian Nights?" —Blanche DuBois, in *A Streetcar Named Desire*.
The Crowd: Youngish men and those who pursue them. Women welcome.
The Space: Five bar areas, including the cruisy main front bar, an intimate garden area, a room with pool tables, and a dance floor. Outdoor patio serves food during summer months.
When to Go: Any night is good.

Just across the street from Sidetrack is the other Chicago gay megabar, Roscoe's, and when Robert's fave cousin from Atlanta brought her 24-year-old best gay buddy to town recently, this was the bar that he wanted to see. Despite her admonishment to "totally not hook up," the young man in question did get lucky at Roscoe's and, scandalously, did not stumble into his hotel room until after 6 in the morning. The crowd here tends to be around 24, plus or minus a few years, and the bar attracts tourists from the suburbs and beyond. A friend from Belgium once ran into an acquaintance from his very small town at Roscoe's. It's a bar with a bit of something for a lot of folks. There's a dark and roomy dance floor, a cruisy front bar, pool tables, and several smaller rooms for quieter conferrals. Evening entertainment ranges from a weekly drag competition to the ever-popular monthly wet boxer short contest. Check out their Web site or call to find out what drink specials and attractions they might offer on a given night. The dance floor does not get hopping until late—but be warned, on Saturdays there's a $5 cover to get in the place after 10 P.M. Our personal favorite times at Roscoe's are 5 P.M. on a weekday, for the laid-back (and more mature) businessman-having-a-civilized-martini vibe, or a sunny summer Saturday on their outdoor side patio, where you can enjoy a burger and a beer and watch the world go by.

Cocktail

3359 N. Halsted St., 773/477-1420

The Vibe: Spiffy, snappy casual.

The Crowd: Men, women welcome, all ages.

The Space: Dark comfy bar with a long window facing Halsted. Strippers featured on selected nights.

The smallest of the gay bars at the Halsted-and-Roscoe ground zero of gay nightlife in Chicago is this succinctly named drinkery. We don't have too much to say about it because it is what it is: a nicely appointed, pleasant place to have a drink. The crowd gets a bit crazier on the nights when go-go boys are in residence on their dance boxes. As far as the dancers go, think gym-buff to the point of Congressional steroid investigation, as well as plucked and shaved in the body hair department. If that doesn't do it for you, or it's a night when the dancers are not in residence, grab one of the primo window seats—the proximity to the sidewalk and the constant flow of foot traffic between **Sidetrack**, **Roscoe's**, and **Cocktail** makes for a fine vantage point to observe strolling gays in their native habitat. Kathie would like to add that even though Cocktail might not feel like the most lezzie-friendly bar when the male dancers are onstage, this is the bar where she made a love connection with her girlfriend-for-life, Nikki, so it will always hold a lesbo-loving, special place in her heart.

Bucks

3439 N. Halsted St., 773/525-1125

The Vibe: VFW hall meets hunting lodge, with shots of Jägermeister.

The Crowd: Bears, blue-collar types.

The Space: A long bar, lots of wooden surfaces, a pool table, outdoor seating seasonally.

If anyone complains one more time that Halsted Street is only for the twinks and baby dykes, we are going to bring them to deer head–decorated Bucks. You'll discover a crowd of hard-drinking gay men a decade or more older than the typical **Roscoe's** or **Sidetrack** patron, with their dress less designer and more T-shirts and flannel. Bucks boasts a good jukebox selection and plenty of prime window seating to watch people pass by (as well as

Miss Foozie, in a rare daytime appearance.
~Photo by Jon Peterson

to place oneself on shameless display). The various dead animal heads on the walls are festively decorated according to the season. Robert recommends spending a sunny late afternoon on their back deck, a peaceful hideaway off of Halsted.

Hydrate
3458 N. Halsted St., 773/975-9244. www.hydratechicago.com
The Vibe: Let's take off our shirts and dance!
The Crowd: The sort of guys who look good taking their shirts off to dance. Girls, too, for that matter.
The Space: The blue entry bar, quieter with more of a lounge feel, and the back red bar, louder and dance oriented.
When to Go: The later the better.

In the dog days of summer, Hydrate lives up to its name by misting pedestrians walking by with a soothing spray of water. Chicago old-timers may or may not lament the transformation of this space, formerly the Manhole, into the much less innuendo-laden Hydrate. Robert and his friends Solveig (lesbian) and Kathy (straight) popped in here on a weeknight not too long ago, and any reservations Robert might have had that he was too old to feel comfortable here or that the place was too

We Won't Dance, Don't Ask Us

Well, that's a lie. We both love to dance, but we are allergic to pricey nightclub cover charges. When we polled our friends, and friends of friends, and their friends, asking where queer people should go bust a move, our correspondents generally suggested the cover-charge-less **Big Chicks** (p. 145) on a Friday or Saturday. Our friend Neil says, "I do not dance or like to dance, but it is so cheerful there, the dance floor so tidy and gemütlich, that even I find myself dancing." Others suggested **Berlin** (p. 134), and there were a few mentions of **Neo** (p. 135) as well. GLBT peeps bump and grind in Chicago nightclubs, especially on designated "gay" nights, which change from club to club depending on the promoters, the DJs, and the whims and trends of the market. Check the local gay weeklies for current hot spots. Two of the longest-running club nights specifically courting the gays are Sundays at **Crobar** (1543 N. Kingsbury St., 312/266-1900, www.crobar.com) and Monday night's omnisexual "Boom Boom Room" at **Green Dolphin Street** (2200 N. Ashland Ave., 773/395-0066om). In addition, scenesters may want to check out downtown's **Sound Bar** (226 W. Ontario St., 312/787-4480,www.sound-bar.com). Sunday is also the GLBT night here. The **Funky Buddha Lounge** (728 W. Grand Ave., 312/666-1695, www.funkybuddha.com) has the motto "celebrating diversity since 1996," and by diversity they do mean *everybody*. Diverse styles of music (no techno) and an ethnically, racially, and sexuality mixed crowd are the standard at **Club Reunion** (811 W. Lake St., 312/491-9600, www.clubreunion.net). On the Halsted strip, booty shakers can be assured of a gay crowd and get their rhythmic movement fix at **Spin** (p. 123), **Roscoe's** (p. 125), **Hydrate** (p. 127), and **Circuit** (p. 129).

ultramale to bring some chicks along were quickly put to rest by the friendly staff and clientele. Miss Foozie, one of the more active drag entertainers on the Halsted strip, was in stacked-wig residence and made Robert and friends welcome with a special Foozie shot. The sturdily frocked and dashingly baubled Miss Foozie is quite the busy gal—by our count she currently works her Foozie magic at four area gay nightspots weekly. Who knows how long she can keep up this demanding pace? Check her out online at the sensibly named www.missfoozie.org.

Hydrate is divided into two spaces, the blue bar, which has a more laid-back, lounge and chat vibe, with open windows allowing for both holler and gaze opportunities, and the louder red zone, with a dance floor that was nearly empty when we were there. We had arrived far too early for the serious dancers—Hydrate is open until 4 A.M. daily except for Saturdays, when they stay open until 5. It's not at all uncommon for a line to form at the door at 2 A.M., when many other Halsted bars close up shop, and then the fun truly begins inside. A roster of acclaimed DJs from Chicago and beyond spin the late-night tunes. The Web site will tell you who spins when and what drink specials you can enjoy.

Dancer.
~Photo by Mel Ferrand

Little Jim's
3501 N. Halsted St., 773/871-6116
The Vibe: No, don't leave—have just one more beer.
The Crowd: Men, locals, 35 and up.
The Space: Dim, porn on one video screen, darts, and pinball.
When to Go: After the other bars close.

One bright spring day at about 3 P.M. Robert was sitting in the Caribou Coffee shop on Halsted Street, supposedly writing in his journal but mostly staring out the window. Across the street he saw an old man with a W.C. Fields nose stagger, obviously intoxicated, and walking with the help of a cane, into the doorway of Little Jim's. Robert thought about what the bar must be like at 3 in the afternoon, with the old, the lonely, and the downtrodden drinking their sour beers. He thought it was strange that no one escorted the old man out of the bar and called him a cab. He did not write much that day, but he did write, "Please, God, when I am an old man, do not let me end up drinking my afternoons away at Little Jim's." That being said, Little

Jim's comes into its own after 2 A.M., when many of the other Halsted bars close, and several friends of ours like the place for its unpretentious historical dive-bar charm. It's a more racially mixed crowd here than elsewhere on the strip, and as mentioned, the age range is older than most Halsted bars—"Somewhere between forty and death," as Auntie Mame might say. Given the late-night, past last-call crowd, hooking up is a goal of many guys here. Of course, in all instances you should be wary of going home with a stranger, especially when you and he are under the influence. And be aware that in at least two unsolved murders of gay men in recent years in Chicago, the last place they were seen alive was here, chatting someone up. At Little Jim's or anywhere, be alert, trust your gut instincts, and, gosh darn it, be sensible.

Circuit
3641 N. Halsted St., 773/325-2233
www.circuitclub.com
The Vibe: Let the music, the pretty lights, and the dancing take you away.
The Crowd: Mixed men, women, all ages (more 24 to 30, but older, too).
The Space: Gigantic dance floor and kick-ass sound-and-light show.
When to Go: For women, it's all about Chix Mix Fridays (info follows). Otherwise Thursday nights for Latin music, Thursday through Saturday nights for the biggest crowds.

Don't you hate it when you go to a nightclub you haven't been to in years (you feel you owe it to the club, as you are in the process of researching a GLBT travel guide) and first of all, when you enter, the butch-girl doorperson says, "Hey, good to see you again," in a very chipper personal way, which is confounding, as you have not been inside the club since before she was old enough to work there, and you are reasonably certain you have never seen her before. Ever. Then the first person you *do* recognize in the crowd is an ex. Except you don't recognize him definitively at first. He looks like your ex would look if the ex got very trim and muscled and tanned. And that's exactly what has happened. As you make small talk with the buff ex (the buffness accentuated by his shirtless, leather vest–clad state) and note that his white jeans are unzipped enough in the front to show that he is wearing striped briefs, you begin to recall what feelings and urges and thoughts led you to sleep with him in the first place, and your view of the unzipped jeans is giving you a tingly feeling "down there." This is when he tells you that he would introduce you to his friends, but he has forgotten your name. The tingly feeling promptly ceases. You suddenly remember that you broke up with him via an e-mail, a missive that was fun and chatty right up until the sentence that started, "I think it might be better . . ." Paybacks are a bitch. The evening at Circuit is not going your way. None of that is, of course, the fault of Circuit. It boasts the largest dance floor on Halsted and, from what Robert has seen, the most impressive and high-tech light-and-sound system as well. Several intimate conversational nooks are tucked away to the far sides of the dance floor, and three serving areas mean not much waiting for the next beverage. One cautionary budget-minded note: a single Sapphire and tonic was $9 without tip. Check the Web site or sign up for the e-mail list, because coupons for free cover charges are common, and given the drink prices, free cover is a good thing. Robert attended Circuit well after midnight on a Saturday night, and the crowd was about 50-50 men and women, the women not all lesbian and generally a bit younger than the men. With the exception of the jock boys dancing in cages, the vibe of the place does not shriek "gay," and Robert imagines that this is a club you could bring straight guy friends to—they would have some straight girls to chat up in the crowd. Circuit's popular Latin nights make it the premier North Side nightclub destination for gay Spanish speakers, and not just on nights designated as Latin. The whole of the club was refreshingly mixed in terms of race, age, and ethnicity. Not to mention it was refreshingly tidy—the men's room smelled very comfortingly of freshly scrubbed walls and floors. As Robert left Circuit, the nearly ubiquitous Miss Foozie, drag hostess for the evening and charming as always, said, "Come back, honey. Your stamp is good until we close at 5."

Kathie has also ventured into Circuit, but she goes on Fridays. On the third friday of the month, **Chix Mix** takes over the nightclub, installing their own staff, including bartenders and sexy go-go dancers. At "Traffic Jam" parties you get a glowing wristband in green, yellow, or red, indicating your availability status. "Wild On" nights feature Coyote Ugly types of hijinks, such as silly string, whipped cream, and upside-down gravity shots. The mix gets mixing after 10 P.M., and there's a $7 cover charge. In 2005, Chix Mix producers Julie Mosier and Kathleen Ulm had just celebrated the five-year anniversary of Chix Mix Productions, which got its start producing and hosting the annual Black Bra Party—a local women's answer to men's circuit parties. After a stint producing special parties for lesbians in a variety of venues, Chix Mix finally landed in what seems to be a permanent gig at the nightclub Circuit—and on a Friday night, no less! Check the Web site (www.chixmixproductions.com) for the schedule. Ulm and Mosier have instituted the "M.A.D." (making a difference) credo for Chix Mix Productions. Each year designated charitable groups benefit from a portion of Chix Mix proceeds. Recent beneficiaries have included Amigas Latinas and the Illinois Gender Advocates. They also offer two $500 M.A.D. annual scholarships to local students who are making a difference in the areas of gay and lesbian visibility and/or GLBTQ rights. Silly string and social change— quite the winning combo!

Cellblock

3702 N. Halsted St., 773/665-8064
The Vibe: Neighborhood feel, with leather on top.
The Crowd: Mostly men, 30 and older.
The Space: Cozy, clean, with multiple dartboards, a pool table, a jukebox.
When to Go: Weeknights for companionable chat, weekend late nights for leather naughtiness.

The wall behind Cellblock's bar features three pairs of plastic hands grasping their diminutive prison bar cells, as if some hapless Sears sportswear mannequins had been drugged, kidnapped, and bricked in. Call us wussies, but we find the effect more creepy than sexy. That being said, Cellblock has a lot going for it: it rules the roost as Halsted's only leather bar, the daily drink specials make this one of the cheaper places in the area to catch a buzz, and a rotating roster of leather interest clubs hosting parties means that cigar aficionados, foot worshippers, fisting devotees, women in leather, Christians in leather, bears in or out of leather, black men in leather, etc., all have their evenings to meet and greet and discuss all things bound and beautiful. Check out the Web site for a full calendar of events. For all of the leather overtones and strategic jail bar placement throughout the club, the general vibe of the Cellblock (at least in the front bar) is one of a neighborhood bar. On a recent Wednesday visit the focus was on buzz cuts and cigars. But thankfully (cough cough) no cigar smokers were in evidence, there wasn't a pair of leather pants or harness in the place, and neither the cute gent giving the buzz cuts or the earnest men receiving them looked like they were experiencing the transaction as erotic. Weekends the focus is firmly on leather, and you have to be wearing some kind of approved gear (leather or rubber) to get into the back bar area, with its naughtiness. You may not want to bring your dewy fresh cousin from Topeka back there, unless you are tired of his dewy freshness.

Bobby Love's

3729 N. Halsted St., 773/525-1200
The Vibe: I know Bobby Love, do you?
The Crowd: Locals, regulars, generally over 30.
The Space: Smallish, pleasant enough.
When to Go: Fridays for karaoke.

Various online reviewers have compared Bobby Love's to the Cheers bar of TV fame because of its regular, friendly crowd. Robert has ducked in here twice recently for a restorative cocktail, and, while the gin was fine, and he was happy the bartender and chatty crew of regulars got along so famously, he ended up feeling like one of the extras on the set, someone who never got to talk to Norm or Woody. Like Bucks, the patrons here tend to be somewhere from 35 to beyond retirement age, and a gym body is not a requirement for entry. On Fridays the crowd of regulars is both boozy and friendly, and the karaoke songsters, with an appreciative audience, can be surprisingly accomplished.

North End

3733 N. Halsted St., 773/477-7999
The Vibe: Spacious zone of beer-drinkin' unpretentiousness.
The Crowd: Blue-collar and blue-collar wannabes. Mostly men, but women welcome.
The Space: Two nondescript bar areas, lots of TV screens.
When to Go: Wednesdays, for the free nacho bar and karaoke.

If you seek a lack of pretension and a guy-guy crowd, this might be your spot. You are not going to be struck dumb by the clever décor, and the bartenders here do far more shot and beer requests than martini mixing. The North End is one of the few gay places we know where, when the baseball game is on TV, the folks watching actually know the score and who is playing. It is also one of the few gay bars where the DJ plays REO Speedwagon with some frequency. Because someone requested it. Whether that is a good thing or not is up to you. One of the bonuses of the place is its roominess. Even on a crowded weekend night, you can generally get a seat. Robert was delighted on a recent Saturday night stop to find a crowd of multigenerational guys (including a 50-year-old on his right and a 22-year-old on his left) in a friendly, chatty atmosphere. The four pool tables mean less waiting for your game, dude.

Charlie's

3726 N. Broadway St., 773/871-8887
www.charlieschicago.com
The Vibe: Like a rhinestone cowboy.
The Crowd: Men, women welcome, 30ish and older.
The Space: Barnlike, as if the Amish had a dance club.
When to Go: Wednesdays in the early evening for line dancing and two-stepping, Thursdays through Sundays after 2 A.M. for contemporary dance music.

Not officially on the Halsted strip, Charlie's is situated at a point where Halsted and Broadway come so close together that it's illegal in some states. You'll find the bar mere paces from **Bobby Love's**. It's tempting to say that the folks at Charlie's like *both* kinds of music, country *and* western, but in fact this oasis of gay country sensibility also moonlights late night as an after-hours dance club, with all the disco diva tunes. The spacious dance floor, ringed by wooden fencing to lean against and set one's drink upon, amplifies the corral effect created by the down-home wooden bar tops and the exposed brick walls. One wall of the dance floor is all mirrors, so the newbie line dancers can see their reflections and the late-night boogie bums can catch sight of how hot they look. Our friend Owen dated a line-dancing dude for a time, and before hearts got achy-breaky broken, he went here quite a bit. Owen says this about Charlie's: "Very friendly, and very embracing of out-of-towners and women, with all ages and levels of two-stepping and line dances. With *free* lessons on Monday and Wednesday, it's a wonderful way to meet people, since it's such an intrinsically social evening. Plus since you are busy, you have a tendency to drink a lot less, so it's cheaper and good exercise to boot (no pun intended)."

On Saturday nights, Charlie's is open until 5 A.M., and any night after 2 it becomes a polyglot party central—everybody and anybody, all races, creeds, genders and sexualities, join in the sweaty, shimmery dance. If country dancing is what you seek, keep in mind what the bartender told us: "Country folk all work for a living, they get here early, they go to bed early." At 10:30 on a recent weeknight visit, the huge space was nearly empty, waiting for the night owls who would arrive later. The dance floor belonged to a slim couple in their 40s—two men in blue jeans, gingham shirts, and cowboy boots—gracefully waltzing to the song "Cowboys Like Us." They gazed into each other's eyes, smiling the whole time, and for them Charlie's was obviously the best place in the world.

A Walk or Short Cab Ride from the Halsted Strip

From closest to farthest …

The Closet
3325 N. Broadway St., 773/477-8533
The Vibe: Smoky little den of lesbian love.
The Crowd: More women than men, locals, and regulars, generally over 30.
The Space: Smallish, pleasant enough.
When to Go: Early evenings for a quiet time, after 2 A.M. for crowded madness.

The Closet is the most dyke-friendly bar in Boystown, just a block away from the Halsted strip. Kathie and Robert love this place for heart-to-heart chats or business talks in the early evening. After 2 A.M., when much of Halsted closes up shop, the Closet begins to feel as crowded as the name might indicate, when everyone who wants a final drink or three walks the block over from Halsted or cabs in from elsewhere and crams through the door: lesbians, gay boys, and adventurous straights. Getting a drink at this hour can be difficult, and if you plan on going to the bathroom, expect a lengthy wait. But we'd recommend a visit even so, for the celebratory nature of the place. A plus for us is the mix of music videos. Some have remained comfortingly the same since we first started coming here, some of which are brand-spanking new. Say hello to Lisa, the no-nonsense doorperson, and Karen, the heartbreakingly handsome bartender.

3160
3160 N. Clark St., 773/327-5969
The Vibe: Quiet bar on a busy street.
The Crowd: Mostly men, varied age range, women welcome.
The Space: Cozy, clean, with multiple dartboards, a pool table, a jukebox.
When to Go: Anytime you want to escape the main Boystown rush and hear live music.

Until January of 2006, this bar was called "Annex 3," and one of the unsolved mysteries of queer Chicago was the question of what exactly the Annex 3 was an annexation *of*? And what happened to Annexes 1 and 2, for that matter? Now it's called 3160, cunningly named after its street address, and Jim Flint, the owner, is instituting a program of live music. We went here in the Annex 3 days. On a quiet Wednesday night we struck up a conversation here with John, a 29-year-old interior designer (the oldest of nine kids in a Mormon family), who called the place "awful." What is so awful about it?, we wondered. It's true the place wasn't packed, but the patrons who were in attendance were not the bleary, slumped-down-on-the-bar career drunks that one might expect from an out-of-the way unfashionable gay bar. Small Tiffany-style lamps at the tables and evenly spaced along the bar gave the place a homey feel. And our hostess, Ikey, who has been slinging drinks at one gay bar or another since days of yore, could not have been friendlier. She memorized our names, chatted us up, bought us a shot, and emptied the ashtray after the first sling of ash from the first cigarette. So what was so awful? "Well," said John, "Nobody comes here, it's too quiet, it's not cruisy, and there's no dancing." We pointed out for some people that a quiet, noncruisy, no dancing gay bar might be the very definition of a good place to be. But John knew that already—he's here all the time! Call or check out local gay papers for a schedule of 3160 events and performers.

Berlin

954 W. Belmont Ave., 773/348-4975
www.berlinchicago.com
The Vibe: Would-be Weimar Republic era.
The Crowd: Men, women, gay-bi-straight, 20s and up.
The Space: Smallish for a club, dark, industrial.
When to Go: Any evening. Most hopping on Thursdays through Saturdays.
Getting There: Virtually underneath the Belmont stop for the Red, Brown, and Purple lines, #77 Belmont bus. Cabs plentiful.

Ah, Berlin! Dance club of our youths, close-quartered, full-floored omnisexual thump-thump bass beat delight! Robert and Kathie have spent many late-night hours here. Wednesday nights at Berlin were once the hottest women's action in town. While many other women's nights at otherwise gay boy or straight bars have came and went like the tide, Berlin's Women's Obsession (R.I.P.) persevered for more than ten years running. Kathie has very many fond memories of Women's Obsession night that include dancing, flirting, and ogling (and tipping) the girlie strippers. Robert recalls with pleasure special Disco, Prince, and Madonna nights, with dancers, impersonators, and a tightly packed dance crowd with lots of semi-innocent smooches with strangers right on the dance floor. We both thought that perhaps memories were all that Berlin was good for. A recent visit seemed more tame—at 10 P.M. the club was dead, the air conditioner blasted frigidly cold air, and nary a soul gyrated on the dance floor. However, by 11, the place was slowly filling up, the temperature was rising, and the night seemed to hum with the potential for fun, which makes us acknowledge that maybe we are the ones who have gotten tamer and lamer over the years, because we had to leave. In an unofficial polling of just about everyone we know in the known universe, they *all* mentioned Berlin as a place they would suggest to queer visitors seeking a dance club in the city. So, Wilkommen. Everyone in our entire known universe can't be wrong.

Neo
2350 N. Clark St., 773/528-2622
www.neo-chicago.com
The Vibe: "Don't ever say that the '80s are over!"
The Crowd: Pansexual mix of men and women, all ages, punk, Goth, heavy on the black eyeliner.
The Space: Dark and cryptlike, one long bar, large dance floor.
When to Go: After midnight on Thursdays.
Getting There: #22 Clark bus. Cabs plentiful.

While nightclub Neo, a fixture in Lincoln Park, is always what we could call gay-friendly, it's really on Thursday nights, from 10 P.M. to 4 A.M., when **Planet Earth** (www.planetearthchicago.com) with DJ Dave Robert takes over, that the queers come out in force. And we do mean queers, of all stripes and types. Neo on Thursdays is a haven for the bisexual, the questioning (Kathie's gal pal Nikki did a lot of her coming out here), the open-minded, and anyone, basically, who finds antique rosaries to be the perfect necklace or wristband for any occasion and owns ripped tights, sleeveless gloves, and oodles of black clothing. On a recent visit, Robert was amazed at how many men and women still had mohawks or multihued dreadlocks. Some folks looked like Madonna did in 1984, some went for the neo-pirate look popularized by Adam Ant, and many, many people in the multigendered and multigenerational crowd found heavy black eyeliner and heavy-handed eye shadow application a must to complete their

At your service at Neo.
~Photo by Mel Ferrand

ensembles. With all the Goth and punk action, Robert was faced with a dilemmasimilar to that created by today's metrosexual phenomenon: who was gay? Generally you might assume that the dude wearing all the mascara is light in his Doc Martens, but in this retro crowd, it ain't necessarily so. An affectionate butch lesbian couple befriended Robert because one of the women dropped a glass and Robert, trying to helpfully catch it as it bounced off the ledge, cut open his finger. They apologized and chatted a bit before he had to go and wash the blood off his hand. In the bathroom Robert could not help but stare at the tall, pale, shirtless, lanky Mohawk-sporting punker who oh-so-carefully reapplied his black lipstick to his bee-stung lips.

Neo's cement interior, combined with the catacomb-style arches, makes it resemble the lower levels of an abandoned cathedral. Blondie, New Order, and classic David Bowie tunes kept the enthusiastic crowd moving their feet to the beat. As Robert was getting ready to leave (with his hand still bleeding, which felt appropriately punk), he heard one woman say to her friend, "Hang on, I'm going to introduce you to a *very* odd man." There seemed to be quite a few candidates to fit that description in the nearby vicinity. Early birds beware: Robert left Neo at 1:30 A.M., and things were really just getting started, with a line of black-clad folk queued up to pay their $5 cover.

Manhandler Saloon
1948 N. Halsted St., 773/871-3339
The Vibe: *The Secret Garden* rewritten by Phil Andros.
The Crowd: Regulars, men, 20s on up, with the emphasis on older, bears, some leather.
The Space: Smallish, comfortably disheveled.
When to Go: Thursdays through Sundays after 11 P.M. Best in warmer weather.
Getting There: Red Line North and Clybourn stop, #8 Halsted bus. Cabs plentiful.

The first time Robert tried to go to the Manhandler, he thought it was closed: no lights, dark windows, ivy vines grown up all over the front—it looked abandoned. He walked across the street to get a cab back to more familiar haunts, when he saw two men stroll up to the door and walk in. Robert darted across and followed, entering a bit of a time warp. Once upon a time, the Manhandler was smack dab in the middle of the gay neighborhood. But time passes, neighborhoods change, the main gay strip traveled north, and now Manhandler is a bar smack dab in the middle of Lincoln Park's yuppieville, with college kids and recent graduates crowding the nearby bars and restaurants. It's tempting to simply write the place off as a relic and say something glib about the patrons being the same men who frequented the place several decades ago. There's some truth to that, but there's also something very refreshing to be in a gay bar talking, as we did the other night, to a man in his 70s, an urbane, witty, and wealthy art collector, who spoke passionately of his collection and also managed to fit in some flirty, "come up and see my etchings" kinds of comments.

And let's not leave you with the impression that everyone in Manhandler is on the far side of 40. Quite a few younger men were in evidence. And if they weren't there for the stacked beer box ambience and tatty disarray, not there for the bathroom doors that don't lock and also don't fully close, not there for the porn on the TV or the undeniable friendliness of the bartender and his laughing cronies, what is the attraction? Three words: the back forty. "The back forty" is what those in the know call the outdoor roofed area behind the bar. Walk through the bar's back door, and you enter a Japanese-style garden with a small fountain—the Japanese style interrupted a tad by the addition of several Adirondack chairs. Walk through this garden, which is about the size of the bar inside, and you'll reach the back forty, an area that, were it well lit, would seem to be a regular outdoor beer garden, with built-in tables and benches, a floor of white pebbles, and a wooden fence to keep out the prying eyes of the neighbors. Were it well lit. But the back forty is not well lit—in fact, it is not lit at all, except by the occasional flare of a match as someone lights a cigarette. If the prying eyes of the neighbors could see through the fence, they would see a lot of men standing apart from each other, mostly in silence. And every once in a while some of the shadow men move toward one another, the shadows meld, and onlookers gather in close and strain to see what might be happening. Patrons enter the back forty as strangers and leave as strangers who have amused themselves with other strangers, if you catch our drift. Whether you come to the Manhandler to do the back forty meet and greet or just to have a beer, don't forget to ask for Manhandler's *free* souvenir poster. We don't know of another gay bar in Chicago that offers this amenity.

El Gato Negro
1461 W. Irving Park Rd., 773/472-9353
The Vibe: Hombre looks like a lady.
Getting There: Brown Line Irving Park stop, #22 Clark bus. Cabs plentiful.

So here's the thing. For years and years, whenever the subject of El Gato Negro, the Lakeview bar just a tad west and north of Wrigley Field, has come up among our friends, invariably two things are mentioned. One, the Latina girls in the club weren't born as girls. Two, the knife fight. *What* knife fight?, you may well ask. Well, generally the story goes something likes this: "Ah, man, El Gato Negro? Dude, this friend of mine was walking by there [or was inside the club] and these two drag queens were on the sidewalk fighting, and one of them totally pulled out this knife. Man, a fight between drag queens—it was vicious." We have had variants of this story told to us by self-proclaimed witnesses, as well as by plenty of people who heard it from the fabled friend of a friend. At a recent party we heard the story as, "You will *totally* get a beer bottle broken over your head if you go there." For all the times we have heard about the cutting, you'd think El Gato Negro was more of a ginsu demo stand than a bar where transsexuals and men in drag perform and hang out. Still, when researching this guide, we would say to a friend, "Hey, want to go check out El Gato Negro next week?" And the friend would tell the tale of the knife fight. His friend's friend got stabbed. Or a drag queen was bleeding in the street. Or there was no knife, but a lot of face clawing. And the friend would say, "Anyway, I'm busy on . . . what was that night you wanted to go? Yeah, I'm busy then." Now, we recognize an urban legend when we hear one. You don't see the Latina boy-girls of the city all walking around with stitched-up faces. And a quick perusal of the Web site (www.rottenfruits.com) for local queer punk rockers Rotten Fruits—"Chicago's favorite drunken faggots," as they like to call themselves—yields a photo gallery of the band performing at El Gato Negro but does not mention any fights, with or without cutlery involved. We asked Rotten Fruit guitarist Mark Frietas (a.k.a. Ears) about his El Gato experience, and he says, "I've not seen knife fights at El Gato, but I have seen 'em at similar bars. Usually it's a fight over drugs or a man, and usually around the bathrooms. They add to the ambience. Anyhow, I don't doubt that there have been knife fights. But not when we played, just a drunken guy in his underwear (not me—I think he saw me playing in my undies and decided to follow suit as a way to get a date)." We don't know about the drunken guy, but Mark looks mighty fine in his undies, as pics on the Web site will prove. And we don't mean just for the underwear photo seekers among you. You can also check out the band's tunes, look at their schedule, and sign up for e-mail propaganda.

The *Chicago Tribune*, in an online review of bars that "tourists won't go to," describes El Gato Negro simply as a "Latino working-class gay bar in ethnically mixed gentrifying neighborhood, low-to-the-ground atmosphere. Queens, butches, nerds, bears, flames, closet cases—the works. Has been around forever." Perhaps there was a fight once, and the tale got amplified and altered, as tales will. Perhaps the knife fight tale was put out there by the ladies of El Gato Negro, to toughen up their image and keep out the scaredy-cats. Ladies, we salute you.

Bars in Uptown, Andersonville, and Other Points North

Scot's
1829 W. Montrose, 773/528-3253
The Vibe: Howdy, neighbor!
The Crowd: Men, women welcome, 30ish and older.
The Space: Small, narrow neighborhood bar. Two dartboards. Wicked cool jukebox.
When to Go: Any evening. Most hopping on Thursdays through Saturdays.
Getting There: Brown Line Montrose stop, #78 Montrose bus. Cabs fairly common.

Robert has to admit he loves the expensive satellite-linked jukebox at Scot's. There is something magical about a machine able to find just about any song out there in the universe. For an extra fee, you can even bump your song ahead of that tired Celine Dion mega-ballad in the lineup. It was worth it, to put a dent in the diva song cycles and hear the creepy deep tones of Johnny Cash's version of "Hurt." Scot's is an intimate space, with not a lot of seats. You might have to stand if it's at all busy. The crowd, though a tad cliquish, is friendly. As one acquaintance, a newbie who'd been dog-sitting for friends in the area, said, "If you just meet one person here, he introduces you to half the bar." The bartenders are all longtimers and generally gregarious. Girl patrons are more than welcome. On a recent visit, we watched a hot butch-femme duo engage in an hour-plus session of slow tongue kissing while grinding up against the wall by the door. It looked like fun. None of the menfolk got anywhere near as frisky—although some of them did seem a bit jealous. Straight peeps are more than welcome, too. One of Robert's straight friends threw his Cubs Opening Day party here for many years, and a glorious mix of worlds it was: all sexualities united in their enthusiasm for baseball and Bloody Marys. We can't imagine any gay-friendly straights feeling at all uncomfortable here. Scot's skylight serves as home to some gloriously fluffy Boston ferns, while the walls serve as a mini-art gallery for the community. We did find something we wanted to bring home and put in the bedroom: the paintings of Bruce Noel (www.brucenoel.com) that graced the walls on our most recent visit recalled both Keith Haring and Salvador Dali.

Clark's on Clark
5001 N. Clark St., 773/728-2373
The Vibe: Where the party people at?
The Crowd: Late-night partiers and Drunky McDrunks, 20s and up. Men, women welcome.
The Space: Boxlike room, pool table, darts.
When to Go: Any evening that you want to hear the birds sing as you stumble home.
Getting There: Red Line Argyle stop, #22 Clark bus. Cabs plentiful.

It took a straight girl to get Robert into Clark's the first time. He was out with his friend Jenny, the 2 A.M. bars were closing, and she wanted to keep the party happening. So they went into Clark's, which is open until 4 A.M. on weeknights and 5 on Saturdays. They both got a crick in their neck from looking up at the gay porn that constantly plays on the TV screen above the door. Early in the evening Clark's is the realm of career drunks and the locals. Robert's ex (not a career drunk, merely a talented amateur) recommends it as a good quiet place to play pool. As other bars get closer to last call, Clark's begins to fill up. The bathrooms are icky (the toilets often don't flush), but the drinks are cheap, and the general booziness of the joint means people are willing to chat. At its best, on a Thursday or Friday night, there's a fascinating social soup: Latina lesbians, leather guys (overflow from the nearby **Eagle**), drag queens, former frat boys three sheets to the wind, bartenders from other gay bars now off their shifts—a festival of fun with all sorts of folks. At its worst, well, Robert once saw an overserved gent keel over backward from his barstool and hit the ground, out cold. It must be true that God watches out for drunks and little children, because the man was basically unhurt. After he'd been coaxed awake, helped to his feet, and led like a zombie out to a cab, the bar crowd cheered, and a round of shots was ordered. Clark's is the habitat of the species known in Latin as *Drunky McDrunkus,* make no mistake.

Chicago Eagle
5015 N. Clark St., 773/728-0050
www.chicagoeagle.com
The Vibe: Are you my daddy, or am I
yours?
The Crowd: Men, leather, 30ish and
older.
The Space: Large square bar in front
room, Etienne murals on the walls.
Dark back bar and play area.
When to Go: Any evening. Leather-
only code in effect for back bar on
Tuesdays, Fridays, and Saturdays.
Getting There: Red Line Argyle stop,
#22 Clark bus. Cabs plentiful.
Parking lot across the street.

~Photo by Jon Peterson

The Eagle is a leather bar in the
proud lineage of Chicago's Gold
Coast Leather Bar, one of the
country's first leather bars. Legendary leather man Chuck Renslow, who owns
the Eagle (along with **Man's Country**, the bathhouse next door), opened the
Gold Coast in 1958 with his lover Dom Orejudos, also known as the erotic artist
Etienne. Etienne's fantasy murals of those hot leather men so good at being bad
still adorn the walls of the Eagle, and the tradition of a space for men who like
leather gear continues. Today's Chicago Eagle consists of two bars: the front bar,
large and square, where anyone is welcome to come in and have a drink, and
the clubroom area, which is smaller, darker, and, at least on Tuesdays, Fridays,
and Saturdays, restricted to those dressed in leather gear. If you don't know
what constitutes proper leather gear, you probably don't own the right stuff to
get back there. The official Web site provides guidance: "Major Article of
Leather, Rubber or Uniform (including Military Camouflage). No Gym Shoes,
Sandals, Sweaters or Perfumes." *Major article* means just that, gentlemen. Your
cute leather wristband is not gonna cut it. And what is the attraction of the
clubroom, beyond its dimness, lit for the most part by two pinball machines and
a television screen playing porn? The clubroom has its own (ahem) restroom,
but no one does much resting there, if you catch our drift. A lanky 24-year-old
friend says, "The Eagle on Saturday nights after 2 A.M. is an experience
everyone should have at least once" (the back room, that is). But he goes on to
warn, "It should be noted that the Eagle's back room is so very dark that it's
wise to pick out whom you'd like to get to know better before you go thither."
In other words, if you wait until you get to the back room to hook up, you might
not be so thrilled with Prince Charming in the harsh light of day. It's also dark
enough that at least two gents of our acquaintance have found their wallets

missing after various distractions and amusements. You might want to just bring ID and some cash and leave the bulging temptation of the wallet at home. One thing we love about the Eagle is the music that bartender Dan plays on Wednesday and Thursday nights: an awesome mix of old-school punk and rougher-edge new wave—it'll make you feel like you got your nose pierced only yesterday. Dan himself is someone to love. We know of several friends who hold a torch for Dan's hirsute, tattooed, leather-clad attractiveness. (We won't mention any names, Patrick.) The budget-minded, whether leather-clad or not, will appreciate the Tuesday special, when all well drinks and draft beers go for one slim dollar.

T's Restaurant and Bar
5025 N. Clark St., 773/784-6000
The Vibe: Comfort food, with alcohol accompaniment.
The Crowd: Men and women, mostly locals, varied age range.
The Space: A loudly yellow exterior with a roomy but homey inside, featuring two bars, table seating, couches for lounging, a pool table, and dartboards. Outdoor seating seasonally.
When to Go: Busy most evenings. Weeknights in the summer, get a seat outside.
Getting There: Red Line Argyle stop, #22 Clark bus. Ample cabs.

T's is a rare hybrid of a place. Gays and lesbians both consider it their own, while straight folks from the neighborhood might come here weekly for the hearty food and say they have never in their lives set foot in a gay bar. Two boys on a date is a common sight here, but so are two lesbians, or big mixed groups, for that matter, and everyone gets along just swimmingly. The food (served until late at night) comes in ample portions—the $5 burger special on Monday nights features a logjam of fries, and burgers are as big as your head. Twelve bucks on Fridays nets you all the fish and chips you can eat. Our baseball caps are off to owner Colm Tracy, who, with traces of his Irish brogue still in evidence, personally presides over a place where your parents would feel comfortable, and so would the tranny-boy nephew who used to be your niece. In fact, tranny boys have somewhat adopted T's as a home base. One nod to this are the gender-neutral bathrooms, each one just saying "restroom." The staff, a hardworking mix of men and women, gay and straight, remains the same friendly faces year after year.

Atmosphere

5355 N. Clark St., 773/784-1100

www.atmospherebar.com

The Vibe: Low-key for a dance bar.

The Crowd: Women, men, 20s to 30s.

The Space: Dance space, bar, and calm lounge area in the back.

When to Go: Weekends are the most happening.

Getting There: Red Line Berwyn stop, #22 Clark bus. Cabs plentiful.

Atmosphere may have started as a place for the boys, but in a great twist on the usual way the boys find a girl bar and take it over, the lesbos have invaded here, and any given evening the crowd is about half and half. Management has obviously noted and courted the girl crowd—on a recent Friday visit, two sexy but slightly tawdry-looking girl go-go dancers alternated shaking their groove thangs on the dance box, and they certainly had not been hired for the benefit of the guys in attendance. In some way Atmosphere seems to have been casting about for an identity. When it first opened it was a dance bar, plain and simple. Perhaps its close proximity to the lesbian bar **Star Gaze** has made young dyke overflow inevitable. And the older, less prone-to-dance GLBT population in Andersonville may mean that the bar has not been able to sustain a pure DJ-and-dance club. Atmosphere has had various theme and party nights, including a Wednesday cabaret night. Check out the Web site for a current schedule. The bar's search for an identity (and an audience) means nightly lure-you-in drink specials that are easy on the wallet. Robert has very much enjoyed grabbing a drink here on quiet weeknights. Large windows that open onto Clark Street allow for easy people-watching as well as chat and flirt sessions with folks walking by.

Star Gaze

5419 N. Clark St., 773/561-7363

www.stargazechicago.com

The Vibe: No pretensions here.

The Crowd: Mostly women, blue jeans and sweatshirts.

The Space: Paneled and mirrored. Small dance floor.

When to Go: Fridays and Saturdays for dancing. Weeknights for chatting.

Getting There: Red Line Berwyn stop, #22 Clark bus. Cabs plentiful.

The fact that Star Gaze posts flyers supporting women in labor unions attests to their blue-collar lesbian leanings. Not every dyke who comes to Star Gaze can route your drain or calibrate your brakes, although if you like that kind of gal, you will not be disappointed. As one of the few nearly exclusively women's bars in the city, Star Gaze is popular with local lesbians who want to grab a beer and a pool game in a friendly, casual environment. Friday nights feature Salsa music and dancing, and the Latina butches and femmes come dressed to the nines. On Saturday nights, the DJ spins a hodgepodge of music to shake your hips to. Any other time, there are the two televisions, a pool table, and the jukebox to keep you entertained. Star Gaze also has a kitchen that specializes in Puerto Rican fare and bar-food standards.

Joie de Vine
1744 W. Balmoral Ave., 773/989-6846
The Vibe: Urban hipster hangout on a quiet side street.
The Crowd: Women, men, GLBT and straight, 30s and up.
The Space: Small, animated space with an ultramodern minimalist flair. Outdoor seating seasonally.
When to Go: Weeknights for a quiet date, weekends for crowded fun.
Getting There: Red Line Berwyn stop, #22 Clark bus. Cabs plentiful. Some street parking.

This lesbian-owned hidden treasure is three short blocks from Clark Street, tucked away on a small stretch of modest commercial spaces surrounded by single-family homes and six-flats. The green lawns and mature shade trees will make you feel like you have left the city and arrived in a peaceful Midwestern town, until you enter the hip and glossy-surfaced Joie de Vine, where you'll feel firmly back in a world city. While other forms of drink are available, the focus, as you might guess, is firmly on wine—by the glass, by the flight, or by the bottle. Their wine list doesn't go that deep, but they offer plenty of nice bottles for reasonable prices. Robert got lazy the other night and told the bartender to just pick him out a nice summery white and ended up with one of the best California chardonnays he's ever had. He went there with two lesbian friends, and he and

Star Gaze girls.
~Photo by Mel Ferrand

the girls both had lots of scenery of the male and female variety to look at. Their only problem was feeling a tad underdressed—on this warm summer night the men all had on trousers instead of shorts, the women were wearing what Robert's friends referred to as "*L-Word* chic," and the only T-shirts in sight were on our heroes. Next time they'll know to be a bit more presentable, although we've heard that this is a popular postsoftball hangout for the lezzie crowd, and we can't imagine they arrive all perfumed and designer-clad for *that*. Joie de Vine offers a modest but accomplished menu of cheese flights, olive flights, and meat nibblies to go with the wine, and the outdoor seating is obviously very popular. Robert also found this to be a primo date spot on a quiet winter's night. Oodles of atmosphere, but quiet enough for get-to-know-you conversation.

Crew

4804 N. Broadway St., 773/784-2739
www.worldsgreatestbar.com
The Vibe: Hey, batter batter, swing out, sister.
The Crowd: Men, women welcome, varied age range.
The Space: A restaurant and bar with a fresh elegant design and sports memorabilia décor. Pool table, dartboard.
When to Go: After the big game or any evening.
Getting There: Red Line Lawrence stop, #36 Broadway bus. Cabs plentiful.

Not many people actually *watch* the various sporting events that play on all 16 of Crew's TV screens, and the sound is not on for any of them—you'll have to squint at the writing at the bottom to find out the score. But Crew is a popular after-the-big-game destination for queer Chicago athletes. A relative newcomer in the world of Chicago bars, Crew opened in July of 2004 and was an immediate success. Part of that success, we think, is the post-gay feel of the place. There's none of the hidden shame that some gay bars hold on to. You can see in through the front windows (in fact, they open up to let in the air in warmer weather), and the lighting, while dim enough to be flattering, is not that oh-we-are-gay-and-dirty-and-must-live-in-the-dark nonillumination favored by so many other establishments. It's entirely possible for concertgoers to leave the nearby Aragon or Riviera theaters, wander in to Crew, and not realize they are in a gay bar until they see the signed Greg Louganis photo in the (delightfully pristine) swimming pool–themed men's bathroom. The girl's restroom has a Billie Jean King theme, no lie. Crew's menu leans to the all-American, with burgers, chicken strips, salads, and lots of items dipped in the deep fryer. The chicken sandwich with goat cheese and spinach pesto was particularly yummy. The crowd here (and it's generally fairly crowded) is a diverse mix, with more men but a welcoming environment for women and an age range from 21 to 55. As you'd expect from a sports joint, jeans are the typical fashion choice. A word to the singletons: Crew is a destination for groups of friends and teammates or people on casual dates, so if you are a solo traveler, this might not be the place to meet new companions—they'll be occupied already. Robert sends kudos and air kisses to the lanky-boy waiter staff, *especially* the guy who always wears funky fun caps and was at the Martha Wainwright concert at Schubas. (Hi! You are quite the hottie!)

Big Chicks

5024 N. Sheridan Rd., 773/728-5511
www.bigchicks.com
The Vibe: Homey joint with extraordinary art on the walls.
The Crowd: Men, women welcome, locals, 25 and up.
The Space: A long narrow bar, side salon room with extra seating turns into a dance floor on weekends. Pool table, darts.
When to Go: Weeknights to chat, Fridays and Saturdays to dance, Sunday afternoons for free buffet.
Getting There: Red Line Argyle stop, #151 Sheridan bus. Cabs plentiful.

Kathie and Robert have long enjoyed the comfort zone that is the neighborhood bar Big Chicks. One of the main attractions of the place is owner Michelle Fire's impressive collection of contemporary photography and outsider art. You owe it to yourself to visit at least once during an early evening, so you have the space and time to wander and view. Our friends often describe the Chicks crowd as being among the most friendly and least pretentious around. The salon room is cleared for dancing on Friday and Saturday nights, and the mix of Madonna, Prince, and other big gay faves generally

Art at Big Chicks.
~Photo by Ianni Grammatis

has the floor full and hopping by midnight. Speaking of midnights, one of the treasured traditions of Chicks is the free midnight shot, one per customer. And speaking of free, here's one of the best deals going: the Sunday free buffet. We're not talking some cheap-ass free stuff—in the summer there's an entirely satisfying barbeque with brats, burgers, veggie burgers, and all the sides and fixings, while winter fare ranges from lasagna to fried chicken to beef. There are always options for the noncarnivore. If you go to the Web site and sign up for the e-mail list, you'll get a notice telling you what the Sunday buffet will be and also have a chance to win a $10 bar tab—Michelle currently gives away two of these every week. As if that weren't enough, you *always* get a $10 bar tab e-mailed to you on your birthday.

A relatively recent addition to Big Chicks is the chance to buy bar food anytime. It's better than the usual bar food, because Chicks shares a kitchen with sister spot **Tweet**, Michelle's restaurant right next door. Everyone seems to single out the French fries as being particularly tasty.

Another item of note about Big Chicks – although Chicago is the latest city to butt out and require all bars and restaurant to gradually become smoke free, Big Chicks is at the vanguard. In January, 2006, the bar voluntarily became 100% smoke free, introducing a heretofore novel concept in Chicago's bar scene – the ability be out at a bar all night and not come home reeking like stale smoke. Who evah heard of such a thing? It's crazy, and yet we think we're in love.

So, What else can we tell you about Big Chicks? Robert has met boys to kiss here, Kathie has met girls—our fondness for the place is deep and abiding.

Far North Bars

Granville Anvil
1137 W. Granville Ave., 773/973-0006
The Vibe: Hey, babe, take a walk on the dive side.
The Crowd: Men, locals, varied age range.
The Space: A nondescript, easy-to-miss exterior leads into a darkish room with an S-shaped bar.
When to Go: We dare you to try it at 9 A.M. (11 P.M. on a Wednesday was good.)
Getting There: Red Line Granville stop, #36 Broadway bus. Cabs not uncommon.

Although we'd heard of the place for years, we only recently ventured into the dark mouth of the Far North Side bar the Granville Anvil. Heart's "Crazy on You" blitzed from the spiffy digital jukebox (the only contemporary touch in the joint), and '80s music seemed to be the patrons' pick of the day, which was fine by us. Also fine was the Wednesday special: $3.50 pitchers of Rolling Rock Light or Berghoff beer. Yes, $3.50!! You can't get a single bottle of beer for that on Halsted Street these days. And this was not some wimpy little mug masquerading as a pitcher. No, sir, these were full on, cleverly chilled-with-ice-compartment pitchers. The décor is nothing to write home about, but if we did, the postcard would say, "Dear Mom, the Anvil is decorated with pencil drawings and prints from the Etienne and Tom of Finland School of 1980s pornography. There's a long bank of mirrors behind the bar. Don't forget to note the two scarily large wooden penis sculptures (complete with wooden scrotums) hanging above the men's room door, like some kind of dildo hunting trophies. Wish you were here." Robert was just about to declare that the Anvil completely defied his expectations of dive-bar scariness. Then he went to the bathroom and saw the barf in the sink. About an hour, another pitcher, and a pleasant conversation with a bar mate later, the cheerful bartender, Frankie, emerged from the bathroom to announce that people washing their hands had flushed away the sins of the unknown barfer, leaving Frankie free to forgo cleaning.

The Anvil is a friendly place. Frankie's cheeriness is infectious, and all of the people around us made sure to say hello and make us feel welcome. One gent followed Robert into the bathroom each time he went, presumably to make sure he did not get lonely.

All in all, we'd have to tell you that if you want a cheap night out (there's some kind of amazing drink deal every night) and aren't too fastidious, try the Anvil! It would be a fun field trip for a group of friends who want to leave Boystown behind for the night. And you might have a supernatural encounter. Frankie the bartender told us that the Anvil has resident ghosts, poltergeists who send lightbulbs flying, and also a "presence" that telepathically communicates "everything is going to be okay." We think we might have seen that ghost, actually—a man dressed in gay clone attire circa 1978: jeans, a red silk shirt open nearly to his navel (exposing his furred chest), a Village People moustache, and long hair parted in the middle and feathered back. This apparition appeared alone, had a drink, and then disappeared as quietly as he'd arrived.

Jackhammer

6406 N. Clark St., 773/743-5772

www.jackhammer-chicago.com

The Vibe: A little bit trashy, a little bit flashy.

The Crowd: Men, women welcome, 20s on up, with the emphasis on older.

The Space: Dance floor up front, rectangular bar in the middle, patio open seasonally.

When to Go: Thursdays for dollar beers or weekends.

Getting There: #22 Clark bus, #36 Broadway bus. Cabs common.

Jackhammer feels to us like a small-town gay bar transplanted into the big city. In a small-town gay bar, everyone who is queer identified goes there because it's the only option, and the microcultures of drag and dyke, leather and lace, jock and bear, young and old, black and white all get along and interact because it's the safe zone and everyone shares it. In Chicago only the **Closet** or **Charlie's** after 2 A.M. equals Jackhammer for its heady mix of ethnicities, social classes, creeds, colors, and fetishistic impulses. All of which makes for good people-watching and bar-chat opportunities. One of the characters-in-residence is a drag queen, a lady of a certain age named Miss Barbie Doll, always a knockout in her platinum wig, totteringly high heels, silver lipstick, and bodacious knockers. If you are lucky, she'll be working the room with her Euro accent and a tray of Kool-Aid shots. Like that small-town bar that's everything to everybody, Jackhammer hosts a lot of specialty nights, from strippers to drag races, from the ever-popular karaoke to porn-release parties. Check their Web site for the particulars. On Thursday nights domestic beers go for just one little dollar a bottle, which may make the trip up north an economically sensible journey. If you do make the trip north, you may as well also pop in at **Touché**—it's right next door, and on busy nights there is a lot of ebb and flow between the bars, as if they were separate tide pools, their populations briefly connected by the salty spray of a potent ocean's waves. Sort of.

Touché
6412 N. Clark St., 773/465-7400
The Vibe: Drunky McDrunk, dressed in leather.
The Crowd: Men, often a leather crowd, generally 35 and up, with a smattering of younger guys.
The Space: Front bar with darts, pinball, and porn, and back bar (info follows).
When to Go: First Saturday of the month for Bear Night, late night on weekends for drunken debauchery.
Getting There: #22 Clark bus, #36 Broadway bus. Cabs common.

The front bar of Touché looks like Any Bar, USA, if Any Bar, USA, played nasty hard-core porn on its TV instead of the ball game. The back bar area, lit in a sort of horror movie red glow and decorated with old tires (don't try this at home), is dominated, so to speak, by a large video screen that also features nasty hard-core gay porn. Taking their cue from the porn, the patrons of Touché have been known to get a bit frisky in the dark alcoves behind and beside the video screen. Touché is a leather bar, and during the annual International Male Leather weekend, it's one of the hot spots for leather folk to meet and greet. "Yeah, it's like Christmas for us," one of the bartenders said. But unlike other leather bars, unless there is a special event going on, there is no dress code enforced in the back bar, and you are as likely to see flannel and blue jeans as leather and rubber. Touché is open until 4 A.M. on weeknights and 5 A.M. on weekends; the backroom action, if that's what you are going for, is more prevalent after 2 A.M. The first Saturday of each month Touché hosts their popular Bear Night, for the big-bellied hairy boys and their admirers, with free eats and drink specials. With all those bears in attendance, capacity is quickly reached, and it's not unusual for a line to form. If you'd rather not wait, go right next door to **Jackhammer**, where Touché's overflow forms a sort of impromptu bear night. An event that makes us warm a bit to Touché is their new "Leather Eye for the Preppy Guy," where young crewneck-clad Biffs and Conrads get made over into Yes-Sir Daddies. Not to put all the emphasis on drunkenness, but you will almost surely meet some overserved men on any Touché sojourn. If we know this, so do the pickpockets, so mind your wallets.

Bars Downtown

Gentry
440 N. State St., 312/836-0937
www.gentryofchicago.com
The Vibe: Life is a cabaret, traveling businessmen.
The Crowd: Downtown workers and travelers who don't want to go to Boystown. Men, women welcome, 20s on up, with the emphasis on older.
The Space: Three bars in one: oval-shaped main bar, intimate cabaret lounge, downstairs video bar.
When to Go: Sundays for open mic, every other night for live performances.
Getting There: Red Line Grand stop. Cabs plentiful.

The downtown Gentry has its share of regulars, from the rare true locals who live somewhere nearby to downtown office workers who stop here before going home. But it also plays host to a lot of travelers and tourists, some of whom have curiously pale bands on their wedding ring fingers. Suit-and-tie garb is common. Perhaps because people are traveling and a tad lonely, we find that Gentry's main bar room is a convivial place, where people are happy to strike up a conversation and not just in the hopes of a hotel room liaison, although *those* conversations happen, too. The comfy cabaret lounge hosts local and nationally known performers. You'll often find chanteuses Kathryn Payne ("pleasure with Payne," proclaims her Web site, www.kathrynpayne.com) and Becky Menzie (www.beckiemenzie.com) in residence. Both women have won After Dark Awards for Best Cabaret Artist from *Gay Chicago Magazine*, and both women know their way around a keyboard and a show tune queen audience. The cabaret lounge does not charge a cover except for special events. Check the Web site for a calendar. If cabaret's not your thing, you can dart downstairs to the darkly appointed video bar. Mirrors make the smallish space less claustrophobic, and snappy contemporary music videos keep the boys' toes tapping.

Second Story Bar
157 E. Ohio St., 312/923-9536
The Vibe: Man, oh man, I need a drink.
The Crowd: Downtown workers in search of boozy comfort. Men, women welcome.
The Space: Itty-bitty space on, you guessed it, the second floor.
When to Go: After work when you have had a very bad day.
Getting There: Red Line Grand stop, Michigan Avenue buses. Cabs plentiful.

Walk up the carpeted stairs to the second story of 157 E. Ohio Street, a mere two skips off of Michigan Avenue, and you'll open a metal portal to enter a small bar that feels more small town than world city. The bartender greeted Robert with, "Hi, I've never seen you here before," which Robert thought an odd thing to say in downtown Chicago, where certainly many travelers must come and go. But Peter and Greg, the two friendly gents sitting next to Robert, told him the place was like TV's Cheers, and indeed they did seem to know a lot of fellow patrons and were quite welcoming to newbie Robert. An anonymous reviewer at Citysearch (www.citysearch.com) says of the Second Story, "This was a big mistake. No one there under 40. Very dark and scary looking." On behalf of the over-40 men, Robert would just like to say, firmly and kindly, that we did not want your pimply young ass *anyway*. As for "dark and scary looking," the anonymous reviewer must scare easily, as this place, while nondescript and possessing a gently seedy air, is no darker than the average bar and about as scary as a box of drunk kittens. On Robert's visit, Peter and Greg were joined by their friend Tom, shots of Jägermeister were imbibed, and everyone got so darn friendly and welcoming that Robert could've had a "second story" to tell in the morning. However, his modest two beers on an empty stomach sent him off in search of a sandwich in lieu of sexual adventure. Maybe next time, guys.

Bars West and South

Davenport's
1383 N. Milwaukee Ave., 773/278-1830
www.davenportspianobar.com
The Vibe: Have a martini, and enjoy the show.
The Crowd: Men, women, 30s on up, dressy attire.
The Space: Swanky piano bar up front, cabaret performance room in the back.
When to Go: Check the Web site to see which performer sounds most appealing.
Getting There: Blue Line Division stop, #50 Damen bus, #72 North Avenue bus. Cabs not uncommon. Street parking available.

You know, there are darn few places left where you can pay good money to go see a professional Judy Garland impersonator perform. Sure, amateurs are a dime a dozen. Pour two martinis down Robert's gullet, and it's quite possible he'll serenade you with "The Man That Got Away." But you probably won't pay him, unless it's to stop. This lesbian-owned nightclub has indeed featured Mr. Tommy Femia (www.tommyfemia.com) doing Judy in the past. Robert went to see him perform with a mixed group of gay and straight folk, and everyone had a blast. Tommy sang (no lip-synching here) songs that Judy made famous, as well as songs she might have sung had the poor dear lived to see the day. The front bar at Davenport's features someone at the piano nightly, tickling the ivories and singing some tunes. Most of the waitstaff will, at some point in the evening, step up to the mic as well, delivering vocals well beyond the amateur range. Certainly you are welcome to remain here, having a cocktail and enjoying the free entertainment. (Be sure and tip the piano player.) But Davenport's main attraction is its rotating schedule of local and nationally known cabaret performers who play the intimate lounge in the back. Miss Debbie Boone of "You Light Up My Life" fame is performing there as Robert writes this. Show prices vary depending on the performers (generally around $25), but a two-drink minimum remains in effect, and the drinks are not inexpensive. Davenport's is not the destination if you are looking for a casual cheap night out. But it's perfect when you are in the mood to get dressy, pretend you are a Rat Packer, and drop a bit of cash. As we said, mixed groups of straight and gay do well here. But we were here once when most of the audience was composed of a straight girl bachelorette party—young straight girls who did not like cabaret music. The bride-to-be was on her cell phone for much of the show and clearly deserved a hearty bitch slapping. The performer that night, bless her heart, did not resort to violence, although she did pull out the sarcasm, sadly lost on the inebriated and none-too-bright bride-to-be. We highly recommend catching Colleen McHugh when she's here or elsewhere in town (check her Web site for info: http://colleenmchugh.com). Her voice is grand, her comedic timing is impeccable, and her version of the Gloria Gaynor anthem "I Will Survive" never fails to bring down the house. Robert and posse particularly enjoyed her annual holiday show, "There's Noel in Chanukah."

Lost & Found
3058 W. Irving Park Rd., 773/463-7599
The Vibe: I'll have a beer and a memory. . . .
The Crowd: Women, 35-plus, a few men.
The Space: Dark and paneled.
When to Go: Tuesdays and Fridays during dart league (winter) or any night for a quiet game of pool. Closed Mondays and Tuesdays except during Tuesday night dart league.
Getting There: It's all about the #80 Irving Park bus, baybee.

Lost & Found is the oldest continuously running lesbian bar in Chicago. We'd wager it might be the oldest in the country. Lost & Found has been serving Chicago's gay women since 1965 (and one may quip that they've kept the same clientele since then). Given its location on a barren strip of West Irving Park Road, you may *think* that you're lost trying to find this place. Only a discreet hanging door sign indicates you are in the right spot, but the friendly confines of Lost & Found paired with a highly recommended Thai restaurant, **Dharma Garden** (3109 W. Irving Park Rd., 773/588-9140), located catty-corner, make this intersection of Albany and Irving Park a welcome oasis in the midst of urban blandness. You have to knock on the door and be buzzed in. Once you're inside, there really isn't much that distinguishes Lost & Found from any other blue-collar neighborhood watering hole. The clock face featuring a sexy lady in a wet swimsuit would be just as at home at Joe's corner tavern as at a lesbian bar. There is a pretty bar, with what looks like original lead-glass details, a pool table, a few dartboards, a jukebox with all the usual suspects, a lot of smoke, and a *lot* of paneling. The crowd is mostly older (but every time Kathie has been there, there have been a few younger gals hanging out, playing pool or what have you) and a smattering of gay male friends. The place isn't very busy during the

week—when someone knocked on the door about 15 minutes after Kathie was
seated on a Thursday evening, a regular commented that it was "a rush."
Business must have been slamming that night, because shortly after that, three
young women came in, bringing the total customer count to about ten. Busiest
nights at the bar are Tuesdays and Fridays in the winter, when dart leagues take
over and the free popcorn machine pops back to life. During other seasons, the
bar is closed on Mondays and Tuesdays and open Wednesday through Sunday,
from 7 P.M. until 2 A.M. (3 on Saturdays) or until business is dead for the night,
which may be as early as 11 on some weeknights, so phone first.

InnExile

5758 W. 65th St., 773/582-3510
www.innexilechicago.com
The Vibe: Fun in your parents' refurbished basement, circa 1979.
The Crowd: Men, 30s on up, women welcome, casual.
The Space: Comfy bar space with video games, dartboard, modest dance floor.
When to Go: Weekends are the most happening times.
Getting There: Cabs rare—you'd have to call one. Ample street parking, parking
lot available.

Robert hitched a ride with his friend Christophe to InnExile on a warm
weeknight in June. To a Chicago North Sider's point of view, the "exile" part of
the name can seem apropos—the bar sits on the outskirts of Midway Airport and
borders a vacant lot, with not so much as a dry cleaner or fast-food joint within
the immediate vicinity. The nearby residential areas are single-family bungalows,
in a neighborhood that feels more suburban than city. One huge benefit of the
bar's remote location is parking. That's right, although close parking is a nearly
impossible dream if you are going to a North Side gay bar, you can pull your ride
up to the door of InnExile and stroll on in. What with the lowered stucco ceiling
right over the bar, the chipped Formica countertop–style bar surface, the algae
blue paint on the walls, and the basketball game pleasantly blaring from two
TVs, Robert felt like he'd walked into someone's nicely done up basement, the
kind where your uncle Joe always keeps a keg tapped and has soda pop for the
kids. Christophe said, not unkindly, that it reminded him of Peoria. After a short
time of having the place to themselves, several other patrons arrived, all men
about 20 years older than Robert and Christophe. The bartender showed off
pictures of a new grandchild. Robert and Christophe's chat was punctuated by
the occasional thunder of a low-flying plane, and also some mysterious clomping
footsteps from somewhere overhead—which reinforced Robert's fantasy of being
in a basement in 1979. This is not to imply that the place was a dive—far from it.
The warm lighting, scrupulously clean bathroom, and complete absence of stale
dive-bar smell made for a comfy, homey atmosphere. The folks at InnExile end
their exile on Gay Pride Sunday—several notices advertised a $5 ride to and from
the parade. Someday, to be fair, the North Siders need to consider staging the

Pride Parade on 65th Street as a nod to their Southwest Side brethren. Robert and Christophe agreed that if they lived closer, this would be a grand spot to grab the occasional beer. At 10:30, just as they were leaving, a group of men in their 30s walked in. It could be that the party was just getting started.

Escapades
6301 S. Harlem Ave., 773/229-0686
The Vibe: Trashy, in the best possible way.
The Crowd: Men, varied ages, women welcome.
The Space: Inauspicious brick exterior, roomy interior with an attempt at tiki décor. Dartboard, ATM.
When to Go: Weekends are busiest.
Getting There: Cabs not common—you'd have to call one. Parking lot available.

It's easy to overlook this unlit brick building, right on the corner of busy Harlem Avenue and 63rd Street. At first glance, Robert and fellow traveler Christophe were not sure the place was open. Look for Mattress World, conveniently located across Harlem to the west, or, more prominently, Mr. Shrimp—no, not a toe-sucking emporium but rather a fluorescently lit fast-foot joint—leaning comfortably smack dab against the Escapades space. The special of the day was chicken tenders, with fries, for $3.99, and yes, they were open late. There's ample parking for both businesses in a side lot. Inside Escapades, you can grab an intimate table for two or belly directly up to the bar, where tap beer, at least, was limited to your choice of Miller Lite or Miller Lite. Someone has attempted a tiki hut theme, with elements including faux bamboo wallpaper, paper fish suspended behind the bar, and paper tiki hut straw right overhead. To Robert's mind this last touch is just one wildly gesticulated cigarette lighter away from newspaper headline tragedy, but he didn't dwell on it because, after all, homos aren't the wildly gesticulating types—well, maybe he should have been more worried. But no fires broke out, and the small crowd was friendly—"He's a real sweet guy," said one patron of another who'd just departed, "he's just not very bright is all." Friendliness might explain the lack of a door on the guy's john. With a mirror in the bathroom *and* a mirrored wall across from the bathroom door, the friendly and inquisitive could probably manage to catch a reflection of the business at hand, so to speak, were they inclined to do so. Located on a major road and close to Interstate 55, Escapades is actually only a 20- to 30-minute car ride from the North Side, at least in non-rush hour traffic. Robert and Christophe feel it warrants a second visit on a weekend, to give the place its proper due. Everyone in the bar called out good-byes as they left. In the parking lot, Robert glanced back regretfully at a beefy proto-bear of a construction worker, who looked alluringly just off the job. The good ones generally arrive when you are departing.

Chesterfield Club

1800 W. Pershing Rd., 773/376-9511

The Vibe: "Another Saturday night and I ain't got no papi."

The Crowd: Men, primarily (though not exclusively) Spanish speaking, women, transgendered folk welcome.

The Space: Large bar with dance floor, pool table.

When to Go: Friday and Saturday nights. Indeed, we are not sure if they are open any other times.

Getting There: Red Line to #35 35th Street bus, #9 Ashland bus. Cabs not common—you'd have to call one. Street parking available.

We tried to visit this primo gay Latino destination. Really, we did. One Saturday night Robert and his friend Christophe arrived at the door around 10:30, only to find a huge long line to get into the place, which spoke well for it as a happening nightspot. *Very* happening, as no one was leaving (why would anyone, early on a Saturday night?) and the line was not moving. They decided to visit a few other places and return later. Later rolled around, and at 12:30 A.M. the long line was still in evidence and still not moving. Robert attempted to go to the Chesterfield on a Thursday night (in a rental car, as there is really not a swift practical CTA way to get from Robert's Andersonville digs to this Southwest Side bar) only to find the bar was not *open* at 10:30 P.M. on a Thursday, something unthinkable for a North Side gay bar, where Thursday is the unofficial Friday. So we conferred with some compadres. Chris Piss, from the band Three Dollar Bill (see our music section, Chapter 15, for more about them), has been to Chesterfield multiple times in the past year. We had heard the bar referred to as the "Latino **Big Chicks**," meaning that it is similar to the laid-back atmosphere and casual dress code favored at that North Side establishment. Chris says that description is accurate: "The space is nothing fancy at all, but it's bigger than Big Chicks. The bar is in the center, so people can hang out on all four sides of it. There are no tables, but there are stools all around the bar and then also around the walls. There's a pool table and there's a dance floor that's almost twice the size of the one at Big Chicks." The crowd, Chris notes, is "predominantly men, but yes there are women there and it's trans-friendly . . . the clientele include both bilingual and monolingual Spanish speakers. Spanish-speaking gay men come from Wisconsin, Indiana, and Michigan just to hang out at Chesterfield on Saturday night. There are also a few male and female college students of various races hanging out there, probably from U of C or UIC, who have opted for Chesterfield instead of Halted Street. Maybe it's closer to where they live?" Some poking around online yielded the interesting fact that female impersonator David de Alba (a Judy Garland specialist) was performing at the Chesterfield Club in the mid-1960s, making it one of the oldest continuously gay nightspots in the city now that Charmers and Legacy 21 are no more.

Robert's friend Charles used to live near the Chesterfield, and it was his neighborhood hangout for a time. Charles speaks glowingly of the Spanish dance music and the atmosphere, which he felt was "relaxed and not all about the fashion." Charles also noted the attendance of what he called "Bean Queens," lone-wolf Anglos in their 40s and 50s looking for younger gay Latinos for boyfriends or "dates." As a small percentage of the younger gay Latinos were looking for older Anglo daddies, the Bean Queens were tolerated. Call us if you are going to the Chesterfield, because we'll go, too, and this time, we'll get there early on a Saturday night, and the length of the line will not dissuade us.

Jeffrey Pub

7041 S. Jeffery Blvd., 773/363-8555
The Vibe: Comfy South Side classic.
The Crowd: Men, women, all ages.
The Space: Small bar with narrow dance floor, great jukebox.
When to Go: Sundays for a boys' night, Thursdays for the girls, Fridays and Saturdays for a mixed crowd.
Getting There: #14 Jeffery Express bus, #15 Jeffery Local bus. Cabs not common—you'd have to call one. Street parking available.

"In Chicago you can't be black and gay on the south side." Or so said J.L. King, author the book *On the Down Low,* in a 2004 interview with the *Advocate.* Activist and writer Keith Boykin and others responded immediately, and one strong refutation they gave to King's comments was the longtime existence of this popular South Side bar. King may not be able to be black and gay on the Chicago's South Side—indeed, he refuses to be labled as bisexual or gay and prefers to remain "a man who has sex with men." Um, okay, Mr. King. At any rate, Chicago has plenty of out black men and women living on the South Side, and one of the places where they socialize is the Jeffrey Pub. Kathie and Robert made their way here one balmy Friday evening. A rainbow sign marked the modest entrance. We were buzzed in by the bartender and joined the men and women sitting at the bar. It was obvious from the conversation and camaraderie that some of the patrons were regulars, well known to each other and the bartender. As the only white folks in the place, we were obviously *not* regulars, and the bartender gave us some insider info on the Jeffrey. Thursday night tends to be the main night for the lesbian crowd, while Sunday is the night for men. Fridays and Saturdays, he told us, the mix was "about half and half," and both nights the dance floor gets full and busy later on (the Jeffrey is open until 4 A.M.). A "two-drink minimum" sign was posted behind the bar, but early in the evening the rule wasn't enforced. The two unisex, single-serving bathrooms don't lock—we can imagine that during busier times you might want to have a friend guard the door for you, to avoid those embarrassing "oops, sorry" moments. Most of the rules posted in the restrooms it would not have occurred to us to break. "No standing on the bar." After just one beer each, not a temptation. "No weed smoking." Even had we wanted to, neither of us was carrying. "No cigarettes or drinks on the dance floor." Having both been victimized by drink spillers and lit-cigarette gesticulators in other establishments, we loved this rule. "No nudity." It was a tad too early for that.

A man to our right watched the Cubs game on TV. To our left, an older lesbian held forth at length about the beauty and desirability of feminist Gloria Steinem: "That woman has managed to age with grace. Damn fine woman." The trim and sprightly speaker, about Ms. Steinem's age, might well have been talking about herself. She only stopped discussing Gloria's charms when the jukebox selection turned to Sarah Vaughan, singing "April in Paris." In one of those wonderful movielike moments, about 30 seconds or so into the song all the busy bar conversation became muted, and everyone, with deep pleasure, listened to the dulcet tones of Sassy.

Not far from the Jeffrey is **Club Escape** (1530 E. 75th St., 773/667-6454). Like the Jeffrey, dance is on the menu, and again like the Jeffrey, Thursday night is women's night here. Oh, and despite J.L. King, you can be black and gay at this South Side establishment. Or white and gay, for that matter.

Don't Try and Stop Me, Mary— I'm Going In: Forays into Straight Bars

Some might argue that the idea of a gay bar—that is, a drinking establishment by and for a strictly homo crowd—is, at least in an urban environment like Chicago, going the way of the Brontosaurus. Indeed, there are plenty of bars and clubs where the patrons—man, woman, gay, straight, everything's just a label—are all part of a glorious polymorphous mix. We know card-carrying members of the homo set who look on a trip to such über-gay places as **Sidetrack** and **Roscoe's** with about as much enthusiasm as a visit to the emergency room. For those queers who don't want to limit themselves to queer-only environments, we do want to remind you that this is (hooray!) the twenty-first century, Chicago is a big oasis of relative tolerance, and with a bar every block or so, you don't have to schlep to Boystown to have a cocktail in comfort. Sure, if you're a boy and you want to publicly dry-hump your boyfriend for hours, the local blue-collar watering hole may not be the place. And if you are a girl and want to make out with your girlfriend somewhere in the yuppie Pickups-ville of Rush Street bars, expect lewd comments and horny male MBA students asking to join you.

Our friend Rod, 35, has lived in Chicago for more than seven years and is, last time we checked, indeed a card-carrying, out and proud fag of the first degree. He's also been known to tip back a pint, more often than not in a straight bar. Rod sports an adorable genuine Arkansas-bred drawl that we can't convey in print. His current favorite watering hole in the city is **Tavern 33**, a sports-oriented bar on Lincoln Avenue near Belmont. Rod likes it because it's close to the "L," the staff and clientele are friendly, and the Pabst Blue Ribbon $2 specials are easy on the wallet. Of his straight-bar forays, Rod says, "My sexuality doesn't define who I am. We have to live and work in a mostly straight world—grow up and drink in one, too. If every faggot would try to spend the majority of their 'bar' time in the straight bar of their choice for a six-month period, they'd meet new and interesting people and, perhaps, introduce a small piece of the rest of the world to a 'real' homosexual. (Plus I prefer to remove alcohol from the casual-sex equation—less room for mistakes and errors of judgment.)"

Amen to that last part, Rod. But what does the charming old codger two bar stools away do when he finds out that (gasp!) the young man he's been talking politics with for the past 15 minutes is one of the gays? "Just about every straight bar I've spent considerable time in has concluded that I'm gay," says Rod. "But by the time they do, they've already grown to appreciate, enjoy, and even (shocker) *like* me as a person. I think I've normalized 'gays' for a small portion of these straight working-class bar folk, and I consider them my friends." Without further adieu, here are some of the straight bars Rod recommends, along with his comments.

Tavern 33
3328 N. Lincoln Ave., 773/935-6393

Robert's been here on several occasions with Rod and always had a great time. It's as straight as a line and completely welcoming. A great place for a mixed crowd of gay and straight friends to gather. No food, but there's a fine burrito stand right next door, or have a pizza delivered, like we did. Rod also recommends the sushi place right across the street.

Village Tap
2055 W. Roscoe St., 773/883-0817

"In the Roscoe Village neighborhood, it has good bar food and Ms. Pac Man!"

Lincoln Horseshoe
4115 N. Lincoln Ave., 773/549-9292

"North of Irving Park, this is a high-style but comfortable rockabilly joint with live music sometimes and great BBQ. The bathrooms are the bomb. Yo, mafia booths, too."

Rose's Lounge
2656 N. Lincoln Ave., 773/327-4000

"The ultimate dive bar, with crappy furniture, a pool table, a predictable juke box, and a great owner (Rose herself). The crowd is mixed between college hipsters and working-class neighborhood old-schoolers and retirees. Cheap drinks, sometimes free pizza, like family!"

AND WE HASTEN TO ADD OUR FAVE WATERING HOLES TO ROD'S LIST
Danny's Tavern
Bucktown: 1951 W. Dickens Ave., 773/489-6457

This dimly lit hipster lounge offers occasional poetry and fiction readings.

The Darkroom
Ukrainian Village: 2210 W. Chicago Ave., 773/276-1411
www.darkroombar.com
This nightclub features DJ-spun music varying from deep house to 1980s retro every night of the week. Nearly as popular with gay men and lesbians as with straights, the Darkroom is a friendly, sophisticated place to sip a martini or a nice glass of wine, hang out with well-dressed friends, pose and be fabulous.

Delilah's
Lakeview: 2771 N. Lincoln Ave., 773/472-2771
Delilah's is an aging punk rocker bar with great drink deals, free movie nights, and DJs spinning punk and alt-country tunes on select evenings.

Gingerman
Lakeview: 3740 N. Clark St., 773/549-2050
If you must go to a bar near Wrigley Field, this is the least odious of your options. For one

The charming Paté at the Holiday Club.
~Photo courtesy of Paté

thing, after ball games they play classical music, to keep away the most drunken of the straight post-frat-boy fools. It's also a good place to play pool on a winter's night.

Grafton Pub
Lincoln Square: 4530 N. Lincoln Ave., 773/271-9000
A fine selection of European beers and tasty comfort food served in a classy atmosphere.

Holiday Club
Uptown: 4000 N. Sheridan Rd., 773/348-9600
www.swingersmecca.com
Don't be put off by the Web site—they mean *swinger* as in Brat Pack swinger, not as in, "Bernice, I'm really interested in getting to know you better, and so is my husband, Rick." For all its brat pack illusions, though, Holiday Club is really just a friendly neighborhood bar appealing to 30-somethings, with free

pool and a decent menu of bar food. On Friday nights, however, local lesbian icon and self-proclaimed *Butchessa* Paté slings drinks in the back bar to a soundtrack of 1980s punk and Goth music for an appreciative crowd of punks, Goths, and queer folk. All this and a photo booth for impromptu souvenir creation.

Hungry Brain
Roscoe Village: 2319 W. Belmont Ave., 773/935-2118
This comfortable, shabby-chic (minus the chic) Roscoe Village bar feels like a hipster's basement. They have an excellent jukebox that gets a lot of use on the nights when they don't feature live avant-garde jazz. Popular with students, alterna-types, and 30-something locals.

Lakeview Lounge
Uptown/Andersonville: 5110 N. Broadway St., 773/769-0994
The in-house cover band offers live music on Fridays and Saturdays in this fun dive bar.

The Long Room
Lakeview: 1612 W. Irving Park Rd., 773/665-4500
It is indeed a long room. Great for one-on-one conversation on quiet weeknights. And they make the best Manhattan Robert's ever tasted.

Rainbo Club
Wicker Park: 1150 N. Damen Ave., 773/489-5999
An alterna-hipster standard since way back when, this is one Wicker Park spot where no one feels the need to get all dressed up and fancy. We have both been here many times, on dates and with groups of friends. Get your photo snapped in the photo booth, or just hang out and drink in the noisy and self-consciously "unpretentious" surroundings.

Simon's Tavern
Andersonville: 5210 N. Clark St., 773/878-0894
Once the sort of place where old men drank away their retirement checks, Simon's, because of its cheap beer deals, has become a hangout as well for 20- to 40-something arty types, including a healthy dose of queers. Snag the little "living room" area in the back with two couches and a fake fireplace, if you can.

Ten Cat Tavern
Lakeview: 3931 N. Ashland Ave., 773/935-5377
Lots of mismatched furnishings from suburban basements circa 1972 give this hipster/working-class bar its funky feel. A gay birthday party held in their back party room was a rousing success.

Creaoke

Love it or loathe it, the karaoke craze is obviously more than a passing fancy. Most of Chicago's gay bars (and many of the straight ones) have a karaoke night, many of them on a weekly basis. And most of the bars that offer karaoke rely on master host and DJ Creagh to provide the equipment, the songs, and the personality to get the job done right.

Creagh has played, as a drummer and a singer, in various bands in his Bridgeport neighborhood. He's also taken improv classes with Second City. "Great," his mom told him. "Music and comedy, two things you'll never make a penny doing." But as the leading personality in gay and lesbian Chicago's ongoing love affair with singing along to prerecorded tracks and a teleprompter screen, comedy and music produce all of Creagh's pennies, enough to support him and employ six other DJs, including a Windy City Gay Idol winner and an ordained minister.

"Do gay people sing better than straight people?" we asked him, and Creagh's hearty "Yes!" was instant. "And they pick a wider variety of music," he adds. "There are more divas in a gay crowd, but they are more friendly. Demanding, but not rude." And what's the bridge between straight and gay, the one artist that everyone at some point wants to cover? Not Madonna, not Prince, not Sinatra. Bon Jovi, according to Creagh, is the great uniter. (Maybe it's the hair.)

Robert first experienced Creaoke at the late lamented bar Buddies, where Creagh was the karaoke DJ on Sunday nights. Robert's song, selected after much deliberation and liquid courage, was "Some Kind of Wonderful," the Grand Funk version. There were several standout singers that first night (Robert not among them), including a lanky gent named Luis, who works for Creagh now. His soaring, almost impossibly high voice can make even Robert feel affection for a Celine Dion song. But the karaoke cosmonauts of kitsch were in residence, too—an alliterative way of saying that some folks plain sucked. A man we'll call Dan, for example, did a version of "Proud Mary" that managed (oh, Mary!) to be off tempo and out of tune for the entire (lengthy) duration of the performance. Robert caught Dan's act again recently—and nope, time has not altered his enthusiastic massacre of the song. The thing is, Creagh is as welcoming and encouraging with Dan the vocally challenged man as he is with angel-voiced Luis, or two drunk sorority girls who want to duet to "Girls Just Wanna Have Fun." He guesses that some of his success comes from his conviction that, for the four minutes a bar patron spends butchering or caressing a song, "you have to genuinely care." Another reason is his amazingly broad selection of songs. Creagh continually solicits requests for new tunes from his audiences and says, "I don't have the most songs, but I have a lot of different kinds of music: country, rock, Broadway, thrash metal, folk, Spanish, French. . . . If you can't find something in my book, you just don't want to sing."

Before he began DJing, Creagh worked as an architectural metal fabricator, and for a while he did both, until sleep started being an item only briefly slipped into his schedule every 48 hours or so. The wake-up call was just that: he woke from a sound sleep to find himself doing 75 miles an hour on the tollway. Something had to give, and that something was architectural metal fabrication. A disagreement with his employer led him to create his own company, and on February 11, 2002, Creaoke was born. The hours were hardly less punishing. For the first two years Creagh did not have a single day off. Not even a holiday. Even now he hosts karaoke five nights a week, mainly at the gay bars where he got his start. And the man has his groupies, "Creaoke-ites." He estimates that he sees 20 to 25 folks three to four times a week at his various gigs. "Take care of the people," Creagh says, paraphrasing McDonald's founder Ray Kroc, "and the business will take care of itself." Business seems to be just fine. Creaoke happens seven nights a week in the Chicagoland area, at 16 different bars and counting. And a happy cross-cultural result of Creagh's loyal following is the fact that gay people are going into the straight bars to sing karaoke, and straight fans are venturing into the gay spaces. And

Creagh of Creaoke.
~Photo by Jon Peterson

shhhh. . . . Sorry boys, it may not be widely known, but the cute and buff Creagh is not himself gay. Not even a little. Which makes his annual participation in the Gay Pride Parade and his continued enthusiasm for the community all the more winning.

We asked Creagh where he goes after hours to unwind. "Home," he said. No, that's not the name of some hip Wicker Park club, he means he goes to his house and works on crossword puzzles, and, he adds, "I don't play music in the car." His advice for delivering a good karaoke performance? "Sing what makes you happy. And remember, it's just for fun. I tell people all the time, relax! No one has ever walked out of here with a record deal." Robert vows to work on "Some Kind of Wonderful." He wants to be the first.

To find out when and where Creagh and his gang will be singing, or to contact him for booking info, check out www.creaoke.com. ✦

All of Life's a Stage: Theater in Chicago

Gay theater? We got it! Gay playwright Tennessee Williams debuted his portrait of the young homo trying to leave home, *The Glass Menagerie*, here in Chicago back in 1944, and Williams maintained close ties to the theater world here until his death. Closer to the present day, the Tony Award–winning *I Am My Own Wife* was work-shopped in Chicago before it went on to New York, and both *The Producers* and *Spamalot* traveled to Chicago before settling in NYC, so it's quite possible you'll be seeing tomorrow's international stage hit today in Chicago. It's also possible you'll be seeing a show that only the actors' families and lucky you happened to catch. Chicago's theater world is wide and varied, and we encourage you to make the most of it. Sure, we have the big Broadway touring shows. But it's still possible here to mount a production with just a few friends, a hot glue gun, and that Judy Garland/Mickey Rooney determination to say, "Hey, kids, come on, we'll put on the show right here in the barn and give this town something better than anything they have ever seen!"

We asked our friend Gary Alexander (who has been seen at Ravinia doing Sondheim with Broadway diva Patti LuPone) why he chose to focus his acting career in Chicago, and he told us, "I realized that Chicago's a great place to get your feet wet and then to dive in. From the tiny storefront to some of the finest theater on the continent, you can find it here. And unlike New York, most Chicago theater is not-for-profit, so companies can be more adventurous with their programming. There is also a huge professional, non-Equity scene in Chicago. That's not really the case in any other city in the United States. Again, it means smaller companies can take chances. Chicago is really a place for actors who are stage actors first."

At any given time dozens of small companies are staging original works and gutsy interpretations of the classics. For about the price of a first-run movie and a popcorn, you can see prime live theater in Chicago any night of the week. And, of course, there are the larger, established companies (who generally got *their* start as little storefront shoestring operations). We'll start with the downtown big-house theater options, followed by a quick overview of the *really* gay theater choices— although come to think of it, that's a lot like saying the *really* gay florists or the super homo flight attendants, because theater has, since the time of Shakespeare (at least), been a haven and home for queers of all stripes. We'll also tell you what theater opportunities, gay and otherwise in the city, that we recommend to friends and family, discuss some dance company options, and offer up some resources you can use to find something you want to see when you visit.

Theater Downtown

Broadway in Chicago
www.broadwayinchicago.com
Information hotline: 312/977-1700

Well, it's official, Clear Channel owns the world. Or at least a healthy chunk of it, including much of Chicago's downtown theater district. There are three main venues to see big Broadway-style shows downtown: the **Cadillac Palace Theatre**, the **Ford Center for the Performing Arts** (a.k.a. the Oriental Theatre), and the **LaSalle Bank Theatre** (known as the Schubert Theatre until very recently). Each and every theater has been renovated and upgraded in the past few years. The fixtures and lobby of the Cadillac Palace Theatre are particularly stunning. But you are probably going to choose a show based on what it is, not the venue. So if you need to see *Cats* or *Les Miz* again for the 14th time (God help you), or you're looking to see a show before it makes it to NYC, Broadway in Chicago is the place to look. Shows such as *Sweet Charity* and *Mama Mia* graced Chicago before heading for even bigger acclaim in New York, while *Chicago*, *Rent*, and *Joseph and the Amazing Technicolor Dreamcoat*, for example, turn and return here with (depending on your point of view) alarming or exciting frequency. The biggest ticket in town recently, of course, has been *Wicked*, the musical based on Gregory Maguire's novel, which imagines the life of the Wicked Witch of the West before that rotten little Dorothy skipped onto the scene with her bucket of water.

Just as a fun side note, we feel we have to share with you show tune queens the fact that it was at the Oriental Theatre (where *Wicked* plays nightly as of this writing) that Frances Gumm of the Gumm Sisters took on her legendary stage name and became Miss Judy Garland. Even without the Oz-Garland association, you have to expect that a show about a talented woman who is scorned for a quality she was born with and has no control over—in this case, green skin— would resonate with GLBT audiences. *Wicked* proved so popular in Chicago that the producers decided to base a company here and let the touring company go on touring. Tickets as of this writing are being sold months and months in advance, and we have high hopes that the good and bad witches will be dueting onstage downtown for a long time to come. If you are in Chicago and want to try for a deal on *Wicked* tickets, there is a drawing held daily for the chance to win a seat in the first two rows for a mere $25—check out the Web site for details. If you are not in town and cannot get to a box office for any of the Broadway in Chicago venues to buy your tickets in person, then alas, you will be forced into the tender arms of Ticketmaster (also owned by Clear Channel) either online or by phone. Tickets for *Wicked* run from the aforementioned $25 deal to well over $100 a seat (not counting the Ticketmaster fees), depending on location and other amenities. Other shows may be slightly less expensive.

The three main downtown venues again are:

LaSalle Bank Theatre
22 W. Monroe St.
Ford Center for the Performing Arts (Oriental Theatre)
24 W. Randolph St.
Cadillac Palace Theatre
151 W. Randolph St.
    For all three of these theaters, call 312/977-1700 for more information.

Auditorium Theatre
50 E. Congress Pkwy., 312/922-2110
www.auditoriumtheatre.org
    The beautiful Auditorium Theatre, a historic national landmark designed by architect Louis Sullivan, is a jewel among theaters. Mr. Sullivan was himself one of the gays, although not so out and proud about it. More like closeted and tortured. But hey, it was another era. Sullivan and his partner (business partner, not life partner) Dankmar Adler created a state-of-the-art performance space when the Auditorium was built in 1889, and it continues to be impressively beautiful and acoustically wonderful—truly a great space to see a show. Political figures such as Theodore Roosevelt and Booker T. Washington gave speeches here, and Janis Joplin and Jimi Hendrix rocked the house back in the day. Currently, touring shows with Broadway in Chicago are part of the Auditorium's offerings, but the theater is also home to Chicago's own Joffrey Ballet, and many dance touring companies, including the world-famous Bolshoi Ballet, pirouette and plié at the Auditorium when they are in town. The theater also hosts pop music concerts and jazz shows throughout the year. There are only two ways to get your tickets to Auditorium events: bite the bullet and contact Ticketmaster (312/902-1500, www.ticketmaster.com), or travel in person down to the box office (50 E. Congress Pkwy.) Monday through Friday between noon and 6. (For weekend box office hours, call 312/922-2110.)

Drury Lane Theatre Water Tower Place
175 E. Chestnut St., 312/642-2000
www.drurylanewatertower.com
    This Magnificent Mile venue for Broadway-style plays and musicals is the newest kid in town, a sibling to the suburban Drury Lane Oakbrook Terrace Theatre. Following its older sibling's lead, the Drury Lane Theatre in Chicago plans on staging plays and musicals with high production values, using both nationally known and locally grown talent. The inaugural show here was *The Full Monty*, the musical about regular working stiffs taking off all their clothes to make money. You have to like a musical with full male nudity and a homosexual love story subplot. Well, *you* don't, but Robert does. And the dapper Christopher Piatt (we love his *Time Out Chicago* theater reviews) said, "The new Drury Lane is going to get credit for a lot of things: the spanking new, well appointed space

is Mag Mile posh; the programming is a notch or two more provocative than its suburban competition of the same size; and if the production values of this, its first production are any indication, we're going to see musicals on par with those of another theater town we can't mention here." We are keeping our fingers crossed that this new kid flourishes—the price is right. Drury Lane has vowed to keep its ticket prices under $50 a seat. Look at the Tuesday night and Wednesday matinee performances for even better deals.

Companies That Specialize in Gay Theater
(and a Few We Feel Are Extra Special Even if They're Not "Specialists")

About Face Theatre
773/784-8565
www.aboutfacetheatre.com

For more than a decade, About Face has been the premier GLBT-focused theater company in the city. The Tony Award–winning play *I Am My Own Wife* was part of the company's New Works program before it went on to New York. About Face excels in several ways. They do adaptations of contemporary novels extremely well and have brought to the stage vivid productions of Jim Grimsley's *Dream Boy*, Carol Anshaw's *Seven Moves*, and Rebecca Brown's *The Terrible Girls*, among others. The company also networks well with other theater companies and individuals, whether mounting a coproduction with **Steppenwolf** or **Lookingglass Theatre**, producing a play at the **Museum of Contemporary Art**, or seeking out talent like Chicago performance poet Cin Salach to amplify and expand on her work. Another thing we appreciate about the Face folks is that their commitment to gay and *lesbian* theater does not sell the women's experience short. And a really great part of the company's work is the About Face Youth Theatre, which gets GLBT youth involved in creating and performing in new productions. Look on their Web site for an inspirational video that explains their youth program in depth.

About Face's mission statement reads in part, "Through our projects, we strive to challenge our artists' and audience's intellects, imaginations, self-conceptions, moral expectations, and ideas about gender and sexuality in contemporary and historical contexts." If that sounds a tad too dry and intellectual for you, we hasten to add that productions such as the bodice-ripping *Pulp* and the sword- and breastplate-full *Xena Live* plays have been campy hilarious fun. And we've never seen a play directed by artistic director Eric Rosen that was not visually stunning. Speaking of visually stunning, if you get a chance to catch cofounder and actor Kyle Hall onstage, take it. Perhaps it's just the answer to the fervent prayers of gay boy theater queens everywhere, but generally there seems to be a place somewhere in the script where he has to take off his shirt or, in the case of the recent *Take Me Out*, everything. God bless a good shower scene.

GayCo Productions
312/458-9400
www.gayco.net

The comedy troupe GayCo got its start as a Second City workshop in 1996 and quickly racked up a bunch of accolades and awards for their irreverent, fast-paced, and political sketch comedy and improv. Sapphic sisters, don't let the *Gay* part of GayCo fool you into thinking it's yet *another* tool of patriarchal comedy—the women in the troupe get as much stage time as the men, and the troupe's gender mix offers a lot of opportunity to reveal the often uneasy alliances between gay men and lesbians (in a funny way, of course). GayCo's focus in the past has been on live stage productions, with irresistible titles like *Weddings of Mass Destruction*, *99 Bottles of Queer on the Wall*, and *Don't Ask, Don't Teletubby*. Lately the troupe has also been branching off into film and video. The multitalented ensemble has been shopping their wares in L.A. and New York, but founding GayCo member Andy Eninger assures us they will not forget their Chicago roots: "We will be running a summer show in 2006 (at the same time as the Gay Games) as a collaboration with Second City. Beyond that, we intend to mount a new show each year in Chicago—so we indeed will be active in the city for the foreseeable future. (At least until we're picked up by one of these fancy new gay TV networks and forced to be famous.)" Well, if you're forced, you're forced. One cast member, the yummy John Bonny, is already famous in Robert's circle of friends, for being yummy. The *Chicago Free Press* calls him "the best joker in any deck," and in GayCo's full house of jokers, that's saying something.

Bailiwick Repertory Theatre
Bailiwick Arts Center, 1229 W. Belmont Ave., 773/883-1090
www.bailiwick.org

Bailiwick has been around for nearly a quarter of a century. At first the company was one of those small can-do groups that put on plays wherever they could rent a cheap space, but after years of struggle and success, Bailiwick has resided in its current home on Belmont Avenue since 1995. They have received a slew of awards, including about a billion *Gay Chicago* magazine's After Dark awards, and induction into the Chicago Gay and Lesbian Hall of Fame. Productions notable for their GLBT content in the past include *Jeffrey*, *Fairy Tales*, Larry Kramer's *Just Say No* (which featured Olympic diver Greg Louganis in all his buff glory), the recent *Planet of the Bisexuals*, and, of course, the crowd-pleasing and long-running *Naked Boys Singing*, a play that delivers exactly what the title promises, nude men and tunes, together. Many of Bailiwick's shows are not specifically queer—but we don't at all discourage you from broadening your horizons by seeing a play without gratuitous nudity. Unlike some other theaters in the city, Bailiwick continues to mount and run new productions throughout the summer months, when other theaters are dark. They also rent space in their building to other companies, offering many a queer-themed show. Tickets tend to run between $20 and $40. Call the box office or see the Web site for current info.

Hell in a Handbag Productions
312/409-4357
www.handbagproductions.org

Don't be fooled by Hell in a Handbag's mission statement, which says they are "dedicated to the preservation, exploration, and celebration of works ingrained in the realm of popular culture via theatrical productions through parody, music, and homage." Eloquently spoken as far as mission statements go, but it hardly conveys the over-the-top, dragtastic, and hilarious experience that is a Handbag show. Whether they are parodying the animated Rudolph Christmas special, *The Poseidon Adventure*, *Whatever Happened to Baby Jane*, or the telekinetic teen Carrie, the jokes are fast and furious, the songs a blast, the gender-bending and sexual hijinks a given. David Cerda and Steve Hickson, the talented men holding the straps on the handbag, love the shows they skewer, and in every production Robert has seen, the cast enjoys themselves so much that the audience can't help but second the emotion. For an extra-fun peek into a boy genius's mind, check out Cerda's blog at www.handbagproductions.blogspot.com. It's like you are right there with him on the set, having a meltdown. Handbag's *Rudolph the Red-Hosed Reindeer*—with the cross-dressing title deer, a Herbie the elf not gay enough for the other elves, and a big dyke of a Yukon Cornelia—has been running during the holidays for seven years now. Let's hope it becomes as much a part of the Chicago theater tradition as *A Christmas Carol* at the Goodman. God bless us, everyone. Handbag mounts shows at various venues in the city, and tickets run about $25.

The Baton Show Lounge
436 N. Clark St., 312/644-5269
www.thebatonshowlounge.com

We weren't quite sure whether to put the Baton in the drinking section or theater, but we decided that while you have to be 21 to get in the door of the Baton (an argument for the bar section), the female impersonators performing at the Baton are on a *stage*, baby. They don't forget it, and neither should you. Celebrities ranging from Carol Channing to Madonna and from Dennis Rodman to RuPaul have all taken in a show here. And so has Kathie, on multiple occasions. In fact, statistically you are *more* likely to see Kathie here than you are Madonna. While you might think that a Baton audience would be made up of admiring dragster wannabes, Kathie's discovered that straight girl bachelorette parties, lesbian group outings, and "straight" businessmen make up most of the audience of this bawdy cabaret showcase (although surely there are plenty of would-be Eve Harringtons, estrogen-enhanced, waiting breathlessly in the wings). The Baton enforces a two-drink minimum in addition to the cost of admission. Look for the handy-dandy two-for-one Sunday night show coupon that you can print off the Baton's Web site. The girls perform Wednesday through Sunday at 8:30 P.M., 10:30 P.M., and 12:30 A.M. As of this writing, you can't make reservations online—in a retro move on the Baton's part, you have to talk to a real live person, at 312/644-5269.

Too Much Light Makes the Baby Go Blind
Neo-Futurarium, 5153 N. Ashland Ave., 773/275-5255
www.neofuturists.org

Robert has taken a lot of friends, relatives, and dates to *Too Much Light Makes the Baby Go Blind*, the long-running late-night show from the Neo-Futurists in Chicago's Andersonville neighborhood. What is a Neo-Futurist? Well, their Web site explains the intricacies of the movement, but what we can tell you is that on a nearly bare stage, cast members, wearing their regular street clothes and playing themselves, do "30 Plays in 60 Minutes." The short plays range from the poignant to the hilarious, from the personal to the political. The show starts Friday and Saturday at 11:30 P.M. (and Sundays at 7 P.M.), but for the Friday and Saturday shows, you'll want to get there at least an hour early, as they nearly always sell out, and you can't make reservations. One fun Neo-Futurist tradition is the fabled "when we sell out, we order out!"—a pizza order that gets called in right onstage. If you are quick you can grab a little nibble at the end of the show. How queer is *Too Much Light*? Well, since the various plays (which change somewhat every week) are written by the current cast of five to eight ensemble members, it depends on how queer the cast is. We can't promise, but often there is "family" in the show. And the straights tend to be lefty sensitive struggling artist types. We can't imagine anyone, gay or straight, not liking at least most of the plays—part confessional poetry, part *Saturday Night Live*, a dash of Dadaism, a portion of inventive low-budget stagecraft. Many, many friends of ours told us we had to mention this as a fun evening out in Chicago. Every June for Pride month, the Neo-Futurists perform an all-gay edition of *Too Much Light*, with the proceeds going to a noble queer cause. In the summertime, when the living is easy, the Neo-Futurists team up with other theater companies to offer hilarious staged readings of very bad movies in their do-not-miss (and often queer-tinged) It Came From the Neo-Futurarium series. You can make reservations for Neo-Futurist mainstage shows. These full-length original productions follow Neo-Futurist guidelines and offer a similar blend of humor and seriousness. Robert recently caught a performance of *The Last Two Minutes of the Complete Works of Henrik Ibsen*, written and directed by *Too Much Light* founder Greg Allen. Yes, it delivered just what the title promised, in such a varied and inventive fashion that Robert and his date pretty much wanted to have Greg Allen's babies by the time it was all over. Mainstage shows run around $15, with discounts for students and seniors. The summer movie series is $10 ($5 with the discount), and for *Too Much Light*, you'll go through the ritual of rolling a six-sided die and paying $7 plus whatever you roll—because that's the kind of zanies these folks are. The changing cast and quick rollover of skits keep this show fresh. We highly recommend it.

That's Weird, Grandma
Barrel of Monkeys at the Neo-Futurarium
5153 N. Ashland Ave., 312/409-1954
www.barrelofmonkeys.org

Barrel of Monkeys ensemble members go into Chicago Public Schools, teach writing workshops to underserved third through sixth graders, and at the end of a residency, celebrate by dramatizing the work the kids have written and bringing in the entire troupe to perform at an all-school assembly. Now, lest all that effort get lost in a single performance, they put together the best of the best of the plays and formed the long-running *That's Weird, Grandma*. If you have a free Monday in Chicago, we cannot think of a better recommendation for an evening of theater. As Christopher Piatt wrote in the *Chicago Reader*, "This group is funnier than anything at Second City, more genuinely creative than anything at Lookingglass, and does more good than all the other nonprofit theaters in town put together. If you don't have a good time, there's something wrong with you." As far as gay content, there's nothing overt, but casting of the plays tends to be delightfully gender-blind, and Robert has it on very, very good authority (okay, he smooched the guy) that at least one cast member is, you know, *funny*. Tickets are $10 for adults and $5 for children. Don't say you read it here, but in the past there's been a coupon for $2 off the ticket price on the Monkeys' Web site. Call their hotline before heading out, because the show, though long running, has taken a few breaks in the past.

Live Bait Theater
3914 N. Clark St., 773/871-1212
www.livebaittheater.org

Live Bait specializes in intimate one-person shows, as highlighted in their annual Fillet of Solo Festival. Among the best of those shows, in our humble opinion, are the works of David Kodeski and Edward Thomas-Herrera, excellent writers and performers who are also partnered in real life. The two of them also happen to be friends of ours, but we hasten to assure you that we would recommend their work if we didn't know them from Adam (and Steve). Kodeski's haunting and humorous solo shows explore how the remains of another person's life, a diary, a scrapbook, can intersect and impact our own. Thomas-Herrera's solo outings use his doppelganger Edwardo to wonderful comedic effect, while his full-length plays skewer (and pay homage) to celebrities and their mythology. Both gents also do shows with their group BoyGirlBoyGirl, which teams them up with fabulous straight gals Susan McLaughlin Karp and Stephanie Shaw. The troupe performs monologues centered around a common theme. Robert has caught two of the BoyGirlBoyGirl shows and can't wait for more. While the boys' solo shows never are *about* gay identity, they organically incorporate the simple fact of their authors' gayness, without grandstanding or polemics.

Queer Burlesque in Chicago

*W*e asked our friend and burlesque aficionado JT Newman (a.k.a. Miss Bea Haven) to give us the lowdown on an alternative form of queer, lesbian-friendly nightlife that's been shaking up more than just a few tassels in the Windy City of late. JT was happy to oblige us, and she had this to say:

What is sex-positive, saucy, political, and a whole lotta fun? Two words, baby: queer burlesque. What is **queer burlesque**?, you ask. Well, I'm glad you did, because there really is no other topic I like to discuss more. . . .

Queer burlesque is an offshoot of the neo-burlesque explosion that's been happening all around the world for the last decade. In essence, it is a revival of vintage stripping. It's an homage to the original peelers of days gone by and a reclaiming of women's bodies of all types. Queer burlesque is one part Bettie Page, one part go-go girl, and one part queer theorist. Now before you go all Andrea Dworkin on me, queer burlesque, by its very nature, frequently features acts that both celebrate sexuality and women's bodies and impart a political message, like feminist body art, which swept the country in the 1970s. (Anyone remember Carolee Schneeman? Anyone?)

It's all happening right here in the middle of the Windy City, girls and bois! So dust off your pasties, pull out your kitten heels (or wing tips, you big, bad butches), and join me on a whirlwind tour of Chicago's queer burlesque scene.

The Sissy Butch Brothers and Gurlesque Burlesque

Red and Gwen, the Sissy Butch Brothers, started it all. Inspired by research for his dissertation, Red took a trip to the Exotic World Museum and the annual Miss Exotic World pageant to work on a documentary on the history of burlesque. What he and his film crew saw blew them away! In July 2002, Red and Gwen produced their first Chicago Gurlesque Burlesque event, and dykes all over the city have been twirling their tassels ever since. Red and Gwen host semiregular burlesque shows at the Abbey Pub (generally in the summer), headlined by out-of-town burlesque stars and local favorites. The show often includes side features (such as a peepshow and intermission acts) and usually has a queer political flavor. Generally thought-provoking and always titillating, this is one show not to miss. Check out www.sissybutchbrothers.com for the next show dates.

The Hellcat Hussies

The Hellcat Hussies are Chicago's only queer, fat burlesque troupe. The Hussies are often featured as a group and solo in Gurlesque Burlesque and other shows throughout the city and beyond. The creators of the Mobtown Moxie tour, this group toured the Pacific Northwest in the summer of 2005 and show no signs of stopping anytime soon. Doing important work by showing the world that fat ladies are dead sexy and can definitely shake it, these gals "put the ass back in sass," as their motto boasts! Check out www.hellcathussies.com for upcoming show dates.

🐦 *In Girlie-Q Burlesque, theater can be as simple as shadows, seduction, and a lone woman dancing.*
~Photo by Nako Okubo

Girlie-Q, Dago-T, and Heartless B!tch

Three other events that happen on a semiregular basis are the Girlie-Q Variety Hour (www.girlieq.com), the Dago-T Variety Show, and Heartless B!tch Entertainment productions. Girlie-Q takes burlesque, infuses it with a multitude of acts, and creates a vintage-style variety show that combines multiple drag, burlesque, and performance art acts. Dago-T's and Heartless B!tch's shows are similar and frequently occur as fund-raising events for various artistic ventures. The best way to find out about these shows is to keep your eye on the Queer Eventers Yahoo! Group for postings or check out the event listings at Dyke Diva (www.dykediva.com, Chicago's best alternative lesbian site), as neither Dago-T or Heartless B!tch has a Web site yet.

—JT Newman

Burlesque of the Nonqueer Variety

Ray Batmo

Okay, so let's say that the groups just listed don't have something going on *this weekend* and you just *have* to see some burlesque. Well, don't fear, little darlings, for hetero neo-burlesque abounds in the Windy City. For the latest in burlesque postings, visit *the* source, Ray's Guide to Chicago-Area Burlesque. Ray, a nice soft-spoken guy and burlesque aficionado, posts his reviews of shows and show dates on his Web site (www.batmo.com/burlesque/). He keeps the site really current, so visit it if you're looking for burlesque on the fly.

Backstage Girlie-Q.
~Photo by Caldwell Linker

Michelle L'Amour, Frankie Vivid, and the Sugarbabies' Lavender Cabaret

Just crowned Miss Exotic World 2005, Michelle L'Amour is the queen of Chicago burlesque. Her acts are not necessarily political (or feminist, really), but she and Frankie put on a fine show of Broadway-ish burlesque numbers set to remixed burlesque classics mixed with Electro (they call it Burlectro!). They also do a variety of other kinds of shows, including the occasional striptease open mic at the Funky Buddha Lounge. They have something going on at least once a month, and Michelle also teaches burlesque classes (in case you're starting to get inspired!). You can find info on shows, classes, and more on their Web site (www.lavendercabaret.com).

Chicago Burlesque and Vaudeville

Dante, one of Chicago's first neo-burlesque performers, puts together a semiregular show of burlesque and vaudeville. I caught Dante's show back in 2002, and it consisted of a variety evening with fan dances, songs, comedy, tableaus, and an emcee straight from the olden days. Her loose configuration of performers (and news of their next show) can be found online (www.voodoocabaret.com). They are worth seeing.

Belmont Burlesque

Now I haven't seen it, but word is that Belmont Burlesque has a decent vaudevillian-style show with some striptease. Hosted by Jack Midnight and featuring the Belmont Bombshells, this show happens once a month at a quarter past midnight at the **Playground** (3209 N. Halsted St.), a local improv theater. Go online (www.belmontburlesque.com) for specific show dates and more information about the Bombshells and the host.

—JT Newman

Some Theater Choices That May or May Not Be Overtly "Gay" but Will Almost Certainly Be Enjoyable

Lookingglass Theatre
821 N. Michigan Ave., 312/337-0665
www.lookingglasstheatre.org

Robert's been a fan of this energetic and innovative company since their 1991 production of *The Secret in the Wings*, a haunting adaptation of fairy tales. While Lookingglass has come a long way from that bare-bones production, the company, formed by a core group of Northwestern University theater students, continues to focus on original plays that meld text, music, and highly athletic stage movement. Director and company member Mary Zimmerman's *Metamorphoses* brought Ovid's telling of the Greek myths to the stage, using a gigantic pool of water to full effect. *Metamorphoses* played to sellout crowds in Chicago before it moved to the Big Apple for its Tony Award–winning run. Celebrity-struck folks take note: one of the founding members of Lookingglass is none other than David Schwimmer (Ross from *Friends*). He is still highly involved with the company and has directed several of their productions in the past. You can generally expect a Lookingglass show to be boisterous and funny at times, as well as to demand a lot of athletic ability from the cast.

Chicago Shakespeare Theater
800 E. Grand Ave., 312/595-5600
www.chicagoshakes.com

Our actor-singer-gourmand friend Gary Alexander says, "Chicago Shakespeare Theater is a great venue for seeing a show. The acoustics are amazing, and don't forget the view from the lobby." From humble beginnings in a North Side pub, this company has become one of the premier places in the country to see Shakespeare, in a state-of-the-art space that mimics the theaters of Shakespeare's day while using the most contemporary technology. A classic Shakespeare play is always a good bet here, but the company performs other work as well. While the main season runs from September through the winter months, the Navy Pier location means that something is always being staged— they aren't going to miss out on all those tourists! Robert recently caught a rowdy, Cabaret-influenced *A Winter's Tale*, which cost about $65 for a prime seat. Summer shows and plays on the secondary stage are considerably cheaper. And Gary's right, the theater's home at Navy Pier offers a magical view of Lake Michigan and downtown Chicago. At intermission, take in a quiet moment with a glass of red wine and the view.

Goodman Theatre

170 N. Dearborn St., 312/443-3800

www.goodman-theatre.org

The Goodman Theatre has been around in one form or another since 1925. Originally associated with the Art Institute, it's been an independent entity since 1980, and moved from its longtime home beside the Art Institute to its glamorous new digs in the downtown theater district in 2000. In its long history the Goodman's stage has been graced by many of the great theater artists of our time, with everyone from Lillian Gish to Harvey Keitel, from James Earl Jones to that amazing Tony Award–winning lesbian thespian Cherry Jones acting up a storm. Gay playwright Scott McPherson debuted his play *Marvin's Room* at the Goodman in 1990. Like most places where theater thrives, the Goodman has been welcoming to works and artists who challenge and expand social and sexual norms. Robert recently saw the triumphant return to Chicago of the Tony- and Pulitzer-winning *I Am My Own Wife*, a one-man play where actor Jefferson Mays portrays Charlotte von Mahlsdorf, a German transvestite who survives and thrives under both the Nazi and Communist regimes in twentieth-century East Berlin. Mays also plays all 34 *other* roles in the play. If you get a chance to see him in this production, you will have seen the performance of a lifetime. The Goodman boasts two stages, the beautiful Albert and the more intimate Owen theaters. You can save a bundle by getting season tickets, which run from less than $100 to nearly $300 for five plays in the Albert or $45 up to $85 for three plays in the Owen. Individual tickets can range from $15 to $60, depending on the day you are seeing the show and the theater it is in. Don't forget to check the Web site for dinner-and-theater deals and for group rates.

Steppenwolf

1650 N. Halsted St., 312/335-1650

www.steppenwolf.org

Yet another Chicago theater that started with a small band of actors, Steppenwolf, 30 years and about a zillion awards and accolades later, is a theater institution. Because much of the work is generated by the company members, the script quality varies widely, but Robert's never seen a play here that had anything but top production values in terms of sound, lighting, set design, and all-around stagecraft. And the acting is always top-notch, just what you'd expect from a company that includes John Malkovich, John Mahoney, Joan Allen, Martha Plimpton, Gary Cole, Laurie Metcalf, Gary Sinise, Kevin Anderson, and other names perhaps less well-known outside of Chicago theater circles but no less talented. There is a thrill, we admit, to seeing an actor you've seen on TV and in the movies right there in front of you, 40 feet away, breathing, sweating, acting up a storm. Robert is a special fan of director and ensemble member Frank Galati, who has won a Tony Award for his work, has nurtured a new generation of directors in his role as professor of performance studies at Northwestern

University, and, incidentally, is a member of the Chicago Gay and Lesbian Hall of Fame. Galati has long had an affinity for the work of postmodern big mama Gertrude Stein and continues to champion this lesbian icon's work and bring it alive on the stage.

If you are in town and see a lot of theater, subscribing is the way to go, with a five-play season running between $160 and $275, depending on where your seats are and when you go. Like the Goodman, Steppenwolf also has a smaller stage, the aptly named Garage Theatre, for less mainstream fare, often more limited runs, and always for less per ticket—sometimes as low as $12. Mainstage productions run from between $20 and $60. Select performances are half price for students of any age with a valid ID, and there are dinner-and-theater combo deals to be had. Check out the Web site for details.

The Second City

1616 N. Wells St., 312/337-3992
www.secondcity.com

Robert had his doubts. Some straight friends were in from out of town, and they'd gotten him a ticket to the mainstage show at Second City. A gay couple in their 60s were also part the excursion. Now, yes indeed, Second City is the place where comedy legends such as Dan Ackroyd, Bill Murray, John Belushi, Gilda Radner, and John Candy got their start. Closer to the present day, the wry and wonderful Tina Fey and *Strangers with Candy* creator Amy Sedaris have done their stints in the City. But given that it's located in the heart of Chicago's Old Town neighborhood (Straighty McStraightville these days), Robert was bracing himself for a night of improv comedy heterocentric to the point of pathological and perhaps offensive to the gays as well. Wrong! There was indeed some homo content in the show, but it was presented in a way that made fun of the hets and their hang-ups, while still giving a pointed social commentary on gay life. Robert's straight friends laughed, the older gay guys in the group loved it, and Robert even spotted a couple of other gayish groups in the audience, when he thought he'd be going alone into the lion's den. Tickets for the mainstage shows currently run from $12 to $20, depending on when during the week you want to go. (Mondays are the cheap nights.) The Second City e.t.c. shows on the secondary stage also run around $20, but Second City Unhinged evenings, featuring current and former students from the training center, can be had for as little as $5, and student-run shows in the Skybox theater are also inexpensive. Second City shows are first come, first seated, with table service, bar-food eats, and mildly overpriced drinks. So even if you have advance tickets (highly recommended), arrive early to grab a good table. If you have the performance bug yourself, check into class possibilities. This is where the fab kids of **GayCo Productions** got their start. It could be your launching pad to fame, tabloid notoriety, and multiple stints in rehab, followed by a season of *The Surreal Life*.

Other Theater Options Worth Mentioning

This is by no means an exhaustive list of other worthy mentions, but we offer up some Chicago theater picks drawn from the varied theater world of the city.

Black Ensemble Theatre

4520 N. Beacon St., 773/769-4451

Under the guidance of actress and director Jackie Taylor, this North Side company specializes in bringing the biographies of notable African-American singers and entertainers (such as Jackie Wilson, Dinah Washington, and Etta James) to the stage in dramatic musicals. Another of their mainstays is the beloved *Other Cinderella*, a musical version of the fairy tale performed with an all-black cast.

Athenaeum Theatre

2936 N. Southport Ave., 773/935-6860

www.athenaeumtheatre.com

Not a theater company per se, the Athenaeum is a building that plays host to a host of small performances throughout the year, including dance, performance art, plays, and music. Many queer-specific plays are staged on one of the Athenaeum's three studio theaters, and the mainstage space sees everything from opera to dance to the Chicago Gay Men's Chorus over the course of a year. Our good friend Richard Fox calls this his favorite theater venue in Chicago.

Court Theatre

5535 S. Ellis Ave., 773/753-4472

www.courttheatre.org

Robert has enjoyed his season tickets to this University of Chicago–associated institution in the past. Court specializes in classics, from Shakespeare to Beckett. The Hyde Park location may be off the beaten path, but the theater is a great place to see a show, and production quality, from acting to all aspects of design, is generally superb.

Curious Theatre Branch

www.curioustheatrebranch.com

Founded by Jenny Magnus and Beau O'Reilly in 1988, Curious has gone from outsider status to validation from foundations, institutions, and periodicals of all sorts. While not queer theater, Curious's work still comes from an outsider point of view. Robert is fond of Ms. Magnus's solo shows, which often put her hauntingly beautiful singing voice to good use. As of this writing, Curious does not have a permanent home. Check their Web site for upcoming show information.

Light Opera Works
847/869-6300
www.light-opera-works.org

Robert's seen several of this Evanston-based company's shows, such as *H.M.S. Pinafore* and *The Merry Widow*, both because in a former life he edited their *Stagebill* program and because his actor friend Gary has been performing with LOW fairly regularly. "They have been around for 25 years now," says Gary (obviously not an impartial party, but still). "In the past, they mostly focused on late nineteenth– and early twentieth–century operetta. Lately, they've been updating, with more classic musical theater. In terms of musical theater with full orchestra and well-trained voices, it's one of the only games in town."

Redmoon Theater
1463 W. Hubbard St., 312/850-8440
www.redmoon.org

The Redmoon folks are masters of putting their hands up into bottoms. Of puppets. Using masks, puppets of all sizes, and actors, Redmoon specializes in pageants and street theater. Our bud Ianni recently saw one of their open-air spectacles and described it as "*The City of Lost Children* meets Cirque du Soleil. Impressive, visually appealing, and a bit on the surreal side, especially since all the actors were speaking a made-up language." Redmoon does slightly more conventional work, also puppet-based, indoors.

Stage Left Theatre
3408 N. Sheffield Ave., 773/883-8830
www.stagelefttheatre.com

The commie pinkos at Stage Left like theater that looks at political and social issues of the day. In the gay community they are perhaps best loved for their musical parody of the Hardy Boys books, *The Secret of the Old Queen*. They have been around for nearly 20 years now. Just as a point of interest (to Robert, at least), when Robert first moved to Chicago he lived right above their old digs on Clark Street, and the actors used to knock on his door and ask him to limit how much he walked around during the performances.

Teatro Luna
773/878-5862
www.teatroluna.org

In a shameless grab from the Luna girls' Web site, we can tell you that "Teatro Luna performs original works created from the Ensemble's individual experiences of being Latina in the United States. [Their] pieces cover issues dealing with family, racism (within and outside [their] communities), color, women, sexism, and body image to name a few." They are not specifically lesbian oriented, but they are womyn centered and way gay-friendly.

The Theatre Building

1225 W. Belmont Ave., 773/327-5252

boxoffice@theatrebuildingchicago.org

The Theatre Building's been a homo haunt for many years, with the homo-rific **About Face, Hell in a Handbag,** and many others presenting shows on the multiple stages of the space. And you have to love the spaghetti colander chandeliers in the lobby. The last show we saw here was a kick-ass remounting of *Hedwig and the Angry Inch*. It's always worth looking at what's going on here—they specialize in nurturing and helping to birth new musicals. Careful of the afterbirth!

Wade Out of the Mainstream!

Maybe, like Chicago performance group **Cupola Bobber,** you feel that "narrative is too comfortable and easy." Maybe you want your visit to Chicago to stretch the boundaries of what you think an evening of theater could be. Maybe it's just that if you have to hear "Memory" from *Cats* one more time you are going to scream until your eyes bleed. Award-winning Chicago poet Richard Fox, a buddy of ours, has never, in this incarnation, seen a Broadway musical, but the man attends more poetry readings, multimedia performances, performance art, and dance shows than just about anyone else. When asked what performance groups and collectives in the city he felt were essential, he told us, "**Lucky Pierre** (www.luckypierre.org) always surprises me in their performance work. There is real 'heart' and a rigorous commitment to what they do. They don't pander to or talk down to their audiences. They work hard to connect to 'community' (however one might define that)." Richard also recommended the work of performance scene veterans **Goat Island** (www.goatislandperformance.org), **Dog** (www.dogtheater.com), and the aforementioned **Cupola Bobber** (www.cupolabobber.com). While none of these groups have overt homosexual themes and agendas, we can pretty much guarantee that they are not going to be working to reinforce typical mainstream norms and mores. And yes, there are 'mos among the members. Mr. Fox is also a fan of performance power couple David Kodeski and Edward Thomas-Herrera (see our **Live Bait Theater** listing, p. 170), and he suggests looking into the schedule at Boystown-adjacent **Links Hall** (www.linkshall.org) for performance, dance, and theater work. For poetry readings, Richard is a fan of the Sunday evening series at Wicker Park's wonderful used bookstore **Myopic Books** (p. 88) as well as Scott Free's weekly Wednesday **Homolatte** series (see our music listings, p. 186). To Richard's list, we will also add a shout-out to queer performance poet **Dave Awl** and his *Partly Dave Show*, a zingy theme-related evening of theater, spoken word, and music that Dave describes as "more fun than a Winnebago full of lemurs. Guaranteed not to stain or wrinkle." The *Partly Dave Show* goes on hiatus with alarming frequency but happily resurrects itself, too. You can read about the show, enjoy Dave's writings, and find useful links and other info at his Web site (www.ocelotfactory.com).

Well, You Can Dance if You Want To: Some Chicago Dance Companies

The major dance companies in the city generally produce two short seasons each, one in the fall and one in the spring. Venues for the performances vary, as do the timing and length of a season, so we are providing you with Web addresses for further info. Vying for the post of best-known dance troupe in the city are the world-renowned **Joffrey Ballet** (www.joffrey.com) and **Hubbard Street Dance** (www.hubbardstreetdance.com). For more than 40 years the **Giordano Jazz Dance Company** (www.giordanojazzdance.com) has been jazzing it up around the world and on Chicago stages, while the modern dance mistress **Chicago Moving Company** (www.chicagomovingcompany.org) is only slightly younger, having just celebrated its 32nd year. Jazz dance specialists **River North Chicago Dance Company** (www.rivernorthchicago.com) like the gays so much that they recently hosted a party/performance, *Summer Fling*, specifically to woo the GLBT audience. Choreographer Molly Shanahan's **Mad Shak Dance Company** (www.madshak.com), founded in 1994, is a relative newcomer. **Muntu Dance Theatre** (www.muntu.com) celebrates and promotes traditional and contemporary African dance and music, while the **Columbia College Dance Center** provides Chicago with the most eclectic and comprehensive contemporary dance performance season in the city, hosting companies and choreographers from all over the world. The Dance Center has a permanent home at 1306 S. Michigan Avenue. You can learn about their full schedule by calling 312/344-8300 or clicking your browser over to www.dancecenter.org. The aptly named **Links Hall** (www.linkshall.org) links dance performances to text, sound, and voice and is the place to see dance work that defies easy classification. One of our fave Links regulars has to be the dance troupe The Seldoms (www.theseldoms.org). And it's not just because company member Doug Stapleton is a total hottie, as well as a swell all-around Wiccan art fag kind of guy. As you might guess from their name, these dancers don't perform all that frequently, but they are well worth seeing when they do. Maybe we shouldn't call them dancers. The Seldoms say, "Although dance is central to our work, we consider what capacity movement, location, image, sound and text have in offering both nuance and clarity to the whole composition."

This is not an exhaustive list of staged dance goings-on in Chicago. Check out the listings in the *Chicago Reader* by either picking up a (free) copy or looking at the listings and reviews online (www.chicagoreader.com). Do we even have to tell you that dance performances are queer comfort zones? Men in tight leotards, divinely muscled women who sweat in public, plus music and rapt onlookers? You do the math.

Other Theater Resources

The *Chicago Reader* (www.chicagoreader.com) is also where we'd suggest you look for the most complete listings of theater and performance events around the city. Both the *Chicago Tribune* (www.chicagotribune.com) and the *Chicago Sun-Times* (www.suntimes.com) offer reviews, but for our money the most reliable theater reviewer in the city is *Time Out Chicago's* Christopher Piatt, who in addition to his erudite commentary on the world of the stage is also an accomplished writer of poetry and prose. Plus he's family. The *Reader's* critic Justin Hayford, also coincidentally one of the gays, favors work that is challenging and new.

For day-of-show half-price theater deals, we urge you to try **Hot Tix** (www.hottix.org). The Web site will tell you what shows may have half-price tickets available, but you have to buy the tickets in person, on the day you want to go, either downtown at the **Chicago Tourism Center** (72 E. Randolph St.) or at the **Water Works Visitor Center** (163 E. Pearson St.). Both outlets are open Tuesday through Friday from 10 A.M. to 6 P.M., Saturday 10 A.M. to 6 P.M., and Sunday noon to 5 P.M. There is also a Hot Tix booth in the **Lincoln Park Tower Records** Store (2301 N. Clark St.). This location only accepts cash for theater tickets. If you are in the north suburbs, you can hoof over to the Hot Tix booth in the **North Shore Center for the Performing Arts** (9501 N. Skokie Blvd., Skokie). Contact the theaters themselves to look for deals. Even relatively small companies offer dinner-and-theater packages in conjunction with local restaurants, special discount nights, or deals for seniors and students. If you don't ask, you won't know. The **League of Chicago Theatres'** Web site (www.chicagoplays.com) offers all sorts of useful information, from what is currently playing in town to job listings and audition opportunities for those of a theatric vocation. While the league's Web site is fairly comprehensive, you can also call 312/554-9800 and talk to a helpful real live person, if you prefer.

Sing Out, Louise: GLBT Music in Chicago

So, gay music in Chicago. By this do we mean music *performed* by GLBT folks or music *enjoyed* by GLBT folks? Do we mean opera, or alterna-pop? Do we mean grassroots guitar-strumming womyn-centric tunes, or a chamber quartet? Do we mean Broadway divas holding notes longer than anyone thought humanly possible, or the sweat-fueled thrash-and-burn rage of queer punk? The answer to all these questions, of course, is yes! Yes to it all. Chicago has many options to offer anyone seeking live music, and in this chapter we'll provide a sampling of venue options and music festivals to watch out for, as well as give you the heads-up on some of the city's most talented and visible out performers. While you have to consider venue and the primary audience, if you are seeing a pop show, classical music, opera, folk, or what have you, no one in the audience is going to give a second thought to a gay couple or group in their midst. Between the two of us, we have seen an awful lot of live shows, and our tastes are pretty eclectic—we've slammed and sweated at punk rock shows, and we've nibbled cheese and sipped wine at a civilized outdoor concert. So while we can't tell you everything about music in Chicago (that would require a much bigger book than this, and we're sure you would not want to lug the damn thing around), still we can give you some names to look out for and offer resources to find out what's going on around town before you get here.

Speaking of womyn strumming guitar music, this seems like the place to sadly report the end of the Mountain Moving Coffeehouse, an institution in the Chicago lesbian-feminist community. The oldest womyn-born-womyn and girl-only coffeehouse in the country presented the top lesbian and feminist folksingers, poets, and activists to Chicago's "womyn's" community on Saturday nights in various church basements for 31 lavender years. Mountain Moving was inducted into the Chicago Gay and Lesbian Hall of Fame but did not exist without controversy—in the early 1990s a local gay male journalist raised a brouhaha over its womyn-only policy. Still, for the most part the coffeehouse and its habitués were able to fill up and spill over in peace. Sadly, fall of 2005 marked their last season of performances. Now on to artists and venues that are still active.

Lola, LA LA La La-LO-La: Rock, Pop, and Folk

Handsome singer-songwriter Dylan Rice won the 2005 Outmusic Award for Outstanding New Recording Debut-Male for his album *Wandering Eyes*. Dylan's currently very active in the Chicago live music scene, playing with his band

and also doing solo acoustic shows, and we thought of him immediately when we wanted to talk to someone about music in Chicago. And indeed, he had a lot to say:

> *Chicago is a fabulous place for original live music if you look at the sheer*
> *volume of clubs and coffeehouses and beer gardens that feature bands on any*
> *given night. Just pick up the* Chicago Reader *and you'll see—sometimes the*
> *number of options can be daunting. I perform primarily in the rock and folk*
> *scenes, so I can speak to the fact that the gig opportunities for musicians in*
> *those genres are many and often. As far as being gay is concerned, I've never*
> *had a problem getting a gig because of that fact. Most talent buyers don't care,*
> *as long as you sound good live and can bring a crowd. Sometimes if the club is*
> *hosting a gay night or a gay fest, it can work to my advantage. But overall,*
> *it's a non-issue, and it's great to see a growing number of clubs featuring*
> *openly gay musicians as well as drawing mixed gay/straight audiences.*

The *Chicago Tribune* calls Dylan's voice "sort of like Chris Isaak via Morrissey." Dylan himself calls his music "folk-rock crooning" or "torch-song rock." For a sample of his tunes, or to find out where he's playing his next gig, you can check him out at, you guessed it, www.dylanrice.com.

MEET SOME OF THE PLAYERS

As Dylan indicated, you can catch out-and-proud rock musicians at gay-specific venues, but most of them play shows at mainstream venues as well. Happily, the mere fact of being a queer no longer relegates a musician to the fringes. Here is a list of some of the more prominent out Chicago rock performers.

Both of these neo-folkies have solo albums, but lately **Andrea Bunch** and **Aerin Tedesco** have been partnering onstage and off at venues like the Alt Q festival, Homolatte, and Estrojam. In addition to their music, which blends folk with electronica, they are also activists for animal rights and work to get recycling happening in the city. More info at www.andreabunch.com.

It's been a while since Robert's seen **Ripley Caine** live (she's a frequent Homolatte guest artist), but she's as busy as ever around town. He does recall that her rendition of the Doors' "Light My Fire" has been known to get the girls (and boys) in the audience a little moist. See www.ripleycaine.com for a schedule and more.

Flesh Hungry Dog's monthly shows at **Jackhammer** have lately become showcases for queer rock in Chicago. Many of the other bands mentioned in this list have shared the stage with the Dogs. While the band itself is fairly new, the members are not teenyboppers, and their accumulated years of experience pay off. In the *Chicago Free Press*, the Dogs compare their sound to the B52's, Blondie, and the Ramones and their guitar work to that of the early Pat Benatar singles. Before you put another notch on your lipstick case, check them out at www.fleshhungrydog.com.

Kimi Hayes and her band play, no lie, every dang summer street fair in Chicago that we have ever attended. And you can also catch her on select summer evenings at Navy Pier. If you are willing to brave the Straighty McStraight Navy Pier crowds, by all means let Kimi be the reason. She's been called a cross between Etta James and Janis Joplin. Dylan Rice adds, "Kimi Hayes is a great roots-rocker with a wonderful voice. I try to catch her live whenever I can." Or catch her at www.kimihayes.com.

Robert preferred Super-8 Cum Shot, the original name for the band **Jinx Titanic**. But Jinx Titanic is now the band's name and also the alter ego for composer-frontman John Kamys. Who wouldn't at least be curious about a band whose new EP is called *Anal Sunshine*? Their live shows, we can report, feature everything from disrobing dancing boys to a woman vigorously fisting a watermelon onstage. After the latter, the watermelon and the first two rows of the audience look a tad worse for the wear. Dylan says, "I really admire Jinx Titanic—he's been able to put camp and wit back in punk. He's got this rich, strong voice, and a knack for a catchy melody, but on top of that he's a real force of nature onstage. There's something beautifully ironic about throwing jock straps out into the audience as take-home freebies." (Robert, to his deep regret, did not catch a jock strap at the last show he attended.) You'll find audio, video, and more at www.jinxtitanic.com.

Cathy Richardson has the summer street fair and festival market all tied up. A look at her schedule will show that all summer long she's jamming out on one stage or another, in the city or the surrounding area. Theater fans may recall her from her stint as Janis Joplin in the Chicago and New York productions of *Love, Janis*. In a *Chicago Tribune* interview, Richardson said the role fit her well: "How (Joplin) felt . . . how she kind of found a home on stage, getting that love and acceptance from people. I experienced that growing up. I was lonely. People teased me, and made fun of me. I definitely used music to get people to like me, to try to make friends. I was pretty much born to do this." No one is teasing her now. Her site? It's www.crband.com.

Chicago native **Ellen Rosner** has opened for Sophie B. Hawkins and Joan Armatrading, headlined all over town, and won kudos for her blues-tinged rock performances at Austin's famed South by Southwest music festival. And Robert has to say that she has those wise eyes that make you believe in reincarnation. (One of those doomed-from-the-start gay boy on dyke girl crushes.) There, he said it. And yes, learn more at www.ellenrosner.com.

The **Rotten Fruits** play honest-to-betsy old-school punk. You can read more about the self-styled "Chicago's favorite drunken faggots" (and Lord knows there's a lot to pick from to find the favorites) in our bar section under **El Gato Negro**, or click on to their Web site, the sensibly named www.rottenfruits.com.

The **Stewed Tomatoes** call themselves "an all girrl psychedelic pop trio that pulses with a soft groove and pounds out a hard edge. Harmonic vocals, sexy riffs, and hot bodies make stewed tomatoes a meal you can't miss!" You can read more about Kathie's adventures with the her friends the Tomato girls in her account of an afternoon of dyke softball in our sports section, or listen to them at www.stewedtomatoes.com.

Three Dollar Bill are veterans of the Chicago punk scene, and they play a mite too infrequently around town for our tastes. Their shows are such raucous fun. And they are pretty great people to boot. Find their info, tunes, and merchandise at www.threedollar.net.

Singer-songwriter Dylan Rice.
~Photo by Emily J. Nelson

With music, it's more about the artist than the venue. Here's a list of some of the most queer-centric pop, rock, and folk venues, with a bit of commentary. For a nearly complete listing of live music in the city (not only pop but also jazz and classical), we'll echo Dylan and highly recommend the free weekly *Chicago Reader*, either in paper form all over the city or online (www.chicagoreader.com).

Homolatte

We may be biased, but we think Homolatte is the best queer stage for writers and musicians in the city. *IN Magazine* described Outmusician of the Year and Outmusic Best Song award winner Scott Free, the master of Homolatte, thusly: "Think Rufus Wainwright with a Mohawk or Cole Porter wearing an ACT-UP T-shirt." Homolatte's format is simple: after a brief performance from the talented, ever-affable (and built like the proverbial brick shithouse, if a brick shithouse had killer pecs and abs) Mr. Free, the guest writer reads for about a half hour, and then the musical guest (or guests) make some music. While the audience is encouraged to donate $5 into Scott's fabled IKEA tip jar, none of the collected money goes to Mr. Free or the hosting location—it's all for the guest artists. For the struggling musicians this cash can mean enough gas money to get to the next stop on the tour. For writers, who almost never get paid for readings, it's a breath of fresh air and a nice little bar tab fund after the show. Another aspect of Scott's tireless generosity is his continual support of other queer artists and performances. On his Web site and in person, Scott makes Homolatte into a communal space for queer folks in the arts to meet, interact, promote, and celebrate one another. And all of this while making no money himself from these worthy efforts. Homolatte has been running at one venue or another for more than five years now, with Scott hosting a wide variety of nationally known GLBT artists, including The Prince Myskins, Alix Olson, David Trinidad, CC Carter, lesbian icon Alix Dobkin, Nedra Johnson, and *Ms. Magazine* woman of the year Nomy Lamm, as well as yours truly, the authors of this book! The small stage format seems to work best for solo artists, but certainly Homolatte has seen its share of bands as well. The queer punkers often do an "unplugged" set. If you yourself are a writer or musician, you might want to contact Scott about the possibility of performing at Homolatte whilst you are in our fair city. The fourth Wednesday of each month, Scott turns hosting duties over to another of our fave indie rock fags, Lars Von Kietz, for the Outmusic Open Mic, where everyone gets their chance to shine. You can learn more about Scott Free and get in touch with him via his Web site (www.scottfree.net), which also displays the upcoming Homolatte schedule. The site is a great resource for finding out about other queer performance series, readings, and concerts of all kinds, in Chicago and beyond.

An outgrowth of the Homolatte series is Mr. Free's **Alt Q** festival formerly known as the "Queer Is Folk" festival. Scott changed the name to show those afraid of the word *folk* that queer music is not all about granola and hugs. These concerts are not all granny campfire songs—no way. Every spring, Scott gets a stellar assemblage of queer performers of all kinds for this annual bash. Every year we are delighted with and astounded by the amazing performances from people we know and love, like the butch and hilarious Phranc and Jill Sobule with her heartbreakingly good lyrics of "I Kissed a Girl," as well as from performers first introduced to us at Alt Q shows, like Melissa Ferrick and her rocking out good times. Each and every Alt Q concert has been a stellar evening, and we're not sure why this show is not a sacrament by now. They are *that* good. As of this writing the venue isn't set for 2006. Check his Web site for updates. E-mail Scott and request his weekly update. He only sends one e-mail out a week, a Homolatte missive packed with info about all things queer music in Chicago, including Alt Q, and his list doesn't get traded around, so you won't be piling junk on to your junk mail in-box. The Alt Q concerts have been held at the **Old Town School of Folk Music** thus far, so it seems natural to talk about them next.

Scott Free man-handles a guitar.
~Photo by Gene Hendricks

Old Town School of Folk Music
4544 N. Lincoln Ave., 773/728-6000
www.oldtownschool.org

The Old Town School is not just a performance venue. It's (duh) a school, for children and adults. Classes range from beginning guitar to doo-wop singing, from drawing classes to dance. (Robert dated a guy who took flamenco dance lessons here.) Our homo friend Dave Short reports that while the school is not a hotbed of gay male action, the classes certainly have their share of lesbians. And how did he know the guitar classmates in question were lesbian? "It becomes clear after she's learned yet another Indigo Girls song," said Dave.

While being a school is the biggest part of Old Town's mission, it also boasts one of the coolest performance spaces in the city. As Dave puts it, "Every seat is comfy, performers love it, the sound system rocks, and the space manages to be intimate but larger than some tiny smoky bar." As we said, the Queer Is Folk Festival has graced the stage in the past. So have The Magnetic Fields, Catie Curtis, and Patty Larkin, to name just a few of the GLBT types who've recently performed here. A look at a season of Old Town concerts will show you they have quite a bit of variety, with jazz, world music, and alterna-pop alongside the sandals, sing-along, and ponytail-type stuff.

Some of our other fave venues for rock, pop, and folkie shows in the city include the **Metro**, **Double Door**, **Martyrs'**, the **Empty Bottle**, the **Hideout**, and **Subterranean**. Dave, who has attended more shows in this city than anyone

Stewed Tomatoes: a band that's both nutritious and delicious.
~Photo by Mel Ferrand

outside of a music critic, says, "Most bands playing these places already read as 'alternative,' so as a gay audience member you are already home free. I might not hold hands with my date, but at least you know you are not at the (way-straight) Cubby Bear in Wrigleyville, with the beer-bellied Bruce Willis types." (Yes, we know, some of you boys have a weakness for just such types. Proceed with caution, we say.) Another spot to find the Mr. Willis types would be downtown's **House of Blues**. They host a lot of different kinds of acts (more pop and rock than true blues), including up-and-coming touring-on-their-one-hit-so-far groups and some way-past-their prime '80s bands (Devo and Pat Benatar spring to mind), and you'd think this would be great for camp value, but a friend's recent bad experience at a Dolly Parton show, where she felt the place was entirely overbooked (her short girlfriend was nearly trampled) and mostly homophobic, has made us a wee bit leery of the spot.

Martha Wainwright Performing at Schubas
3159 N. Southport Ave., 773/525-2508
www.schubas.com

Okay, Robert loves seeing shows at Schubas. In fact, it's his favorite place to see live music in Chicago. There's the space, a barnlike room that manages to be both churchlike and intimate; there's the sound system and sound guys—at every show he's seen, the artists say how they *love* the sound here; and there's the over-all vibe—regardless of who is playing, Schubas is a fairly gay-friendly place. And their well-organized Web site makes it easy to find out about upcoming artists and hear some of their music. Oh, and let's not forget the Harmony Grill, the attached restaurant that serves completely yummy comfort food. There's generally some kind of free appetizer or wine special for diners with tickets for the evening's show. Ask your server, as they say. Speaking of tickets, here's another savings tip: you can buy tickets for most of Schubas' events on their Web site for a modest $1.50 service charge, as opposed to the evil "convenience" charges lobbed on by most major venues these days. Shows run from a mere $7 to $17, depending on who is headlining. The music tends toward the folk or alt-country independent rock, which as a field certainly has its share of GLBT performers and devotees. A final nod to the Web site: if you sign up for their e-mail list, you get calendar updates but no attendant junk e-mail or bull crap. Yay, Schubas!

The audience for Martha Wainwright was queerer than most, probably because she's partly known as the sister of famously queer brother Rufus. As soon as Robert walked in the door of the bar before the show, he spotted a cute waiter from gay bar Crew, and they did the shy smile of recognition. His dyke pal Jennifer arrived, and in the concert space they both found eye candy and acquaintances among the audience, including music journalist Gregg Shapiro. (You can check out his interviews and reviews at www.chicagofreepress.com.) Opening for Ms. Wainwright was Chicago alt-country diva Kelly Hogan, whose powerful voice and winning stage presence are always a treat. As Gregg said to us, "Okay, now why isn't this woman a superstar?" A bonus for the gay boys in the audience was her cover of "Papa Was a Rodeo," a song she aptly introduced as a "homoerotic love song" from Stephin Merritt of Magnetic Fields fame.

And then Martha Wainwright took the stage and used her aching strumpet trumpet of a voice to keep us in her pocket for the rest of the evening. A highlight had to be her don't-piss-off-a-singer-songwriter song, "Bloody Mother Fucking Asshole," widely rumored to be about her father, the folksinger Loudon Wainwright III. Why doesn't it get more radio play?

Two cautionary notes about Schubas. First of all, unless they are expecting a very small crowd, they won't put out chairs. You either have to arrive right as the doors open and grab a seat on the church pews that line one wall or resign yourself to standing all night. Second, please remember not all the slouchy cool emo boys and flannel-wearing buzzcut girls are queer. Talk to someone a bit before you hit on him or her, to avoid awkward misunderstandings. On the other hand, those indie rock types are generally pretty easygoing and flexible, and Midwesterners are known for our politeness. You might get laid because they are too shy to tell you they are not "that way." As a favorite T-shirt of ours reads, "Ten percent is not enough, recruit, recruit, recruit." ✦

Street Fairs and Music Festivals

Free is a price hard to argue with. During the summer months in Chicago, every weekend means another street fair, neighborhood festival, and art fair (or three) in various neighborhoods of the city, all of them jamming with live music, in addition to the food, frolic, people-watching opportunities, and arts and crafts. **Pridefest**, **Northalsted Market Days**, and the **Andersonville Midsommarfest** are the street fairs that feature the most overtly gay crowds and music, but **Retro on Roscoe**, **Summer on Southport**, **Taste of Lincoln Avenue**, and **Ribfest** all host live music, from hometown heroes to nationally known acts. The street fairs generally ask for a "donation" at the gate, but if you're really broke, keep in mind you always have the right to refuse to donate. Most fests will advertise the lineup of acts in the *Chicago Reader*; you can also peruse the *Free Press* and *Windy City Times* for music options at the homocentric ones.

While the street fairs are all over the dang city, tucked into this neighborhood and that, nearly every weekend from June through September there is one constant spot for free music: Grant Park. First comes the **Chicago Blues Festival**, the first weekend in June, followed in turn by the **Gospel Music Festival**, the **Country Music Festival**, the **Taste of Chicago** (with pop and rock acts in addition to the eats), the **Viva Latin Music Festival**, the **Jazz Festival**, and the **Celtic Music Fest**. Count us among the many Chicago natives who are *not* big fans of these large outdoor fests. The price is right, being free, and we are happy the city offers them, but they tend to be crowded and uncomfortably raucous, in a heterocentric manner. Unless you are very close to the stage, you will not be among the people who are attending in order to listen quietly to the music. And if you are very close to the stage, you will be jammed up way too close to fellow audience members—this is fine for a basement rock club venue but both unexpected and uncomfortable when you are sweating out under the stars. Given the choice, we go with the smaller and more local street fairs every time. The Grant Park festivals draw artists from all over the world, and many play local club and concert venues in the city before and after their Grant Park appearances. For a complete schedule of free city festivals, get thee to a computer, visit http://egov.cityofchicago.org, and click on "Events."

Of course, you can also opt for the outdoor venue where you pay for tickets. The **Ravinia Festival** offers an outdoor classical, opera, jazz, or pop concert nearly every night of the week in the summer. Lawn seating, where you can enjoy your own picnic costs as little as $10, but you can also purchase seats in the concert pavilion, eat dinner on-site at a table with real silverware, and avoid the damp ground. Don't let the suburban Highland Park location deter you— Metra trains (from downtown or North Side stops) deliver you to and from Ravinia's gates. During any given Ravinia season, one or two concerts—the B52's, Rufus Wainwright, and the Indigo Girls spring to mind—become de facto gay events. Ravinia also offers show tune queens the chance to see Broadway legends like Patti LuPone, Audra McDonald, Betty Buckley, and Barbara Cook do their diva thing. To view a schedule, get driving directions, or purchase tickets, see www.ravinia.org or call 847/266-5100.

An *indoor* music festival with decidedly queer leanings is the annual **Estrojam Music and Culture Festival**. Founded by women but open to all, this fest celebrates and promotes women in the arts, offering workshops and panel discussions in film, music production, and so forth. As the *jam* part indicates, the emphasis is on music, with out artists like Indigo Girl Amy Ray and Scream Club (*Punk Planet* calls them "the next queer punk rock rap legends") participating in the tune making. The main Estrojam Festival takes place in the fall, but benefit concerts and events take place year-round. See www.estrojam.org for all the fine print and estrus details.

Chicago Cultural Center
78 E. Washington St., 312/744-6630

Lest you think us ill-mannered louts who live only for rock and roll and beer, let us assure you that while that is quite true, we still want to tell you about some chances to see music that does not showcase the electric guitar. The architecturally splendid **Chicago Cultural Center**, located near **Millennium Park**, at Washington Street and Michigan Avenue, not only hosts free art displays, lectures, and theater, it also has perhaps the most interesting and diverse music series in Chicago. And the price? That oh-so-easy-on-the-pocketbook free. The 12:15 Lunchbreak series includes classical music, jazz, pop, rock, and folk, as well as lectures and forums. A Sunday salon features classical music as well. We urge you to take advantage of this unique opportunity; when you're downtown, work a free concert into your itinerary. In September the Cultural Center is the focal point for the **World Music Festival**, which brings in artists from all over the world in a feast of styles, rhythms, beats, and feats. The World Music concerts in the Cultural Center are free, but other venues around the city also host various events and jam sessions, most of them modestly priced. We love to see our tax dollars at work in this fashion. You can call the World Music Festival Hotline (312/742-1938) or surf your way to more info at the City of Chicago's Web site (http://egov.cityofchicago.org). For all things arts and culture in town, including events at the Chicago Cultural Center, contact the Department of Cultural Affairs (312/744-6630).

Nice Vibrato: Classical and Orchestral Music

Chicago Symphony Orchestra

Symphony Center, 220 S. Michigan Ave., 312/294-3333
www.cso.org

It's not bragging when it's true—Chicago has one of the best civic orchestras in the world. The Chicago Symphony Orchestra has achieved kudos, acclaim, and renown, not to mention Grammy Awards. If you attend a CSO concert, we promise you, cross our hearts, you won't be the only homos there. After all, who do you think *plays* many of those instruments?

Established in 1890, the Chicago Symphony has been a well-respected world-class orchestra for much of its history, with an influence and reach on Chicago's cultural and musical life that is difficult to underestimate. The symphony's regular season runs from October through June, but in the summer months they are far from idle, with free concerts in **Millennium Park** and a busy schedule at the **Ravinia Festival**. With an array of special series featuring piano, chamber music, guest conductors, jazz concerts, lectures, and more, Symphony Center has something for just about anybody.

Even reluctant classical music listeners can find a Symphony Center pop concert to be excited about. Guest artists performing with the Chicago Symphony include every big name in classical music, as well as stars from Broadway and pop. Buying a whole series will save you money, and there are a lot of options, from modest three-concert packages to lengthier commitments. Single concert tickets may be

The Jay Pritzker Pavilion in Millennium Park.
~Photo by Sebastian Pinon

purchased online at their Web site or by calling the box office (312/294-3000). Bear in mind that if you are in Chicago in the summer months, there are ways and means to see CSO concerts for free (that delicious word again!) as part of the Grant Park Music Festival.

The Chicago Park District's **Grant Park Music Festival** was the idea of then-Mayor Cermak, who thought Chicagoans could use some cheering up during the Great Depression. The first concert was performed in July of 1935. What with the bread lines and rampant unemployment, free tickets seemed to be the way to go.

Today this classical music series is housed in the **Jay Pritzker Pavilion** in **Millennium Park,** with a few concerts still performed at the **Petrillo Music Shell** in **Grant Park.** If you don't want to be on the lawn, it's possible to purchase tickets for Pavilion seating. But with the state-of-the-art sound system at the Pritzker, why buy? We recommend a summer night, a blanket, a cooler of goodies, a hot date, or good friends. On Robert's last date here, he and his companion were definitely not the only same-sex couple sharing cheese spread on a blanket on the lawn. For the fest's impressive schedule, log on to www.grantparkmusicfestival.com.

Also in the realm of modestly priced music, keep in mind that area universities offer budget-friendly (free or inexpensive) classical and jazz ensemble concerts. It's worth taking a look at offerings from Northwestern University (www.northwestern.edu/calendars/), DePaul (http://music.depaul.edu), Roosevelt (www.ccpa.roosevelt.edu), and the University of Chicago (www.events.uchicago.edu), not only for the performing arts, but also for lectures and workshops open to the public.

If you really go in for the greatest hits of the 1600 and 1700s, you might want to hear Chicago's own **Music of the Baroque.** They play concerts at Chicago-area churches. Our piano- and bassoon-playin' bud Rich and his partner, Michael, are season ticket holders. Check them out (the Baroque folks, we mean, not Rich and Mike) at www.baroque.org, or contact them at 312/551-1414. When Rich and Mike get their own Web site, we'll let you know.

When we asked our friend Gary what music programs or series he felt were hidden gems in the city, he told us that the **Newberry Consort,** based in the ivy-bedecked edifice of the independent but open-to-the-public **Newberry Library** (60 W. Walton St.), "is worthy of mention. If you're into that sort of thing—lots of viola da gamba and lutes." You can subscribe to the three or four concert series for a bit over $100. Students, seniors, and associates of the Newberry Library receive a substantial discount. To consort with the Consort, dial them at 312/255-3610 or cyber-stalk them at www.newberry.org/consort/. The **Chicago Sinfonietta's** mission includes presenting work by composers and soloists of color. Housed in Symphony Center, Sinfonietta's prices range from box seating for $90 to student tickets at $12, with three show subscription passes also available. Call 312/236-3681 or find them online at www.chicagosinfonietta.org. The **Chicago Arts Orchestra's** concerts of historic and new orchestral music take place at the **Athenaeum Theatre.** This relative new kid on the block "seeks to be innovative in its programming and presentation of concerts." Nothing like innovation, we always say. CAO tickets run $15 to $25. Learn more at www.chicagoartsorchestra.org, or dial their digits, 773/562-4921.

When the Fat Lady Sings: Opera

Maybe you like your violins to be accompanied by large women wearing Viking helmets. Maybe you are what is referred to by those in the know as an "opera queen." Our friend Gary sure is. During a performance of Handel's *Alcina* with Renée Fleming he stopped breathing. "Really. I was so taken in with the beauty of her voice that I forgot to breathe for a few seconds." The naked guys onstage were just icing on the cake, so to speak. Gary is a season ticket holder at the Lyric Opera of Chicago. "But I go to see some things more than once. You can almost always get a ticket on the street from people selling them at the last minute. I've found if I explain that I'm an actor, people are more willing to reduce the price even more." We leave it up to you to find your own ways to coax down the price of people selling opera tickets on the street. Just keep it legal. If you have the luxury of choosing where you will be sitting at the Lyric, Gary says, "It's a big barn of a theater—3,600 seats, I think. I like the main floor, but not under the balcony. The sound gets a little muffled back there. Also, if you're on the main floor, sit off to the sides—the sight lines are better. In the center section, even if you're close, you'll spend a lot of time leaning left and right to see the stage. Further off to the side the better, in my opinion. Up in the upper balcony, sight lines are not a problem and the sound is still pretty good."

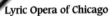

Lyric Opera of Chicago
Civic Opera House, 20 N. Wacker Dr., 312/332-2244
www.lyricopera.org

Robert was lucky enough to chance into tickets to the first two performances of Richard Wagner's *The Ring Cycle*. It was like *The Lord of the Rings* movie trilogy but longer—and with singing. Earlier in the year, an opera-loving straight couple bought him a ticket to *Madame Butterfly*, so he'd become an old hand at the opera-going thing. Although not as old as some of the hands, apparently. One of the first things you'll notice about opera patrons is that the average age of the folks milling around in the art deco entryway is around 65. This might make you depressed about the prospects for opera's audience later in the century, if you choose to dwell on it, but Robert focused on the hopeful thought that all these people, gay and straight, in their 60s, 70s, and beyond, were leading active full lives, replete with opera outings and nights on the town. If you have any problem figuring out who among the older gentlemen is straight and who is not, here is one clear hint: the straight men have ponytails. Grey, often, and sadly cascading down the back in a vain attempt to obscure the lack of any hair at all in the front, but ponytails nonetheless. For Robert's *Madame Butterfly* visit, he'd been on the main floor, seated with grand dames, fur coats, tuxedos, diamonds, and a whiff of old glamour. Robert's *Ring Cycle* friends had more modest digs in the uppermost balcony, commonly called "the nosebleed seats." The excellent acoustics of the Civic Opera House, however, meant the music was lovely in both places. Some purists claim the sound is actually better in the high reaches. You will want to bring those fancy opera glasses in order to see if you sit in the heights. Robert is not an opera buff, but he highly recommends the experience of going to see a Lyric production. You'll hear world-class vocal artists at the top of their game, the production values and orchestra will be top-notch, the people-watching is unparalleled (which of the young men is a paid companion?), you'll eavesdrop on the gowned, the bejeweled, and lesser mortals as they sip wine and promenade during the intermissions, and you'll see opera queens in their natural habitat, their enthusiasm infectious. Individual seat costs depend on the show and the night. You can expect to pay between $30 and $400, depending on what you are seeing, when, and where you want to sit. Season subscribers and donors pay less. The fabled fat lady? Believe us, before it was over, that big girl opened her pretty mouth and *sang.* ✦

While any discussion of opera in Chicago is dominated by the Lyric, the **Chicago Opera Theater**, founded in 1974, has also made its mark. Gary tells us the COT "has become a great opera company in its own right. Several years ago they seemed to have made the decision not to be just a 'little Lyric.' Instead, they started mounting productions of things that wouldn't be appropriate or easy to pull off at Lyric. They mainly focus on early baroque opera. I've seen a stunning *Orfeo* and *L'incoranazione di Poppea*—both Monteverdi. COT is also building a reputation for great twentieth-century and chamber works. Recently they staged two highly regarded productions of Britten operas." The COT just moved into the Harris Theater for Music and Dance in **Millennium Park**. Three opera package deals range from $90 to $315, with additional discounts for students. The COT can be contacted at 312/704-8414, and you can get more info at www.chicagooperatheater.org.

All That Jazz . . . and a Bit of the Blues

Between our limited bebop experience and a bit of scouting around, we can give you the scoop on several fine jazz and blues spots in our fair city. The **Jazz Institute of Chicago** is a great resource. Their Web site (www.jazzinstituteofchicago.org) has a comprehensive list of the city's whoopee spots and who is playing at 'em, and they are the proud programmers of the annual Chicago Jazz Festival and the JazzCity free concert series. Our fave hot jazz joint has to be the Green Mill.

Green Mill Cocktail Lounge
4802 N. Broadway St., 773/878-5552
www.greenmilljazz.com
Getting There: Red Line Lawrence stop, #36 Broadway bus. Cabs plentiful.

The Green Mill Cocktail Lounge in Uptown is a convivial spot for cocktails and for jazz, especially in the form of local lesbian chanteuse and pianist **Patricia Barber** (www.patriciabarber.com), who often graces the stage here on Monday nights. Barber plays both original compositions and delightfully idiosyncratic covers—you have never heard Sonny and Cher's "The Beat Goes On" in quite as dreamy/sexy fashion before. With a mere $7 cover charge, seeing Barber is a deal.

Chatterboxes please note that the Green Mill is all about listening to the music. Enjoy the 1920s speakeasy-era décor, much of it original, enjoy the music and the drinks, but this is *not* the spot to head with a loud chatty group to catch up on old times—the staff will not hesitate to shush you (or kick you out if it comes to that) if you converse at a volume that distracts others from the performance. In addition to jazz, the Green Mill is also home to the original **Uptown Poetry Slam**. Slam originator Marc Smith (www.slampapi.com) hosts an open mic, followed by a featured guest poet or performer and then the Slam—a sort of *Gong Show* meets Jack Kerouac, poet vs. poet competition. In stark contrast to the jazz, audience members are encouraged—nay, exhorted—to loudly vocalize their praise or derision to the poets reciting their work. Local homos **Cin Salach**, **David Kodeski**, and **Dave Awl** have been among the various Slam champs and audience favorites in the past, and the lefty-leaning audience, combined with the Uptown location, makes the Green Mill a fairly welcoming environment for the GLBT crowd, whether they are here for the jazz or the spoken word. The talented Ms. Salach calls the Green Mill Slam "essential," adding, "my poetry soul was raised in the Green Mill Lounge, so that's my number one." Bar hoppers should note that the gay bar **Crew**, a sports-themed spot welcoming to both men and women, is right smack dab next door to the Green Mill, and they serve food, in case the poems or the jazz made you hungry. Or horny.

Jazz Showcase
59 W. Grand Ave., 312/670-2473
www.jazzshowcase.com
Getting There: Red Line Grand stop, #36 Broadway bus, #29 State Street bus, #65 Grand bus. Cabs bountiful.

Years ago, Robert caught the beautiful Diana Krall tickling the ivories here, before her international stardom and marriage to Elvis Costello. Like the **Green Mill**, music is the focus here, and the audience is asked to keep conversation to a muted minimum while the musicians are playing. The club is a mite fancier than the Green Mill, a good reason to get gussied up a bit, and the higher cover charges, generally around $20 to $25, reflect this. They offer discounts to students, musicians, and Jazz Institute of Chicago members at the Sunday matinees. Bargain hunters may also ponder the Italian dinner–Jazz Showcase option. You can call **Maggiano's Little Italy** (516 N. Clark St., 312/644-7700, www.maggianos.com), right across the street from Jazz Showcase, and book a meal and jazz show deal for a tad over $40. For jazz that costs you *only* your dinner tab, the Showcase's little sister, **Joe's Bebop Café** (at Navy Pier, 312/595-5299, www.joesbebop.com), has Southern eats and live jazz seven days a week and no cover charge.

HotHouse: The Center for International Performance & Exhibition
31 E. Balbo Ave., 312/362-9707
www.hothouse.net
Getting There: Red Line Harrison stop, Brown Line Van Buren stop, Blue Line

LaSalle stop, Orange Line Adams stop, Michigan Avenue buses. Cabs not uncommon.

Everyone and their brother told us we had to sing the praises of the HotHouse, and sing out loud and long. Alterna-weekly *New City* named this space the "Best Cultural Gem Downtown" and proclaimed, "One of the most beautiful music rooms in the city, it features great live indie, jazz, soul or world music on any given day and always has intriguing art on display." You can see HotHouse's schedule and purchase tickets online. Shows run $7 to $20. Robert is fond of the house band, Yoko Noge's Jazz Me Blues. Lest you doubt the international flavor here, when's the last time you heard a band led by a Japanese jazz-blues singer and piano player?

We both admit to a passing familiarity with *having* the blues, if not singing them, and indeed, the blues have homo roots. Most of the great blues ladies of the past had bisexual or lesbian "tendencies," including Alberta Hunter, Ethel Waters, Billie Holiday, Ma Rainey, and Bessie Smith. These last two are often rumored to have been lovers. Remember that it was in Chicago, in 1925, that a neighbor called in a noise complaint and the responding cops found Ma Rainey in a room full of naked women doing "intimate" things with each other. Bessie had to go bail Ma out of the klink. Just how noisy was the party for the police to be called? That is a *lot* of moaning going on. And if they were lovers, what do you suppose Bessie said to Ma, when they got back in the car after bail had been posted? Ah, history. The mind reels.

Sadly, contemporary blues clubs in Chicago are not as queer-friendly as we would like. We have not heard any horror stories, but our own experience has been that the blues clubs in Chicago tend to attract a crowd we call "touristy" in the most pejorative way: straight, loud, loaded, obnoxious. (We are not against tourists in general, or we would not be writing a travel guide.) We would not dissuade you from going to a blues club if the blues is what you want to hear, but expect the homo comfort level to be much less than it would at, say, a Madonna concert. All that said, there *is* a club we recommend: **Rosa's Lounge**.

Rosa's Lounge

3420 W. Armitage Ave., 773/342-0452
www.rosaslounge.com
Getting There: #73 Armitage Bus, #82 Kimball Homan bus. Cabs sparse.

Founded by an Italian immigrant who fell in love with the blues and brought his mama, Rosa, along to Chicago with him, Rosa's Lounge bills itself as "Chicago's friendliest blues lounge." Maybe it's the Italian hospitality, maybe it's the club's West Side location, well away from downtown tourist central, but whatever the reason, Rosa's does welcome all colors, creeds, people, and needs. They have been around since 1984 and have been cited as "Chicago's best blues club" by the *New York Times* and as "a blues Mecca for true believers" by *Rolling Stone*. Cover charges for the most part remain in the entirely reasonable $5 to $8 range. For a different kind of blues trek, consider booking a seat on Rosa's Summer Moonlight Blues Cruise. The ship sails off into Lake Michigan from Navy Pier, and for $40 you get snacks, a raffle, blues music, and a view of the Chicago skyline at night. Call them or see the Web site for more.

Sometimes Amateurs Do It Best: Chicago's Queer Social and Music Groups

Several GLBT groups in town get together to make a joyful noise. In addition to adding to the cultural life of the city through their performances, these groups also serve a social function, allowing gays and lesbians to meet like-minded people for friendship and dating. Attend a concert, or consider joining in the musical fun.

The vocal lads of the **Chicago Gay Men's Chorus** have been performing concerts, musicals, and theatrical reviews since 1983. CGMC produces a December holiday season show, a spring production, and an annual Pride concert in June. Tickets to all shows generally sell out (most tickets go to season ticket holders before the general public gets a chance at them), so plan accordingly. Their shows tend toward the over-the-top, more-is-more element you might expect from a bunch of show tune queens putting their heads together. Seasonal shows are at the **Athenaeum Theatre**, but CGMC also performs at civic and community functions throughout the year. You can scout out more about the CGMC boys at www.cgmc.org or via an old-fashioned phone call to 773/296-0541.

The oldest gay chorus in the Midwest, **Windy City Gay Chorus** was founded in 1979, just a few tra-la-las after choruses were formed in NYC and San Francisco. WCGC generally offers three main concerts a year: in December, in early spring, and a Pride concert in June. The men of WCGC have also lent their voices to theater productions and a host of community events. In addition to the main chorus, **Windy City Performing Arts** also boasts **Unison**, a choir for male and female vocalists, and the doo-wop, a cappella sounds of the **Windy City Slickers**. Look at www.windycitysings.org for more information, or contact Windy City Performing Arts at 773/404-9242.

You can spot the **Lakeside Pride Freedom Band** (the marching component of the Lakeside Pride organization) oompah-pah-ing in the annual Pride Parade. The parent organization also includes a symphonic band, a jazz ensemble, and a string ensemble (which got its start in 2005). The band's color guard twirl their flags at parades and appearances locally and nationally. If you want to be one of the boys (or girls) in the band, all you have to do is start showing up to rehearsals—none of that scary auditioning stuff; they are inclusive that way. Check them out at www.lakesidepride.org, or call them up at 773/381-6693.

Artemis Singers, a chorus composed primarily of lesbians, performs only music either written or arranged by women. Membership is open to all women of "lesbian feminist inclination" (as long as you are free on Thursday nights to practice). The group chooses songs collectively. Performances are directed by perhaps as many as six different women at any one concert, as the Artemis gals don't have a paid director. So if what you *really* want to do is direct (and sing while doing it), look them up at www.artemissingers.org or phone 773/764-4465.

WE LIKE TO WATCH: A GUIDE TO QUEER FILM IN CHICAGO

Homos like our movies. Chicago boasts a lot of theaters and screens, with everything from the Hollywood first-run blockbusters to grainy, hardly distributed films in languages so obscure that even the actors don't know what they are saying. We'll give you the benefit of the doubt and act like you can figure out how to find the first-run features playing around town all on your own. (Hint: check out the faithful *Chicago Reader* listings, either online or in print.) But we will fill you in on GLBT-specific film events and venues, give a brief shout-out to our favorite Chicago movie houses, and cap things off with suggestions on some gay film rental options and alternative venues.

Chicago Filmmakers
Reeling, the Chicago Lesbian and Gay International Film Festival
5243 N. Clark St., 773/293-1447
www.chicagofilmmakers.org
www.reelingfilmfestival.org

Reeling, the Chicago Lesbian and Gay International Film Festival, has been an annual event in the city since 1981. This weeklong festival, which takes place in early November, presents everything from full-length queer-themed features to experimental video works by both established filmmakers and first-time directors—that could be you. Reeling is part of the programming of Chicago Filmmakers, a 30-year-old arts organization devoted to the creation and appreciation of film. While Reeling is only one week out of the year, Filmmakers' screening series brings queer-themed programs to the public all year long, for less than you would pay to see a movie at the mall. Screenings take place at Filmmakers' Andersonville offices, as well as downtown's **Chicago Cultural Center.** If you are looking for a date night or a place to meet a potential date, the fine folks at Filmmakers have initiated two programs, the Dyke Delicious series and the Gentlemen's Queer Quarterly series, both designed to screen a movie or series of shorts and afterward have a postflick meet and greet. For aspiring John Waterses, Rose Troches, and Guinevere Turners, Filmmakers offers classes in filmmaking as well.

Chicago International Film Festival
312/683-0121
www.chicagofilmfestival.org

The Chicago International Film Festival is North America's oldest competitive movie fest. You have to love a festival that got its start by honoring Miss Bette Davis. The festival takes place in October each year. Whether they are looking for the next Academy Award winner or a challenging gem, movie buffs can find something to interest them here. The queer quotient, of course, varies year to year, but given the ubiquity of homos in the arts, there's sure to be at least some specifically GLBT-themed work. The festival's parent organization, Cinema/Chicago, offers free movies on Thursday evenings during the summer, downtown at the Chicago Cultural Center.

Women in the Director's Chair
P.O. Box 11135, 60611, 773/235-4301
www.widc.org

Another film-focused arts organization, but with a lesbian slant, is Women in the Director's Chair. As their mission statement puts it, "WIDC is a Chicago-based, international media arts/activist organization which exhibits, promotes, and educates about media made by women, girls, and transgendered people that express a diversity of cultures, experiences, and issues." The WIDC film festival has been showing independent film and video since 1981 and traditionally takes place in March each year. Sadly, we are informed that the organization is struggling, and its future is uncertain. We are sending helpful fund-raising cosmic vibes their way. Heck, if this book makes us wealthy, we'll include a check. Let's hope the angels come to the rescue.

Music Box Theatre
3733 N. Southport Ave., 773/871-6604
www.musicboxtheatre.com

How do we love the Music Box Theatre? Let us count the ways:
1. They have been the main screening zone for **Reeling**, the Chicago Lesbian and Gay International Film Festival, for years and years.
2. They are homo-friendly both in terms of staffing and programming all year long.
3. They are independent, not part of some huge corporate behemoth.
4. On Saturday and Sunday mornings at 11:30, they show classic films, from the camp and quips of *The Women* or *The Thin Man* to the rainbow-liciousness of *The Wizard of Oz*. They also have weekend midnight offerings, including must-sees like *The Rocky Horror Picture Show* and ultraclassics like *Breakin' 2: Electric Boogaloo*.
5. The 800-seat main theater opened in 1929, and the current owners have tried to keep the look and feel of a classic movie palace intact.
6. If you are in town during the December holiday season, the Music Box's traditional double-feature showing of *White Christmas* and *It's a Wonderful Life*, complete with an appearance by Santa and a holiday song sing-along

(with organ accompaniment), is the perfect way to get into a warm yuletide spirit. Every time we've gone, it's been practically a gay pride event.

7. The theater is reputedly haunted by Whitey, the ghost of the original manager of the Music Box.

8. The Southport location is adjacent to a slew of good restaurants, making a movie/dinner date night a snap.

There. We love the Music Box at least eight ways, right off the top of our heads.

Landmark's Century Theatre
2828 N. Clark St., 773/509-4949
www.landmarktheatres.com

Our hearts belong to the **Music Box**, but in terms of the sheer number of queer-themed films showing throughout the year, the Landmark's Century Theatre, nuzzling the edge of Boystown, has the Music Box beat. Operated by a chain specializing in art house and independent film, the Landmark offers comfortable stadium-style seating. It has also hosted some of the **Reeling** film festival screenings.

CinéArts 6 Theatre
Century 12
1715 Maple Ave., Evanston, 847/492-0123
www.cinearts.com
www.centurytheatres.com

Evanston's CinéArts 6 Theatre offers most of the same movies as the Landmark, and is adjacent to Century 12, which shows first-run Hollywood fare on, you guessed it, 12 screens. This gives you an opportunity to nip those potentially atomic arguments in the bud: "That's okay, honey. You go see your crazy subtitled incomprehensible Euro-trash art. I'll catch the new Spielberg flick one theater over. Love you." Both theaters are at 1715 Maple Avenue, easily accessible via CTA's Red and Purple Lines.

AMC River East 21 Theaters
322 E. Illinois St., 312/596-0333

Speaking of Spielberg and the like, here's a brief shout-out to a good venue for first-run features. The AMC River East 21 Theaters downtown offer bountiful, comfy stadium seats, parking if you need it (not free, sadly), and those 21 screens, so you and your friends can probably find *something* you want to see.

Gene Siskel Film Center
164 N. State St., 312/846-2600
www.siskelfilmcenter.org

If it's the not-so-mainstream films you have a hankering for, check out the Gene Siskel Film Center. Associated with the School of the Art Institute, the Center showcases movies from around the world, with programming that focuses on countries, directors, actors, trends, and schools of thought. Tickets are $9 for Jane Public, $7 for any student, $5 for Film Center members, and $4 if you are an employee or student of the School of the Art Institute.

Video Data Bank

112 S. Michigan Ave., 312/345-3550
www.artic.edu/saic/art/vdb/

Another media lovers' paradise associated with the School of the Art Institute is the Video Data Bank. While their primary mission is making the work of contemporary video artists (a queer lot if ever we saw one) available to educational and media institutions, their 15-seat screening room, *free* and open to the public, allows individuals or small groups to view titles from their collection. They also own the rights to some videos for the home market, including the work of lesbian filmmaker Sadie Benning.

Doc Films

Ida Noyes Hall, 1212 E. 59th St., 773/702-8575
http://docfilms.uchicago.edu

If you are down in Hyde Park, hanging out near or at the University of Chicago, take advantage of Doc Films, the longest continuously running student film society in the U.S. of A. All movies show in Ida Noyes Hall for the oh-so-nice price of $4. Sunday matinees are even a dollar cheaper! Doc Films is student curated, so the series varies in its queer-related content. Call Doc's hotline or compute the info at online. We bet you can find something on which to feast your eyes.

Facets Cinematheque

1517 W. Fullerton Ave., 773/281-9075
www.facets.org

Other movie-viewing opportunities include Facets Cinematheque. The Illinois Arts Council (one of their funders) declares that Facets "offers a year-round showcase of premieres, retrospectives, festivals, re-discoveries, and filmmaker visits." If that's not enough, Facets also offers videos and DVDs for rental and purchase—their huge archive includes plenty of homo-tinged experimental work. In Facets Film School classes you can see and learn more about everything from new China masters to the Marx Brothers.

Specialty Video

Boystown: 3221 N. Broadway St., 773/248-3434
Andersonville: 5307 N. Clark St., 773/878-3434

Speaking of rental and purchase, if you want to stay in and see a movie in the comfort of your own home, we give three cheers to Specialty Video. They stock the new stuff but also have a good selection of classic films, and, best of all, they *specialize* in gay and lesbian cinema. That means having pink classics like *Desert Hearts* and *Maurice* on hand, as well as more throbbing fare, like *Powertool* or *Battle of the Big Dicks*. Specialty has two locations, both of them, conveniently enough, in the gay hoods.

Grant Park Outdoor Film Festival

Butler Field in Grant Park, at Lake Shore Drive and Monroe Street, 312/744-3370
http://egov.cityofchicago.org (click on "Events")

To conclude the movie section, we have to declare our love of the annual Grant Park Outdoor Film Festival. On Tuesday nights in the summer, the City of Chicago offers a free movie series on the lawn of Butler Field in Grant Park (at Lake Shore Drive and Monroe Street). Kathie and Robert found this to be a swell date night—in fact, they have double-dated here. Bring a blanket, a cooler with some goodies, friends and loved ones, and Chicago provides the ambience as well as the film. Crowds arrive early, so get there well before the sunset start time to grab a good spot. A word to the dog owners: pets aren't allowed. Open alcohol is forbidden in the park, too, but a little bird tells us that if you are discreet and don't go about guzzling Old Style and disrobing, the police will have better things to do than worry about picnickers with a bottle of wine. The little bird enjoyed a nice pinot grigio. The films selected tend toward the classic and the crowd pleasing. One or more movies a season can be counted on to have camp value, if not an actual gay presence. In our experience, showings of *Some Like It Hot*, *The Wizard of Oz*, and *A Streetcar Named Desire* had enough of a homo audience to make us feel right at home among our homies. No matter what flick you pick, you are not going to be the only fag on a blanket or lesbian on the lawn. In addition to the Grant Park Festival, summer also finds the Chicago Park District screening free kid-friendly movies, like *The Incredibles* and *Harry Potter*, at smaller parks throughout the city. Check out www.chicagoparkdistrict.com and click that mouse on "Events," or call 312/742-7529.

Chapter 17

HOOKING UP: SPORT OF KINGS (AND QUEENS)

How do we get laid? Let us count the ways. "We" in this case referring to GLBT folk in general and not your humble authors specifically. In this chapter we'll let you in on some of the ways, the places, and the areas that queer people in Chicago use to find a date, a love, or a quick anonymous lay. If the information seems heavily testeronic and male-driven, keep in mind that gender differences in approaches to sex, while not universal, do exist. Also bear in mind that men are dogs. (And sometimes bears. Sometimes both.) In other words, we are sad to report that there are no lesbian bathhouses in Chicago. We've placed this "naughty" bit in the nighttime section, knowing full well that lust knows no day or night. Certainly you can avail yourself of many of the following resources anytime you choose.

First the simple question of where to go to meet people. While we're not in the dating guide business, some of the truisms of the genre apply. You meet people by doing activities you love: joining sports teams, clubs, spiritual or social organizations, reading groups, political organizations. You meet people at parties and through friends. But maybe you are only in town for a few days and don't have the time for a relationship. Maybe you already have a relationship, which exists happily in Boston, but this is Chicago and you are in town on business, and you and your partner have an understanding—or you, dog that you are, have a secret. How to meet the Mr. or Ms. Right Now?

A Little Sumthin' Sumthin' for the Laydees . . .

If we had a nickel for every time a frisky femme lamented the lack of a backroom sex scene on par with anything the boys have, well, we still wouldn't be able to retire early. Whether this dirty divide can be attributed to differences between female and male socialization or lesbian versus gay male mating and dating patterns is not for us to say. What we do know is that there are lesbians out there who would like to have a little fun without a two-year relationship, a new cat, en couple viewings of *The L Word*, and matching haircuts. In fact, in the 2004 Pressie Awards from gay paper *Chicago Free Press*, readers voted for the Best Place for Women to Hook Up. The winner, by a landslide: "I wish women hooked up."

One way or another, women do manage to hook up despite the obstacles thrown in their way. In the interest of leveling the laying field, so to speak, we've

Leather gals.
~Photo by Mel Ferrand

surveyed some of our favorite lascivious lesbos to get the down low on where girls find girls to get down and low with.

They frequently cited the Web site **craigslist** (www.craigslist.org). "Some of my most memorable hookups were through them," says our friend Martie. A quick perusal of the site does indicate a lot of hookup potential, albeit mostly from women looking for a first-time experience or for a woman to show her the ropes. Hey, if you're frisky enough, why not? Or straight couples looking for an adventure: "This may sound crazy," some guy writes, "but my girlfriend says she wants to try this. See how sweet I am to oblige her?"

There's also the "Totally horny, totally hot petite blond, 36-24-34, looking for a sexual soul mate. *No men!*" who is, we assure you, a pervy man in a dark room, peering at his computer screen, hoping to wank off to the responses. And finally, there are the all-*too*-lesbian "Let's cuddle and share our secrets" listings encrypted with the reservation number for U-Haul. However, Martie assures us that lesbian and bisexual women who navigate through all of the above without losing their mojo actually manage to find other flesh-and-blood women to get freaky with. And many women just passing through Chicago use craigslist to find a companion for a night on the town. Other Web sites popular for hooking up include **PlanetOut.com** (www.planetout.com) and **Gay.com** (www.gay.com). *Caveat emptor.*

Away from the computer, Martie's also had luck at **Neo** nightclub, especially on Tuesdays (the "gay" night) and Thursdays (the "Goth" night), between 2 and 4 A.M. Her experiences at Neo include "making out on the dance floor for two hours with this totally hot domme" before going back to her place and, well (ahem), Martie had claw marks on her back for some time afterward. Meow.

Many women mention **Chix Mix** as a place to find some action ("Always lots of totally hot women"), as well as the Andersonville bar **T's** ("Right now it's probably the lezziest bar in town"). Our friend Lisa also cites annual events, such as the **Backlot Bash** and **GirlBlast**, for make-out opportunities before and after the **Pride Parade** (see the Pride listing in Chapter 19), as well as big-ticket events such as the LCCP **Coming Out Against Cancer Ball** and Howard Brown Health Center's **A Taste for Every Palate**, which are more "sophisticated," and where she has met women for non-insta-sex "nice dates."

As for those back rooms? Our friend JT recalls, "One time I was trying to get into the back room at the **Chicago Eagle** and my gay boyfriends kept pulling me back. Finally, one of them went in there and saw two dudes going at it, so he came back and described the scene for me, but he still wouldn't let me go back there. I asked him if I were wearing my cop uniform, would he have let me? He said, not at the Eagle, but maybe at **Touché** or **Cellblock**. He went on to describe some hot scenes between girls and guys (girls/girls, girls/guys, guys/guys) during **International Mr. Leather** the previous year." JT adds, "I was only asking because I was writing bar reviews for Centerstage.net and I needed some juicy info." Whatever, JT. We don't judge!

Black Bra party.
~Photo by Mel Ferrand

Where the Boys Are, and What They Are Doing When They Get There

When the nameless hustler narrator of John Rechy's classic man-on-the-prowl novel *City of Night* reached our shores, he said, "Now it will be Chicago—that savage city like a black fortress erected against the blue of the sky, the blue of the lake."

We're not sure just how "savage" the city is these days, but the lake and sky are often brilliant blue, and as for things "erected," well, as a friend of ours put it, "A stroll around Boystown on a warm afternoon will probably produce some sort of erotic frisson. The same may well be true of Andersonville. **Caribou Coffee** for coffee-and-cruising, **Unabridged Bookstore** for reading-and-cruising. **Spin Cycle** on Broadway for laundry-and-cruising. **Jewel** on Broadway or in Andersonville for groceries-and-cruising. The lakefront between Broadway and Hollywood for jogging-and-cruising. The 'L,' last car at rush hours, for transit-and-cruising."

Ah yes, the fabled "last car on the 'L,'" rumored to be a place where the gays go to cruise. We have yet to see personal evidence of this, but urban tales abound. Let us know how it works out for you. But perhaps you don't want to do a bunch of "L" riding and walking around just to *maybe* catch someone's eye and *perhaps*, if you are both brave enough, have a conversation, which *might* lead to sex. Instead of heading out to find some action, you could stay in and score via your computer Internet service. Web sites specializing in hookups for gay men abound. For dating potentials, try the Yahoo! or Match.com personals. Other Web sites, with live chat, tend to be geared toward a date that skips the coffee and heads directly for the bedroom. Or dungeon. Gay.com is probably one of the most popular chat room sites. At any given time there are about 300 gay men in Chicago on the site, looking for action. Some profiles on **Gay.com** will straightforwardly state that the person is looking only for chats or for dates. In years past it was a more social space, with general conversations going on about current events, gossip, and so forth. The site has morphed, however, into what another friend called "that bathhouse in the sky." This being said, Robert has two good friends he met on Gay.com, neither of them in a sexual situation. Most guys chatting on Gay.com will say that they are "looking," and they don't mean bird-watching or looking at the stars. Other hookup sites include **Adam4Adam.com**, popular with gay men of color; the British-based **Gaydar.co.uk**, good for meeting European travelers; and **BigMuscle.com**, good for meeting buff dudes. Robert asked one of his more sexually adventurous friends if he'd ever hooked up via online resources, and the gent replied that he'd had much success with **Manhunt.net**, **BigMuscleBears.com**, and the straightforwardly named **Men4SexNow.com**. Most of these sites are free, although they offer more complete service if you become a paying member.

As with the lezzies, one of the gay hookup sites steadily growing in popularity is **craigslist**, with its free, anonymous listings. You can search for jobs or couches or board game partners on craigslist, but you can also find that special foot fetishist or big bear daddy. Craigslist allows you to anonymously post what you are looking for (and many correspondents are *surprisingly* exacting about just what it is they want) and wait for the responding e-mails to arrive. You only reveal yourself through your true e-mail address if you reply to someone who responded to you, so there's the issue of safety to always keep in mind. Although not "allowed," you will find some hustlers flaunting their wares on craigslist, and Gay.com too, for that matter. Not to mention the models and escorts advertising in the back pages of free weekly *Gay Chicago*. Sorry, guys, we did not research the realm of paying for it—our modest budget simply would not allow it.

BATHHOUSES

So, the Internet can be that big bathhouse in the sky. For those who like their hooking up here on earth and not originating on a computer screen, Chicago does have bathhouses on the ground. The two main bathhouses are **Steamworks**, in Boystown, and **Man's Country**, in Andersonville.

SOME RULES AND CAUTIONS ABOUT INTERNET HOOKUPS

Be aware of the acronyms and lingo. You should know, for example, that *pnp* means "party and play" and generally refers to someone wanting to have sex while doing crystal meth. *BB* refers to barebacking, or anal sex without a condom. *NSA* sex means "no strings attached." In other words, don't send flowers the next day. Someone looking for *friends with benefits* is not looking to be added to your insurance policy. If you are new to the Internet chat scene, read some profiles and listen in on some chat before plunging in.

- Be honest about what you want and how you present yourself. Don't use photos that are ten years old, don't say you are buff if you only wish you were buff, and don't succumb to the mysterious "Internet inch," which seems to attach itself to the profiles of gay men looking online for sex. As someone else put it, "In cyberspace, everyone is good-looking and has a big dick." If you are hoping for a tender cuddle and make-out session, don't answer the ad for the master looking for a submissive slave.

- Assume that there are many liars (and freaks) out there. The Internet inch, misleading photos, and inaccurate self-descriptions are the order of the day, unfortunately. We strongly side with conventional wisdom, which says this: meet your hookup in a public space, and don't look online for hookups while your judgment is impaired by drugs or alcohol. You don't want to end up in little pieces in a dumpster somewhere. We don't want that for you, either.

Steamworks

3246 N. Halsted St., 773/929-6080

www.steamworksonline.com

Steamworks, open 24 hours, seven days a week, boasts amenities such as a 5,000-gallon hot tub, dry saunas, a steam room, public play rooms, a TV lounge, a fireplace, a workout area, and 90 rooms for rent. It's a private club, so you have to pay a $6 membership fee, which keeps you a member in good standing (tee-hee) for six months. In addition to the membership fee, you'll need a place to stow your street clothes (they make you wear a towel); you can rent a locker or get a room. Lockers run $10 to $14, depending on the time of day. And rooms cost from $20 to $50, from just a bare-boner bed, to a room with porn playing on a TV screen, to a full sling-scene setup. Visa, MasterCard, and Amex are all accepted. You need to be at least 18 years old and have a valid ID. Friends have called

Steamworks "very, very clean" and "the best bathhouse anywhere," though one dissenting correspondent told us the place "is to be avoided: too many there are too high to think clearly about your health or their own (to say nothing of getting it up), and the atmosphere is grim and unpleasantly purposeful overall." This particular man, a sweet guy in his mid-20s, prefers the North Side bathhouse **Man's Country**. "Although it is much grittier and its clientele is less golly-gee gorgeous," he says, "it often seems much friendlier and less dangerous (and they let you keep your pants on, if you'd rather)."

Man's Country
5015 N. Clark St., 773/878-2069
www.manscountrychicago.com

Unlike **Steamworks**, where you need to renew membership every six months, you can join Man's Country for "free," with a onetime $10 registration fee. Rooms cost between $20 and $40, depending on what extras you might be looking for, while lockers are $10. They do not accept credit cards, but there's an ATM in the lobby. You can park for free from 9 P.M. to 6 A.M. in the lot directly across the street from the club. Man's Country was founded by Chicago's legendary leather man Chuck Renslow and his late partner Dom Orejudos, also known as the erotic artist Etienne. You can still see the artwork of Etienne on the walls both here and at the neighboring **Chicago Eagle** bar. Open 24 hours, seven days a week, the club on Friday and Saturday nights offers free entertainment in the form of erotic dancers. The stage they grace has seen, in its day, performances from Boy George, the Village People, and the fabulous Divine. The stripper troupe is often joined by special guest stars, including some of the top names in gay porn. Word of mouth has it that Man's Country is not as clean as Steamworks. One friend of ours, when asked about it, said, succinctly, "Ewwww!" But it does have a rep for being a place where men of varied ages, races, and body types can be found, while Steamworks is sometimes seen more as the realm of the buff and the twink.

Man's World
4862 N. Clark St., 773/728-0400

Man's World, a third bathhouse option, is reputedly more the realm of the bearish and mature. This bathhouse is so discreet and off the radar that *nothing* on the outside indicates the contents within. Robert has walked by the place a gazillion times and has never been aware that he was strolling by a bathhouse.

"BATHHOUSES WITHOUT THE WATER"

Just a block away from Man's World is **Banana Video** (4923 N. Clark St., 773/561-8322), a spot a friend of ours calls "a bathhouse without the water." Patrons of the Banana, whose motto is "peel one off," climb up to the second-floor space to browse the selection of videos, DVDs, toys, lubes, and so forth or avail themselves (for a $10 fee) of the private viewing area, where the naughtiness goes on. One guy Robert dated said he'd had the best non-relationship sex of his life at Banana Video. May you be so lucky. Naughty monkeys can go to the Banana Mondays through Thursdays from 4 P.M. to 2 A.M., Fridays and Saturdays from 4 P.M. to 4 A.M., and Sundays from noon to midnight. The Boystown equivalent of the Banana is the **Ram Bookstore** (3511 N. Halsted St., 773/525-9528), right on the Halsted strip. They sell magazines, books, DVDs, condoms, lube, toys, and so forth and also offer a "screening area" with private booths and shared space, where men do things privately and also with some sharing. A friend familiar with the Ram says, "It's hit or miss, could be a handful of hot guys, or a handful of trolls. I hate saying 'troll'—there's someone for everyone, and I enjoy all types—but some guys that hang out there are aggressive, or pushy, and can get grabby if you let 'em. But you can score very hot guys there. Start out in a glory hole booth, trade peeks at each other's cocks, then peek at each other, if it's good, you can continue to a room with a bench, a video monitor, and have a little more fun." The Ram is open 9:30 P.M. to 6 A.M., seven days a week. In the Old Town area, you can catch a flick (and hopefully nothing else) at the legendary **Bijou Theater** (1349 N. Wells St., 312/943-5397, www.bijouworld.com), the oldest gay movie house in the country. View whatever porn masterpiece is currently playing, browse the movies, magazines, and such for sale, or adjourn to the second-floor play area. Their Web site even provides you with a map to help you plan your visit. Will you linger in "The Meat Market" or spend way too much time in "Blow Job Alley"? You can also purchase videos and DVDs online.

All of these "bathhouses without the water" charge a fee to enter the areas of the establishment where the action goes on. But there are other spots in the city where, for the price of a beer, you can be in a sexual situation. The bars **Cellblock**, **Chicago Eagle**, **Touché**, and **Manhandler** all have backroom areas with man-on-man sex action. For bars where you might be able to find sex for carryout, so to speak, as we said, men are dogs, and any bar can be a singles pickup place when the right guys meet at the right time. As one friend put it, when asked what Chicago bars are best for hooking up, "Depends on the guy. For sheer economy, Cellblock and the Eagle are best, since it is possible to meet a guy and hook up with him in the same room. For those for whom hooking up involves baseball caps, muscle gazing, and frozen drinks, **Sidetrack**. For those for whom hooking up involves dancing or being charming, **Big Chicks**. For those for whom hooking up involves no liquor, **Caribou Coffee** on Broadway." Spots with guys more likely to be on the prowl include (but are not limited to) **Clark's on Clark**, the **Granville Anvil**, and **Little Jim's**. Beware of your own beer goggles. Read more about the drinking establishments in our bar section (Chapter 13). It is certainly possible to hook up in the clear light of day. Any walk through Boystown or Andersonville has at least the possibility of sexual adventure, and certain areas of the Chicago lakefront are notorious for cruising. One of our enviably active friends told us, "The lakefront, between Montrose and Foster! If you're in a car, it's pretty cruisy, just watch for cops. I've heard that if you're on foot, Hollywood Beach has some action, some during the day, but mostly at night. If you're downtown, the men's room in the basement of the John Hancock building is pretty cruisy. . . . I can usually get a blow job there any day of the week." Who knew? We always thought people went there for the view from the top of the building.

Many of the men darting in and out of the bushes at the Magic Hedge bird sanctuary at Montrose Harbor are not bird-watchers. But many folks with binoculars in hand are there to look for warblers and swifts. They don't need to be seeing the North American gay sapsucker at work. Bear in mind that grannies and children frequent the park as well, not to mention undercover cops. Our advice: if you meet someone on the nature paths, take your pleasures somewhere private. As in indoors. It's not worth getting arrested, guys. Hollywood Beach and the lakefront area from Hollywood to Foster are also busy with questioning gazes. Robert was walking here just the other day when a scruffy guy made squirrel noises and flicked his tongue, in what he hoped was an enticing fashion. It wasn't. The public restroom closest to Hollywood Beach can become a virtual orgy during high gay summer season, but again, sex there is (a) illegal and (b) getting in the way of the people, some of them kids, who really just need to pee. Meet your stud on the beach, but take him home to take off the speedo.

Sex in Chicago

ASK THE INTERNATIONAL FLIGHT ATTENDANT

Let's say you are an international flight attendant. Or you want to be one. Or be *with* one. Or play one on TV. We asked our friend Sebastian about the mating habits of that sky-high creature, the flight attendant from foreign climes. (Along with the foreign boys who accompany them.) Sebastian does not subscribe to the stereotype that "all flight attendants are whores" but says "even so, I do like the cute names people throw at us, like sky witch, air mattress, trolley dolly, juice pusher (that's German), cart boy, etc." A Texas native himself, Sebastian has lived among the jet-setters in Paris and London as well as Chicago, so we thought he might know a thing or two about where the frequent travelers meet, greet, and get sweet. As far as accommodations go, Sebastian says that, due to the strong pound and euro, "the 'W' Hotel reigns supreme, but pretty much anything near Michigan Avenue, because there is nothing a fag loves more than shopping. Interestingly enough, Euro fags don't seem to want to stay at bed-and-breakfasts the way Americans do." If you want to meet a Euro guy in Chicago, Sebastian tells us they generally only go to the bars on the main Halsted drag, "the numero uno being **Sidetrack**, then **Roscoe's** and **Cocktail**. Do be aware that almost all the international kiddies I know frequent **Steamworks**. The Euros love their bathhouses for no-strings sex!" For sexy locations right at O'Hare,

Sebastian admits, "Seeing as none of the urinals in United's Terminal 1 have dividers, it's very common to catch guys inspecting the wares. But one bathroom every flight attendant seems to know is cruisy is the one between the United terminal and the CTA station, across from the hallway that leads to the Hilton. Also bear in mind that the Hilton has a gym facility, and anyone can purchase a day pass for it. From what I hear, the showers are ripe with cruising and shenanigans." Sebastian also wants to remind you that in the event of an emergency, your seat cushion doubles as a flotation device.

ASK THE WRITER

Kathie and Robert have both been friends with writer and all-around great guy Owen Keehnen for a long time now. He's lived in Chicago for more than 20 years and written fiction and journalism for publications as diverse as *Windy City Times*, *Christopher Street*, and *Penthouse*. He's a man with a lot of irons in the fire, one of them being *Starz*, his new book of interviews with gay porn stars. Among the big-name porn stars living in Chicago, Owen tells us, are Brad McGuire, Adam Wolfe, Brett Wolfe, J.C. Carter, and Brian-Mark Conover. Owen has a bit of porn experience himself, on the *other* side of the camera, as a boom mic operator. Ask him sometime to relate the horror story of the borrowed white couch and the actor not totally "prepared" for the scene.

Are any pornos filmed in Chicago? The first one that springs to his mind is Joe Gage's *Glory Holes of Chicago*. (Thank goodness it wasn't cheaper to film it in Vancouver or something.) In Owen's opinion, Gage is one of the hottest directors in porn. "He's great with sexual tension, with showing the buildup to sex, which is actually more erotic than just watching people in the act of sex." Does he think there's a porn star mentality or characteristic that's typical of the Midwest? "Guys from the Midwest who do porn are almost dualistic—they are more repressed and therefore more wild sexually. On the West Coast they tend to be narcissistic, concerned with the lighting and how they look, while the East Coast guys tend to be more piggy. And Midwest guys are smarter, too." Smarter than . . . ? Well, Owen would not go on the record as stating that Southern porn stars are often several sandwiches short of a picnic, so we'll just have to let that be.

As far as cruisy areas in the city, Owen waxes nostalgic about the lightly wooded area in Lincoln Park, a "sperm burial ground" that's now the site of the Peggy Notebaert Nature Museum. "Thanks, Peggy," says Owen, with a hint of rancor. He also recommends the grassy area next to Belmont Harbor known as the Belmont Rocks. Although much of the cruise factor has moved north to beaches and lakefront areas past Wilson, Owen says you can still catch sight of "the occasional thong-wearing sunbathing hottie on the rocks."

ASK THE PORN STAR

So Big is one of porn star Brian-Mark Conover's favorite titles, along with *Come and Get It*, *One Basket*, *Roast Beef, Medium*, and *Giant*. No, those aren't movies he's been in; they are titles from Brian-Mark's favorite writer, the novelist and Algonquin Round Table wit Edna Ferber—she wrote Show Boat, too. In fact, you are not going to find another man in gay fetish porn more conversant on early twentieth-century American fiction than Brian-Mark; a talk with him is custom made to shatter preconceived notions about porn stars and what they might be like. Brian-Mark is a former Iowa farm boy, a former high school English teacher, and a stage actor; furthermore, he served for many years as executive director for the HIV fund-raising organization Season of Concern. Among the tattoos he sports are twin naked devils bearing festive and gigantic erections (one devil per arm) as well as the words sex pig inked across his shoulders. His first foray into porn, a film called *Leather Buddies*, was shot in San Francisco. "I was petrified," he recalls. "But it was also fun. I think it's hot that people watch me do something that's generally so intimate." Brian-Mark's work has mainly been fetish porn, including barebacking, piss scenes, scat, and bondage. He laughs and says that in his movies "you're not going to find me lounging on the beach and holding hands." But he adds, "I'm not advocating anything. I don't want anyone to be like me. Pornography is not educational, it's entertainment."

"If you don't like it," he adds, "don't watch the video." Brian-Mark's worked a lot for the Chicago-based Oink Video and says that a good rule of thumb is "the nastier the video, the nicer the guys involved. Generally, the clean-cut guys can be divas." You can see some of his work in *What a Pisser*, *Pigs at Play*, and his favorite, *A Pig's Adventure*. "Guess what it was all about? Me!" he says, with a delighted laugh. "When I'm grocery shopping in the Jewel, and someone comes up to me and whispers, 'I saw you,' well, I find it endearing."

So we know where he buys bread, but where does a sex pig go out in Chicago? For a group of friends he recommends dining at **X/O** or **Yoshi's** on the Halsted strip. And for out-of-town guests, "the architectural boat ride tours downtown are great." Oh. But what about sex?

"Well, I'm not an Internet hookup guy." And bathhouses? "Not an option." He adds, however, that "any gay bar is a potential hookup place. And the leather bars are more conducive for talk. If you're into a fetish, you have to talk about a scene before you do it." He recommends the **Cellblock** ("There's always someone from the community to chat with there") and on the North Side, **Jackhammer** ("I love that place").

He also loves something the stripper Gypsy Rose Lee said: "Nobody laughs at me because I laugh at myself first." "Porn stars," according to Brian-Mark, "can be very serious, with this butch, *male* image. Sex should be *fun*. We are all way too serious."

Part 4

WOULD YOU LIKE A SIDE OF RESOURCES WITH THAT?

We have made our list and checked it twice, and hereafter you'll find social sex clubs if you want to be naughty and service and charitable organizations if you want to be nice. And also health and support resources, media outlets, political groups, and informational Web sites. All kinds of things to get you going, get you off, get you thinking, or get you started in this fine city of ours.

Unless noted, all street addresses are in Chicago. Also bear in mind that our categories are broad; for example, you might want to volunteer for one of the organizations listed under "Get Help," or you might get some great advice or a referral from one of the organizations listed under "Get Involved." We end with a sort of queer calendar of events in and around Chicago, featuring in-depth reporting on (and the occasional cursory nod to) events we hope sound enticing enough to inspire you to join in the action.

☠ *Something for everyone.*
~Photo by Mel Ferrand

BEING RESOURCEFUL

Get Help: Health or Social Services and Support Groups

Affinity
773/324-0377
www.affinity95.org
 Affinity is a nonprofit organization founded by and for black lesbian and bisexual women, with services ranging from a singles group to a drumming circle, health programs to peer discussion groups.

AIDSCARE
212 E. Ohio St., 5th Floor, 773/935-4663
www.aidscarechicago.org
 AIDSCARE is a residence and care facility that offers support for people living with HIV.

AIDS Foundation of Chicago
312/922-2232
www.aidschicago.org
 They say, "We collaborate with community organizations to develop and improve HIV/AIDS services; fund and coordinate prevention, care, and advocacy projects; and champion effective, compassionate HIV/AIDS policy." The annual events Dance for Life and AIDS Run/Walk are fundraisers for these folks.

Events like the annual AIDS run/walk give a wide range of queer community members the chance to sweat and stretch while helping a good cause.
~Photo by Marie-Jo Proulx

Ladies.
~Photo by Mel Ferrand

AIDS Legal Council of Chicago

312/427-8990
www.aidslegal.com

Working to promote and ensure the fair treatment of people impacted by HIV, this organization offers legal assistance, provides educational outreach, and conducts fund-raising efforts.

Chicago Commission on Human Relations

740 N. Sedgwick St., Suite 300, 312/744-4111

The commission includes advisory councils on gay and lesbian issues, as well as on Latino, immigrant, veterans', women's, and other issues. Call here for hate crime support or if you believe you have been a victim of housing discrimination.

CENTER ON HALSTED

Halstead and Waveland, 773/472-6469
www.centeronhalsted.org

As of this writing, the center is not yet actually *located* on Halsted. (Ground for the new center has been broken.) This is Chicago's one-stop shop for GLBT services, advocacy, community, health, and resource programs for queer youth, for older people, for women—you name it, and they either have a program for it or can direct you to the right spot. Among the available services are three hotlines:

LGBT Info Line, 773/929-4357, Mon.-Fri. 6 P.M.–10 P.M.
LGBT Crisis Hotline, 773/871-2273, emergency only, 24 hours
HIV/AIDS/STD Hotline, 800/243-2437

Not only for those in dire need, the Center on Halsted has programs for social networking, friendship building, and community involvement. When completed, the new center will be an anchor and beacon for Chicago's queer community. The programming already is.

Chicagoland Bisexual Network

312/458-0983
www.bisexual.org/g/chicagoland/

"By and by we all are bi," a friend of Robert's once said. CBN sponsors discussion/support groups for bisexual men and women and provides social opportunities. They also publish a newsletter, *Bi . . . the way*.

Chicago Office of LGBT Health
333 S. State St., Room 2142, 312/747-9632

Services, referrals, information, and training are available here for health-care professionals.

Chicago Women's Health Center
3435 N. Sheffield Ave., 773/935-6126

www.chicagowomenshealthcenter.org

CWHC embodies everything great about grassroots feminist organizing. Started by volunteers back in 1975, the center offers gynecological care, counseling, alternative insemination options, and more, on a sliding-fee scale kept really, really low due to the fact that all of the doctors and nurses who provide services here do so on a voluntary basis.

CORE Center
2020 W. Harrison St., 312/572-4500

www.corecenter.org

The center provides care for individuals and families affected by HIV and other infectious diseases.

Gay, Lesbian, Bisexual Veterans of America/Chicago Chapter of American Veterans for Equal Rights
P.O. Box 29317, 60629

www.aver.us

This nonprofit group promotes equal rights for current and past members of the U.S. armed forces.

Illinois Gender Advocates
47 W. Division St., #391, 60610, 312/409-5489

www.genderadvocates.org

ILGA provides legislative and legal advocacy for the rights of transgender and gender variant people, with a special emphasis on youth. They say, "The vision of ILGA is to create a community that celebrates the inherent worth and dignity of every person, regardless of gender identity or gender expression." Amen.

In-Touch Hotline
312/996-5535

Hours: Daily 6–10:30 P.M.

This free hotline is for crisis intervention, counseling, and referrals, for issues ranging from depression and relationship woes to sexuality questions.

Legal Assistance Foundation of Metropolitan Chicago's HIV/AIDS Project
312/347-8309
www.lafchicago.org

LAF provides information to and advocacy for people impacted by HIV and those who serve them. These folks also offer legal assistance for underserved and disadvantaged populations on other issues as well.

Lesbian Community Cancer Project
4025 N. Sheridan Rd.,
773/561-4662
www.lccp.org

LCCP was started in 1990 to provide advocacy and support services, in a bias-free and supportive environment, for lesbians dealing with cancer. Among their offerings are support groups, quit-smoking clinics, and various workshops. Their annual fund-raiser, the Coming Out Against Cancer Ball, is one of the highlights of Chicago's lesbian social calendar.

HOWARD BROWN HEALTH CENTER

4025 N. Sheridan Rd., 773/388-1600
www.howardbrown.org

At the Midwest's largest GLBT health-service organization, Robert likes his doctor's plainspoken approach. When he recently went in with a sore throat, his (lesbian) doctor said right off the bat, "Robert, has anyone come in your throat recently?" Don't worry, it was just tonsillitis. As they eloquently say in their mission statement, Howard Brown "promotes the well-being of gay, lesbian, bisexual and transgender persons through the provision of health care and wellness programs, including clinical, educational, social service and research activities. HBHC designed these programs to serve gay, lesbian, bisexual and transgender persons in a confidential, supportive, and nurturing environment." The point is that queer folks can feel comfortable here, and Howard Brown works with the community on everything from HIV treatment and information to fertility options for lesbians looking to conceive (Kathie's goddaughter got her start here), along with mental health support, youth services, and, yes, care just for those regular sore throats. You can get treatment for that odd rash "down there," or you can have a regular checkup when nothing is wrong. Kathie got her vaccinations here when she went back to school. If they can't help you with your mental or physical health issue, they will connect you to someone who can. Fees are on a sliding scale, and they don't turn people away. This translates into fairly lengthy waits—we have never actually gotten in to see a health practitioner at our appointment time. But we have never had a bad experience here with anyone on the staff—from the receptionists to the aides, nurses, and doctors, everyone is friendly and professional, and we are so happy Chicago has Howard Brown.

Mayor's Liaison to the Gay and Lesbian Community
312/744-7911

Might as well go right to the top. Do you have a question, compliment, or complaint about the City of Chicago that involves GLBT issues?

M Group
P.O. Box 315, Lincolnshire, 60069
www.mgroupchicago.org

Suburban-based peer support group for gay and bisexual men married to women, both those who want to remain married and those who are ending their marriage. Meets twice monthly. They emphasize, "We are not, however, a dating group organized to meet other men." Go to Halsted Street for that.

NAMES Project Chicago
773/472-1600
www.namesprojectchicago.org

Sponsors and keepers of the AIDS Memorial Quilt.

New Town Alano Club
909 W. Belmont Ave., 2nd Floor, 773/529-0321

Here you can attend GLBT 12-step AA meetings, as well as meetings for users of crystal meth and other drugs, sexual compulsives, and others.

YOUTH SERVICES

Advocate
6525 N. Sheridan Rd., Box #25,

Advocate (pronounced "like the verb and not the noun") is a student group (formerly BGALA) by and for Loyola University GLBT students.

Café Pride
716 W. Addison St., 773/281-2655
www.cafepride.com

This free coffeehouse, for GLBT and questioning youth ages 17 to 21, is open from 8 P.M. to midnight on Fridays.

Coalition for Positive Sexuality
www.positive.org

Disseminates information for teens on sex, sexuality, HIV, and reproductive issues.

Northwestern University LGBT
Resource Center
847/491-1205
www.lgbtcenter.northwestern.edu

All kinds of referrals, programming, and good stuff for the Northwestern queer and questioning community.
www.luc.edu/orgs/rainbow/

Pride DePaul
773/687-2000, x4041
http://condor.depaul.edu/~pride/

Student group for GLBT students, questioners, and their allies.

Queer and Associates
773/752-6044
http://qa.cs.uchicago.edu

GLBT and questioning student group at the University of Chicago.

UIC Pride
312/413-3036
www2.uic.edu/stud_orgs/pride/

GLBT student group on the University of Illinois at Chicago campus.

Oak Park Area Lesbian and Gay Association
947 Garfield, Oak Park, 60304, 708/848-0273
www.opalga.org
OPALGA provides support programming and advocacy, including "Prism" for GLBT youth ages 14 to 18, "Spectrum" for young adults ages 18 to 24, and "Amigos Latinos Apoyando Siempre" for Latin men ages 18 and up.

PFLAG Chicago/Lakeview
P.O. Box 11023, 60611, 773/472-3079
www.pflagchicago.com
Parents, Families, and Friends of Lesbians and Gays—we love these guys. They say, "We hold monthly chapter meetings where parents, families, friends and gaylesbitrans persons can find a confidential, warm and supportive setting to talk, ask questions and find comfort and reassurance."

Project VIDA
2659 S. Kedvale Ave., 773/522-4570
www.projectvida.org
A range of HIV services for Chicago's Latino and African-American communities, including education, prevention, testing, counseling, and patient care.

Rainbow Families of Illinois
773/472-6469, x464
www.ssgservices.com/RainbowFamiliesIllinois/
If Heather has two mommies, or two mommies are thinking of having Heather, Rainbow Families is the resource, providing peer support, advocacy, and educational programs for GLBT families and GLBT people considering parenthood.

Sexual Compulsives Anonymous
773/935-3573
www.scachicago.org
A 12-step peer-guided spiritual program for when "the girl's gotta have it" thing is getting out of control.

Test Positive Aware Network
5537 N. Broadway St., 60640, 773/989-9400
www.tpan.com
TPAN offers HIV-positive people "peer-led programming, support services, information dissemination, and advocacy. [They] also provide services to the broader community to increase HIV knowledge and sensitivity, and to reduce the risk of infection." TPAN produces *Positively Aware*, a bimonthly newsletter, in both English and Spanish.

Vital Bridges
348 N. Ashland Ave., 773/665-1000
www.vitalbridges.org
   A wide variety of services, resources, information, and help for people impacted by HIV.

Get Involved: Athletic, Social, and Political Groups

Adodi Chicago
312/458-9584
www.adodichicago.org
   Social group for African-American men who love men, with monthly potluck dinners and other events.

Amigas Latinas Lesbianas/Bisexuales
312/409-5697
www.amigaslatinas.org
   Amigas rightly declares itself to be "the only organization of its kind in the Chicago metropolitan area promoting safe space, educational opportunities and resources for the Latina les/bi women's community."

Artemis Singers
773/764-4465
www.artemissingers.org
   Feminist lesbian chorus, singing songs written or arranged by women.

Asians & Friends Chicago
312/409-1573
www.afchicago.org
   A social and advocacy group, not just for gay men of Asian heritage, but also for men who appreciate Asian men as well— they have the decency not to say "rice queens" on their Web site.

Vets.
~Photo by Marie-Jo Prouix

Association of Latin Men for Action
773/929-7688
http://almachicago.org
A member of the Chicago Gay and Lesbian Hall of Fame, ALMA sponsors "community forums, educational workshops, seasonal dances, brunches, and cultural activities" for gay, bisexual, and questioning Latino men.

Bear Naked Chicago
www.bearnaked.org
They say, "Enjoy sweaty, furry men celebrating each other's manliness in a friendly, safe, sexual atmosphere." We say, it's a sex club for bears! Woof.

Chicago Area Gay and Lesbian Chamber of Commerce
773/303-0167
www.glchamber.org
All kinds of info on the Web site about queer-friendly businesses and resources.

Naked Bowling.
~Photo by Mel Ferrand

Chicago Area Naturists Sons
www.cansguys.org
Social group for guys who wanna get naked together but not have sex.

Chicago Gay Men's Chorus
773/296-0541
www.cgmc.org
Singers and socialites, with three major shows a year.

Chicago Gender Society
www.chicagogender.com
Social and educational group for trans, intersexed, and androgynous folks.

Chicago Hellfire Club
P.O. Box 577618, 60657
www.hellfire13.org
For men who like their sadomasochism "safe, sane, and consensual."

Chicago Leather Club

P.O. Box 56115, Harwood Heights, 60656

www.chicagoleatherclub.org

A pansexual social, service, and educational group focusing on . . . well, it's not a sewing club, okay?

Chicago Lesbian and Gay Bar Association

P.O. Box 64933, 60664

www.chilagbac.org

For queer judges, attorneys, and law workers.

Chicago Metropolitan Sports Association

312/409-7932

www.chicagomsa.com

Your connection to all kinds of sporty competition in the GLBT community.

Chicago Prime Timers

312/409-1590

www.primetimersww.org/chicago/

A gay men's social club, sponsoring specific social events like card nights and theater evenings as well as a monthly open social.

Chicago Pro Wrestling Club

www.cpwc.20m.com

Hang out with guys who like to rassle, and while they might get an erotic charge out of it, they don't have sex right then and there. It's not that kind of wrestling.

Chicago Smelts

www.chicagosmelts.org

A gay and lesbian swim and social club. Dive right in!

Chicago Spirit Brigade

773/991-0465

www.chicagospiritbrigade.org

Be, a cheerleader, Be Ee a cheerleader. GLBT community spirit and HIV/AIDS fund-raising.

Chicago Women's Rugby Football Club

312/409-5297

www.cwrfc.org

The name kind of says it all.

Yeah, Team!
~Photo by Jermey Lawson Photography/Gay Games Chicago

Chi-Town Squares
5315 N. Clark St., PMB 167, 60640
www.iagsdc.org/chi-townsquares/
Bow to your partner, bow to your corner! Gay and lesbian square dancing in a smoke-free, booze-free environment. Singles welcome.

Equality Illinois
3712 N. Broadway St., #125, 60613, 888/434-7888, 773/477-7173
www.equalityillinois.com
"Defending the rights of lesbian, gay, bisexual and transgendered persons." Check out the Web site for legislative news, resources, and details on fund-raising events.

Euchre Club of Chicago
312/458-9010
www.euchrechicago.org
Mostly GLBT euchre card game enthusiasts. Meets twice a week to play.

Femme to Femme Chicago
www.f2fchicago.com
f2fchicago-owner@yahoogroups.com
For the girly girls who like girls. Monthly supportive meetings.

Frontrunners/Frontwalkers
312/409-2790
www.frfwchicago.org
They state they are "a club for lesbians, gay men, bisexuals, transexuals and friends who are interested in running and walking together along Chicago's great

open lakefront." Weekly run and walks, social meetings, and sponsors of the annual Proud to Run 10K race/walk in June during Pride weekend.

Gay Games Chicago
www.gaygameschicago.org
   Information, registration, and all sorts of good stuff for GLBT folks wanting to attend, participate in, or learn more about the Gay Games in Chicago in 2006.

Gay Liberation Network
www.gayliberation.org
   Formerly the Chicago Anti-Bashing Network. Fights against all hate crimes.

GLSEN Chicago
773/472-6469, x235
www.glsenchicago.org
   The Chicago chapter of the Gay, Lesbian and Straight Education Network "is dedicated to creating safe elementary, middle and high schools in the greater Chicago area."

Great Lakes Bears
773/509-5135
www.glbears.com
   Sponsors of the annual Bear Pride (www.bearpride.org) on Memorial Day weekend, as well as monthly social outings for bears and bear-appreciative types.

Hearts Foundation
3712 N. Broadway St., Suite 600, 60613, 773/244-6000
www.heartsfoundation.com
   Fund-raising for HIV services and prevention. Hearts Foundation sponsored the now defunct Fireball circuit party.

Human Rights Campaign
www.hrc.org (click on "Chicago")
   Gay and lesbian rights advocacy organization with gala dinners and fund-raising events.

Illinois Gay Rodeo Association
312/409-3835
www.ilgra.com
   Yee haw! This GLBT groups sponsors the annual **Windy City Gay Rodeo** (each August), as well as social and charitable events throughout the year.

khuli zaban
312/409-2753
www.geocities.com/westhollywood/9993/
Social and educational events for South Asian and West Asian women who love women. The name means "open tongue" in Hindi and Urdu. Hehe.

Lakeside Pride
773/381-6693
www.lakesidepride.org
Among Lakeside Pride's musical ensembles are a symphonic band, a jazz ensemble, and a marching band. Join up before the parade passes by.

Lambda Car Club
P.O. Box 268534, 60626, 773/465-5307
For the guys who love guys and also love their classic cars.

Lambda Legal Defense and Education Fund
312/663-4413
www.lambdalegal.org
"Committed to achieving full recognition of the civil rights of lesbians, gay men, bisexuals, transgender people and those with HIV through impact litigation, education and public policy work." In addition to their activist work, they have an online help desk for those with legal questions.

Leather SINS
847/203-8900
www.leathersins.com
They call themselves a "kink friendly social dinner club." Not just for the gays—bring your kinky straight friends, too. Leather SINS (which stands for Social Interaction of the North Shore) sponsors Kinky Kollege, a "pansexual BDSM Institute of Higher Yearning." See if you can get on the dean's list.

Lincoln Park Lagooners
3712 N. Broadway St., PMB #278, 60613
www.lincolnparklagooners.org
The first-ever gay and lesbian social organization in Chicago, and a member of the Chicago Gay and Lesbian Hall of Fame. Events include rafting, camping, bowling parties, and fund-raisers for charity.

Log Cabin Republicans
3712 N. Broadway St., #136, 60613
www.logcabin.org/lcrchicago/
Queer Republicans. We don't get it either. It's like "Nuns for Guns" or "Nymphos for a Sex-Free America." But each to his own.

Long Yang Club

www.longyangclub.org

lycchicago@yahoo.com

Social and support network for gay Asians and their friends. And Long Yang is the name of an ancient Chinese hero—get your mind out of the gutter.

Masters and Slaves Together

www.mast.net/chicago/

These guys meet on the second Friday of each month to discuss issues in master-slave relationships: getting 'em, keeping 'em, proper discipline, knots, and so forth.

Men of All Colors Together

312/409-6916

www.members.aol.com/mactchgo/

Ebony and ivory, living together in perfect harmony—the gay version. Well, that one version had Michael Jackson already, so, oh, never mind.

Mid America Fists in Action

P.O. Box 2230, 60690, 773/841-6234

www.mafiaff.org

No, M.A.F.I.A. is not some Sopranos-style mob group—it's just an organization for your average friendly Midwestern gay male fisters. The club has a meet-and-greet bar night at Touché once a month, plus private meetings. See the Web site for more details, cuz we shant be providing them here.

The Next Generation of Chicago

www.tngc.org

TNGC is a group of 18- to 35-year-old folks interested in getting tied up and stuff. In their words, they're "a support group in Chicago to help the younger adults of the BDSM scene to create a community where [they] can support each other in [their] lifestyle. This is a Pansexual group, all sexual preferences, persuasions, orientations, identifications and kinks are welcome!"

Onyx Men

312/329-6141

www.onyxmen.com

Social club for black gay leather men, with monthly events at Touché and Cellblock as well as the annual International Male Leather conference.

OUTlaw
www.law.northwestern.edu

This Northwestern University School of Law group sponsors lectures, panel discussions, and social outings for queer Northwestern legal folk aiming for the bar. No, the other kind of bar.

Queer to the Left
www.queertotheleft.org

Multiracial GLBTQ group committed to promoting "economic, racial, and social justice." Meets monthly.

Radical Faeries
www.groups.yahoo.com/group/chgoradicalfaeries/

A socio-spiritual and spirited group, they say, "The Radical Faeries in Chicago have a wonderful history of joy, magick and wonder. It is a circle of energetic earth-centered Queer Faerie folk who meet for community. We celebrate solstices, equinoxes, the ancient holidays of the sun and moon and share Heart Circle in Chicago."

Rainbow Lotus Sangha
773/271-8811
www.groups.yahoo.com/group/chicago_rainbowlotussangha/

They describe themselves as "a Chicago-area pan-denominational, lesbian/gay/bisexual/transgender Buddhist meditation group. . . . We seek to form a community with a focus on meditation, Dharma study, social activities, and social activism." They meet weekly.

ROTC
773/405-8189
www.rotcchicago.org

No, not the military group. This ROTC is the Righteously Outrageous Twirling Corps. How many many military synchronized marching/gun corps do routines to "It's Raining Men"? (The Geri Halliwell version.)

SANGAT (South Asian Gays/Lesbians) Chicago
773/506-8810
www.members.aol.com/youngal/sangat.html

SANGAT is a social and activist group for GLBT people of South Asian extraction.

Season of Concern
312/332-0518
www.seasonofconcern.org

A theater community fund-raising organization for HIV/AIDS service providers.

Stonewall Democrats of Chicago
5443 N. Broadway St., 2N, 60640, 773/573-8838
www.stonewalldemocrats.org
A political group that makes a bit more sense than the Log Cabin Republicans, if we say so ourselves.

Team Chicago
P.O. Box 13470, 60613
www.teamchicago.org
Sponsors and promoters of Chicago's Gay Games team, as well as other Midwestern GLBT athletic activities.

Trident International Windy City
Uptown Station P.O. Box 408755, 60640
www.tridentwindycity.com
A gay and lesbian Levi's and leather social and service club.

Windy City Athletic Association
www.wcaa.net
Organizes gay and lesbian basketball, bowling, darts, softball, and volleyball leagues. You know you want to play.

Windy City Bondage Club
312/409-7613
www.wcbc-chicago.org
A guys-only club with regularly scheduled play parties. You know you want to play.

Windy City Cycling Club
312/458-9841
www.windycitycyclingclub.com
This GLBT social and athletic club promotes bike riding, fitness, and socialization. Their Dykes Pedaling Bikes events are specifically geared for (naturally) the ladies.

Windy City Empire
773/334-3296
www.windycityempire.org
GLBT group of queens dressing up like kings and queens, for fun, societal interaction, and charity.

Windy City Gay Naturists
312/494-2654
windycitygaynaturists.org
    Social group for guys who wanna get naked together, and yes, they might
have sex while being naked. Depends on the event.

Windy City Performing Arts
773/404-9242
www.windycitysings.org
    The umbrella organization (a pink umbrella, or parasol, we assume) for the
Windy City Gay Chorus as well as Unison, a choir for male and female vocalists.
Three major shows and many other performances throughout the year.

Get the Spirit: Religious and Personal Growth Resources

AIDS Pastoral Care Network
8321 W. North Ave., Melrose Park, 60160, 708/681-6327
    Dedicated to the spiritual well-being of people with HIV/AIDS.

Archdiocesan Gay and Lesbian Outreach
711 W. Belmont Ave., 60657, 773/525-3872
www.aglochicago.org
    Roman Catholic GLBT-friendly services are held Sundays at 7 P.M. at Our
Lady of Mount Carmel, 690 W. Belmont Avenue. Social hour follows.

Axios
5601 N. Sheridan Rd., #5B, 312/271-1027
AxiosChi@aol.com
    Social and support group for GLBT Eastern and Near Eastern Orthodox and
Byzantine and Eastern-Rite Catholic Christians.

Broadway United Methodist Church
3344 N. Broadway St., 60657, 773/348-2679
www.brdwyumc.org
    Robert's attended services here. As befitting a church in the heart of
Boystown, it's way gay. And the community has a wonderful ally in the person of
Pastor Gregory Dell.

Brotherhood of the Phoenix
773/525-8308
www.brotherhoodofthephoenix.org
This gay men's neo-pagan group says, "We stress a simple neo-pagan principle: Find the Divine within your own experience." In addition to public rituals, the brotherhood sponsors workshops, lectures, and parties.

Chicago Coalition of Welcoming Churches
www.chicagowelcomingchurches.org
The coalition offers a great Web site that will connect you to all the "Christian churches in the Chicagoland area which welcome and affirm all persons, regardless of sexual orientation."

Church of the Open Door
5954 S. Albany Ave., 60629, 773/778-3030
Specializes in ministering to the black GLBT community. Weekly Sunday services are at 4 P.M.

Congregation Or Chadash
5959 N. Sheridan Rd., 60660, 773/271-2148
www.orchadash.org
A synagogue for GLBT folks, their families, and their friends.

Dignity Chicago
312/458-9438
www.dignitychicago.org
Support and activism for GLBT Roman Catholics.

Ebenezer Lutheran Church
1650 W. Foster Ave., 60640, 773/561-8496
www.ebenezerchurch.org
A Reconciling church in the Andersonville neighborhood. Main services are held Sundays at 8 and 10:30 A.M.

Epiphany United Church of Christ
2008 W. Bradley Pl., 60618, 773/281-4144
www.epiphany-ucc.org
Services are held at 10:30 A.M. on Sundays.

First United Methodist Church at the Chicago Temple

77 W. Washington St., 60602, 312/236-4548

www.chicagotemple.org

The oldest continuous congregation in Chicago, established in 1831. Services are held at 8:30 and 11 A.M. on Sundays.

Grace Baptist Church

5253 N. Kenmore Ave., 60640, 773/334-9003

www.gracebaptistchicago.com

We love that they say, "We are learning to follow Jesus (but aren't wrapped up in doctrinal conformity)." Because who needs to be wrapped up in that? Services are Sundays at 6 P.M.

Holy Covenant United Methodist Church

925 W. Diversey Pkwy., 60614, 773/528-6462

www.muralchurch.org

It's probably a good sign when you look up a church online and find a photo on their Web site that shows the pastor marching in the Pride Parade. Services are 10:30 A.M. on Sundays, and they helpfully declare them to be "informal in dress." So wear the good T-shirt.

Holy Trinity Lutheran Church

1218 W. Addison St., 60613, 773/248-1233

www.holytrinitychicago.org

Services are held at 8:15 and 10 on Sunday mornings.

Lake Street Church of Evanston

607 Lake St., Evanston, 60201, 847/864-2181

www.lakestreet.org

They are a Baptist church that is "willing to go on record as welcoming and affirming all persons without regard to sexual orientation or gender identity." The main service is at 10:30 A.M. on Sundays. Plus they offer yoga classes.

The Night Ministry

4711 N. Ravenswood Ave., 60640, 773/784-9000

www.thenightministry.org

This service organization works with people on Chicago's nighttime streets, providing health care, condoms, food, and counseling, especially to the GLBT youth population, homeless and not. They are nondenominational but supported by many congregations of all faiths. Volunteers and donations are always welcome.

St. James Presbyterian Church

6554 N. Rockwell St., 60645, 773/465-6254

www.stjameschicago.org

They declare: "The mission of More Light Presbyterians is the full participation of gay, lesbian, bisexual, transgender people of faith in the life, ministry, and witness of the Presbyterian Church." Plus they offer yoga classes. Sunday services are held at 10:30 A.M.

St. Pauls United Church of Christ

2335 N. Orchard St., 60614, 773/348-3829

www.stpaulsuccchicago.org

Service times vary seasonally. See the Web site for details.

Temple of the Four Winds

www.temple4winds.org

This pagan spiritual-social group says, "We welcome all genders, all races, all sexual orientations and all those differences of life situations; background, physical, emotional, intellectual and Magickal abilities that increase our diversity."

That All May Freely Serve

312/409-4523

www.tamfs.org

Working to create a GLBT-inclusive Presbyterian Church.

Wellington Avenue United Church of Christ

615 W. Wellington Ave., 60657, 773/935-0642

www.wellingtonaveucc.org

They say, "We affirm sexuality to be a gift from God and celebrate all loving relationships." Well, alrighty! Sunday services are at 10:30 A.M. In the Boystown hood.

Get Informed: Media Outlets

Boi Magazine

773/975-0264

www.boimagazine.com

Ad-heavy guide to nightlife for the young and fabulous variety of gay male.

Chicago Free Press

773/868-0005

www.chicagofreepress.com

Weekly free GLBT publication features news, commentary, art and culture reviews, nightlife listings, and more. Find it in street-corner boxes and at GLBT-type places all over the city.

Chicago Magazine
312/222-8999
www.chicagomag.com
　　Monthly magazine with Chicago news, features, and reviews. Not a lot of specifically gay content, but useful for spotting hot new restaurants and shops. Wherever magazines are sold.

Chicago Reader
312/828-0350
www.chicagoreader.com
　　Free weekly alternative paper. We think the *Reader* has the best movie, theater, arts, restaurant, and music listings going. Also a must if you are searching for housing. Plus they carry Dan Savage's "Savage Love" sex advice column. Pick it up at street-corner boxes, book and record stores, and cafés, as well as downtown at the Virgin Megastore.

Chicago Sun-Times
312/321-3000
www.suntimes.com
　　Daily paper with a perhaps more working-class, average-Joe feel than the *Tribune*. Available everywhere.

Chicago Tribune
800/TRIBUNE, x6349
www.chicagotribune.com
　　Daily paper with a slightly right-wing editorial slant. Decent arts coverage. At newsstands and corner stores everywhere.

Gay Chicago Magazine
773/327-7271
www.gaychicagomag.com
　　Free weekly newsprint magazine that's been dishing up news, reviews, a community calendar, and such since 1976. Mostly for the guys.

Homofrecuencia
www.wrte.org/homofrecuencia
　　Spanish-language radio program for GLBTQ youth, Mondays from 8 to 10 P.M., at 90.5 FM on your dial.

Identity
www.wctimes.com/identity.html
　　Published by Windy City Media Group, this free monthly glossy focuses on issues and people of interest to the Latin and African-American GLBT communities.

New City
312/243-8786
www.newcitychicago.com
   Gay-friendly, alternative paper, a slimmer sort of *Chicago Reader*. They sometimes review surprising or eclectic events. It's free, so you could do worse than pick up a copy.

Nightspots
www.wctimes.com/nightspots.html
   Irreverent weekly lil mag devoted to queer nightlife and fun events. Lots of photos. And it's the happy right price of free.

The Onion
312/751-0503
www.theonion.com
   Free satiric humor weekly with good reviews of movies and music. You have to love a paper that prints the headline "Rumsfeld Makes Surprise Visit to Wife's Vagina." Well, you don't, but we do.

OUT! Guide
www.wctimes.com/gay/lesbian/news/OUTGUIDE/
   Whether you want a gay therapist or a lesbian plumber, this is the guide. Every service and shop under the sun is listed, as long as they are gay-friendly: vets, caterers, chiropractors, and much more.

Think Pink
www.wluw.org
   Queer music radio show, made by and for queers, hosted by Eric and Ali, Tuesdays from 6:30 to 8 P.M. at 88.7 FM on that radio dial.

Time Out Chicago
www.timeoutchicago.com
   Weekly guide to everything going on in the city, from film, theater, dance, and music to dining, sports, and more. Good for uncovering hidden gems and unknown treasures. Each issue contains a lesbian and gay interest events listing and highlights one or more of them with a brief article. Wherever magazines are sold.

Windy City Radio
www.windycityradio.com
   Hear them out on Sunday nights from 10 to 11 P.M., on WCKG (105.9 FM), or tune in online, any old time.

Windy City Times
773/871-7610
www.wctimes.com
Free GLBT paper with news, cultural coverage, and a calendar of events. Find it throughout the city at gay-friendly businesses, or look online.

Get Yourself Some Culture: Information and Networking in and About the Arts

About Face Theatre
773/784-8565
www.aboutfacetheatre.com
Chicago's premier GLBT-focused theater company. Stages shows at various venues around town.

Aldo Castillo Gallery
233 W. Huron St., 312/337-2536
www.artaldo.com
This gay-owned Latin-American art gallery declares that they "foster an understanding and appreciation for all cultures and their history through lectures, presentations, live cultural performances, classes and other events, both inside and beyond the gallery walls."

Bailiwick Repertory Theatre
Bailiwick Arts Center, 1229 W. Belmont Ave., 773/883-1090
www.bailiwick.org
The site for many GLBT-themed productions and new musicals throughout the year.

Barbara's Bookstore
www.barbarasbookstore.com
This GLBT-friendly independent small chain of stores has locations near UIC, downtown (inside Marshall Field's), and in Oak Park. They host one of the best author reading series in town.

Blithe House Quarterly
www.blithe.com
An online GLBT literary journal originating in Chicago.

Chicago Artists' Coalition

312/670-2060

www.caconline.org

Check 'em out for Chicago arts community events, workshops, lectures, and the opportunity to buy art from Chicago artists online.

Chicago Cultural Center

312/744-6630

78 E. Washington St., 60602

City visitor information, along with concerts, exhibitions, theater, film, lectures, tours, and more, almost all of it absolutely free. Find them online at http://egov.cityofchicago.org (under "Exploring Chicago" click on "Arts and Culture").

Chicago Filmmakers

773/293-1447

www.chicagofilmmakers.org

Sponsors of Reeling, the Chicago Lesbian and Gay International Film Festival, with additional GLBT programming and classes throughout the year.

Chicago Public Library

312/747-4300

www.chipublib.org

It's a public library, silly. All kinds of info.

Chicago Symphony Orchestra

312/294-3333

www.cso.org

The CSO is a cultural treasure and one of the finest civic orchestras in the world.

Facets Multimedia

1517 W. Fullerton Ave., 773/281-9075

www.facets.org

Facets screens films from all over the world, including works of interest to GLBT types. They are also a great resource for renting or buying such work.

Gerber/Hart Library

1127 W. Granville Ave., 773/381-8030

www.gerberhart.org

Archive and cultural center for Chicago's GLBT community, with titles of interest to academic as well as the general queer public. Gerber/Hart hosts gay and lesbian book discussion groups, art exhibitions, and film viewings.

Homolatte
www.scottfree.net
Weekly queer performance series featuring writers and musicians, and info on the Web on all sorts of queer Chicagoland music and concerts. Read more in our music section (Chapter 15).

HotHouse
31 E. Balbo Ave., 312/362-9707
www.hothouse.net
The place for world music and performance, including jazz.

Hot Tix
www.hottix.org
Find half-price tickets to theater shows around town, or just see what's playing, cheap seats or not.

Jazz Institute of Chicago
www.jazzinstituteofchicago.org
Sponsors of the annual Chicago Jazz Festival. Their online home is a dandy spot to see what's going on in the city's smokin' dens of doo-wop and bebop.

Las Manos Gallery
5220 N. Clark St., 773/728-8910
This lesbian-owned gallery in the heart of Andersonville regularly features lesbian and gay artists.

League of Chicago Theatres
312/554-9800
www.chicagoplays.com
Listings and links to everything happening in the Chicago theater world.

Literary Exchange
P.O. Box 238583, 60643, 773/509-6881
Lesbian-friendly African-American literary group, publishers of the zine *Literary Express.*

Lyric Opera of Chicago
312/332-2244
www.lyricopera.org
Chicago's world-class stage for opera.

New Town Writers
www.newtownwriters.org
Since 1980 members of this GLBT writing group have been workshopping together, as well as producing readings, a journal, and now an e-zine.

Old Town School of Folk Music
773/728-6000
www.oldtownschool.org
The place to learn to strum your guitar or hammer your dulcimer, as well as a fine venue for seeing musical artists of all kinds, from folk to pop, jazz to world music. GLBT-friendly—they are relaxed granola tie-dyed types, after all.

Ravinia Festival
847/266-5100
www.ravinia.org
Suburban outdoor summer music festival features classical, pop, jazz, and opera concerts and dance, too. Sit on the lawn and groove.

Seminary Co-op Bookstore
773/752-4381
http://semcoop.booksense.com
Hyde Park bookstore with a wonderful selection of titles in the humanities, including gender and queer studies. The co-op also has a general bookstore, 57th Street Books, in Hyde Park, as well as a tasteful shop inside the Newberry Library.

Specialty Video
Boystown: 3221 N. Broadway St., 773/248-3434
Andersonville: 5307 N. Clark St., 773/878-3434
Both locations for this independent movie rental spot boast a good selection of mainstream releases as well as indie and GLBT flicks. Oh yeah, and pornos, too—it can't all be subtitles and fancy cinematography.

Unabridged Bookstore
3251 N. Broadway St., 773/883-9119
Gay-owned general bookstore with the largest gay section in the city, plus magazines, calendars, kids' books, and great travel and fiction selections.

Woman Made Gallery
2418 W. Bloomingdale Ave., 773/489-8900
www.womanmade.org
In their words, "Unlike the mainstream art world, we are building an alternative community where the artistic values and criteria are determined by women, for women." They feature lesbian artists frequently.

Women & Children First
5233 N. Clark St., 773/769-9299
www.womenandchildrenfirst.com
   Since 1979 this lesbian-owned feminist bookstore has had a great selection, a dedicated staff, and an active author reading series.

Ann and Linda, owners of
Women & Children First Bookstore.
~Photo by Mel Ferrand

Get Logged On: Web Sites of Note

Andersonville Chamber of Commerce
www.andersonville.org
   The chamber's site presents info on shopping, arts and entertainment, restaurants, business resources, and area history.

Chicago Crystal Meth Task Force
www.crystalbreaks.org
   The sad facts and hard statistics of crystal meth use. Some links to help. Don't do it. Stop if you do. This is nasty, nasty stuff.

Chicago Dyke March
www.chicagodykemarch.org
   Information on the annual Dyke March.

Chicago Gallery News
www.chicagogallerynews.com
   Find out what's showing at what art gallery in the city and when.

Chicago Gay and Lesbian Hall of Fame
www.glhalloffame.org
   Every October, at a formal ceremony hosted by the Mayor, deserving folks are added to Chicago's official Gay and Lesbian Hall of Fame for their contributions to the city as a whole and to the queer community in particular. This informative, official site lists and describes all the inductees. We don't know of another American city that honors its gays in such a permanent and public way.

ChicagoPride.com
www.chicagopride.com
   With reviews, news, an events calendar, personals, interviews, and more, this is the whole Chicago GLBT tamale.

City of Chicago
http://egov.cityofchicago.org
   Whether you are planning a trip to the city, reporting a problem, buying a city sticker for your car, paying a tax bill, or trying to find your alderman's office, this is the place. Arts, culture, transportation, lodging, and a heck of a lot more.

craigslist: Chicago Classifieds
www.chicago.craigslist.org
   Find yourself a new job, a new apartment, a slightly used IKEA couch, or a slightly used sex buddy, all on one free Web site.

Dyke Diva
www.dykediva.com
   The way-cool online guide to Chicago events and resources for the Sapphic sisterhood.

Encyclopedia of Chicago
www.encyclopedia.chicagohistory.org
   A fascinating and comprehensive look at Chicago history, including entries on the gays. Read up before you visit!

Feast of Fools
www.feastoffools.net
   Home of the fab blue-haired Fausto Fernos's queer podcast, for you iPod users.

Gapers Block
www.gapersblock.com
   Great site for gossip, info, musings, and hidden gems of Chicago. Events listings, too. Very GLBT-friendly.

GLBTQ
www.glbtq.com
   An online encyclopedia of queer culture. Good stuff, Mary.

Independent Gay Forum
www.indegayforum.org
   Queer writers, academics, and activists debate and discuss gay-related issues and current events. Not Chicago-specific.

InterPride
www.interpride.org
   All about Pride events all around the world.

Lakeview Chamber of Commerce
www.lakeviewchamber.com
   Links for and info on Boystown neighborhood businesses and resources.

Miss Foozie
www.missfoozie.com
   Hello, Pineapple! Halsted Street's busiest hostess tells where she will be and when.

My Favorite Drag Queen
www.dragtastic.com
   The online resource for drag kings, queens, and fans, with a performance calendar and links. A nationwide site with lots of Chicago drag stuff listed.

National Transgender Advocacy Coalition
www.ntac.org
   Works for equal rights and understanding of transgender and gender variant folks. Links to many resources.

Northalsted Area Merchants Association
www.northalsted.com
   Sponsors of Northalsted Market Days. Links for and info on Boystown businesses and resources.

Queer Cultural Center
www.queerculturalcenter.org
   Text, video, sounds, and images archived. Look for our friend Owen Keehnen's interviews, many of them with queer Chicago's best and brightest.

Queer Day Magazine
www.queerday.com
   This far-reaching blog includes news, culture, and gossip of interest to the GLBT community. They are looking for tips and submissions. Not Chicago-specific.

A YEAR WITH THE QUEERS: HIGHLIGHTS
OF OUR CHICAGO CALENDAR

Something goes on every day and every night in Chicago's GLBT community. Meetings, dates, theme nights at bars, volunteer orientations, drag shows, parties, rock performances, snacks, sporting events, potlucks, circle jerks, political meetings—heck, even the lonely gal or guy staring out the window of their high-rise apartment and watching the rain fall is doing *something*. This chapter presents some of the things that Chicago's GLBT community looks forward to with delighted anticipation. And most of them are more fun than sitting around watching the rain. We offer personal observations and musings on some of the events we have attended, but the lack of a report in no way signals a lack of enthusiasm for any particular occasion.

January

The weather can be wicked in January. We do go out and do things, though, honest. Theater is big this time of year, while the bars are full of specials and events. Mostly indoor stuff, if you catch our (snow) drift. Brrr.

February

The weather can be wicked in February. Luckily, a couple of the social events of Chicago's GLBT season occur to take the sting out of that distinct chill in the air.

Lesbian Community Cancer Project's Coming Out Against Cancer Ball
When: Early February
Where: South Shore Cultural Center, 7059 South Shore Dr., 773/256-0149

Since 1991 women have been going in droves to what has become the lesbian social event of the year. Women in ball gowns and tuxedos tumble out of limos, while others don their best khakis and rugby shirts—such is the lesbian way. Once inside this high-priced affair, you'll encounter a long, cruisy gallery that connects rooms offering various diversions: tables cascading over with hors d'oeuvres in one, a silent auction of items donated by local businesses in another (sometimes including items donated by high-profile celebrities; past examples have included Melissa Etheridge's guitar and the Björk-influenced swan suit worn by Ellen DeGeneres when she hosted the Academy Awards). Yet another room houses a couple of cash bars, tables, and a small raised platform where speeches and performances occur. Finally, a fourth room pulses with a disco beat as a live DJ throws down the latest dance tracks. Past COAC Balls have featured celebrity guest DJs such as MC Lyte and Me'Shell Ndege Ocello, and as the night progresses, the dance floor really gets moving. Check the LCCP Web site (www.lccp.org) for the latest schedule; COAC Ball information (and online ticket purchasing) is usually available by October or November for the next year's event.

March

In March or early April, the **Windy City Gay Idol** competition kicks off. It's not quite *American Idol*, but it is a heck of a lot of fun to either watch (and sometimes wince) or belt out a song, if you are so inclined. Get more info at www.outlineschicago.com.

Windy City Gay Idol Semifinals

This annual contest, both a rip-off of and an homage to TV's *American Idol*, is jointly sponsored by Windy City Media (the fine folks who bring you the gay free weekly paper *Windy City Times*) and the Chicago karaoke industry that is Creaoke, along with some corporate sponsors. Participating bars across the city have their designated evenings to host the contest, and several lucky winners from each initial competition advance to the semifinals. The ultimate winner stands to take the not-at-all-shabby grand prize of $1,000, two airline tickets, and a new bike. Robert and his buddy Gene met at the unlikely venue of the **Chicago Eagle** to check out 20 queer would-be superstars. The Eagle is actually housed in the same building as the bathhouse **Man's Country**, and the contest was held in an event room shared by the bathhouse and the Eagle for special porn star appearances and such. Our hostess for the evening, actress and radio personality Amy Matheny, said, "Ah, you can just smell the poppers and lube in the air." We couldn't really (that would have been distracting), but there was something quite fun about seeing a crowd of gay and lesbian (along with plenty of straight) supporters turning out to cheer for their singing friends in a room that has probably witnessed far more lascivious goings-on over the years. Robert and Gene took advantage of a great special on a bucket of Budweiser (thanks, corporate sponsor!) and settled in for 20 songs by 20 queers. Local celebrity judges offered up their sound bites after each performance, though none displayed the Simon Cowell cattiness that you find on the TV show. Contestants were butch, femme, buff, plump, young pups, and old hands, with only a couple of clinkers in the bunch. Robert and Gene, like much of the appreciative crowd, were well fueled by Bud. They loved everyone with a warm beer love. There's a lot of talk of the GLBT "community" but precious few events that bring together the widest possible range of queers. A-listers, working stiffs, tough chicks, and slick ricks all joined together and cheered *all* the brave contestants, even though most folks were attending to support a specific friend. And you have to admit, it takes balls of one kind or another to work a stage and warble in front of

300 people. Luckily, the Eagle has a good aura for balls. At the halfway point, our hostess Amy gave away a ton of freebies, like theater tickets. Sadly, Robert did not win the grand prize audience giveaway, $1,500 worth of electrolysis, so his back is just going to have to be hairy for another summer at the beach. He did get a Bud key chain, so he still feels special. ✦

April

Finally, the prospect of snow fades. We begin putting away scarves and gloves, heading out onto the bike and running paths, and basically poking our heads outdoors again.

Who's That Girl?
When: Late April
Where: Lately at the Park West Theater, but check the Web site to be sure

This is an annual fund-raising event for Chicagoland HIV services, offering two evenings of drag, impersonation, dance, and music. See www.whosthatgirl.biz for photos and more.

Gabi Atun.
~Photo by Jon Peterson

May

All sorts of heck breaks loose on Memorial Day weekend as the **International Male Leather** convention hits town. Thousands of male, female, and trans leather and rubber enthusiasts descend on Chicago, with everything from breakfasts to dance parties to leather contests as part of the festivities. Just to gruff up the proceedings a tad, this is also **Bear Pride** weekend, for all the hirsute belly boys and their admirers. Dozens of satellite events take place over Memorial Day weekend, too. One of these, the **Grabby Erotic Video Awards Show**, is the gay porn equivalent of the Oscars. Log on to www.imrl.com for more on IML, www.glbears.com for more on Bear Pride, and www.grabbys.com for more on the Grabbys.

IML

Robert's first trip to International Male Leather's Leather Market was as fun a Saturday excursion as he's had in quite a while, and we're talking about a guy who owns nothing more exciting in the leather realm than hiking boots and a couple of belts. International Mr. Leather, or IML to those in the know, is the annual convention (every Memorial Day weekend) for leather men and women. IML started in Chicago—and Chicago remains its home base. Like any convention centered on an industry or a special interest, IML offers workshops, parties, receptions, and opportunities to casually network and meet like-minded folk in the hotel lobby. True, IML attendees are generally going to be outfitted in leather gear of some kind: chaps, pants, vests, shirts, boots, armbands, and, in some cases, all of the above. (Animal rights activists don

🔥 *Crowd at May's International Mr. Leather.*
~Photo by Jon Peterson

pleather and rubber gear, and are equally welcome.) And true, casual networking in this case may mean, "Hey, do you want to come to our JO cocktail party in room 718 at 5 P.M. today?" But even Rotary Club and Tupperware conventions get a mite frisky, we're sure.

The big focus of the weekend is on the International Male Leather contest and its satellites: contests for women, for bootblacks, and so forth. The contest is kind of like a Miss America pageant, with a Pecs and Personality portion in place of the bathing suit strut. The contest is a worthy event in its own right, but everyone we spoke with said that the Leather Market was a must. And so our boy reporter set out to spend a Saturday with daddies and slaves and bears, oh my!

Just getting into the market is an adventure. In a good way. Because a lot of the material in the market is of a sexual nature, you have to sign an affidavit declaring that you are indeed 21 and that viewing sexually explicit materials does not offend you. The IML folks also ask for a small donation to the Leather Archives and collect basic demographic info about you to better woo sponsors and vendors. All of this takes some time, so you'll be corralled into a line that resembles the line for a theme park ride, that back-and-forth incremental zigzag, which happily allows for maximum cruising potential.

Once the donation has been donated and the forms filled out, you get a wristband (black, naturally) applied by a helpful leather-clad volunteer, and you're free to join the strolling throng checking out the thongs (and other items) on display and for sale at the Leather Market. Here you'll be able to find just anything you could ever imagine and then some, including traditional leather jackets, kilts, candles, lubricants, special bondage beds, sex toys, clamps, whips, chains, DVDs, magazines, jewelry (for *all* body parts), artwork, and more—all of this presented in a setting as formal and well appointed as any trade show you've ever attended. You're just going to see more people in leather full-body suits holding their masked and gagged submissives by a spiked leash than you would see at, say, the dental implements trade show in Las Vegas. And lest that scare you, rest assured that among the bears and bikers, the leather man obsessives and the dominant divas in rubber push-up bras and spiked high-heel boots, much of the crowd wears what they always wear—in Robert's case, a black long-sleeved T-shirt and jeans. He promises, not a single person all day pointed at him and called him a loser because of his lack of leather gear. He quickly fell in, actually, with a group of similarly attired acquaintances—including Adam, even a tad more square, due to his green polo shirt, and Ryan, in a purple T-shirt that proclaimed "Dump Her"—and got a lot of attention on the floor, although Ryan, it's fair to say, would probably get attention in a crowd of gay men no matter what he wore. (Not that you are chopped liver, Adam.)

The boys recounted a demo they'd just seen for a very special chair. Imagine a potty chair, but built for an adult, and instead of the potty part, just an oval hole. Someone (the rimmee) sits in the chair, while someone else (the rimmer) reclines below. (We'll include a diagram in the next edition.) What impressed them the most with the display was that the man sitting in the chair continued his spokesmodel spiel, complete with practiced hand gestures and a memorized script about the comforts and features of the rimming chair, while the man below, um, rimmed. "I hope," said Adam, "that the rimmer guy isn't also working the kissing booth."

Like any trade show, the Leather Market is rife with free samples. The astute attendee can leave laden with any number of fun things. If you leave without condoms and lube, you either don't need or don't want condoms and lube, as these items are nearly everywhere for the taking. There were also a lot of opportunities to end up on e-mail lists by signing up for raffles—Robert and company noticed only belatedly that the porn star signing them up for a chance to win a set of his production company's DVDs was the big throbbing star of the film playing on the screen behind him. Another booth had a spin-the-wheel deal, where participants could win anything from DVDs to come towels (each helpfully labeled "cum towel") or, best of all (to Robert's mind anyway), a black rubber duckie. Ryan won a rubber duckie, but when he saw the avaricious light shining in Robert's eyes, he bowed to the inevitable and gave up his rubber duckie. Now it lives in Robert's bathroom, bossing around the small flock of yellow rubber ducks on top of the medicine cabinet.

Sure, the Market has things that shock—sometimes literally, as in the case of the video demo depicting the advantages of electricity applied to the gonads at the moment of orgasm. That and the TV replay of the enthusiastic whomp of a rubber mallet applied at a similar moment (and at the same location) are mental images seared in Robert's brain, possibly for all time. But if the Leather Market only sold fancy bracelets and nice coats, no one would go back year after year. The kinks are part of the fun. Still, when Robert overheard a salesperson say, "And this attachment also doubles as a catheter!" he knew he'd reached the perfect moment to abandon the market in favor of the other great arena of IML, the hotel lobby. IML takes over different hotels in different years, as an estimated 13,000 to 18,000 leather folk arrive in Chicago and make it home. In this case, it was the Hyatt Regency on Wacker Drive. The spacious glass-domed lobby, at 4 in the afternoon, had been transformed into the largest, friendliest leather bar in the world.

People-watching is the great sport here. If you go to the IML hotel lobby to hook up, that opportunity exists, but before you rush off to some form of pleasure in someone's private room, you owe it to yourself to find a good lobby spot and watch everyone go by. You'll be struck by how inclusive the leather community is. You'll see deaf leather men talking in sign language. You'll see all ages, all races, and all body types, from the chiseled to the morbidly obese. While women don't make up a huge percentage of IML attendees, they are warmly welcomed. You might see several blasts from your past, as Robert did: three ex-boyfriends, two tricks, and someone whose name he forgot but they snogged for an hour a few years back at a party. It's part Halloween, it's part Mardi Gras, it's deadly serious for a few (can we please just say ixnay on the SS uniforms?), and it's great fun for many. One cautionary note: there was a whole lotta smoking going on—and not just cigarettes. Those old leather daddies love their cigars, and this particular IML, at least, was not a nonsmoker-friendly space.

One of the underlying messages of IML is that everyone is sexy. From the ultra-studs with their gym muscles to the slack seniors with sagging butts, from the wide, big-busted women wearing leather bustiers to skinny just-legal boys in soccer gear, everyone's gathered to say, "Hey, put this on. You look good. Doesn't it feel good? Don't you feel sexy?" Pleasure being something in generally short supply, we say, Come down to the Leather Market. Hang out at the hotel. At lot of people are smiling there—you should be smiling, too. ✦

June

With all the queer events this month, you'd think there was some sort of monthlong celebration, like a Pride month or something. Pride month in Chicago includes ten billion events, from readings to lectures, vigils to prayer services, fund-raisers, award ceremonies, concerts, and more. If a GLBT social or service group exists in Chicago (check out Chapter 18 for some of those), you can pretty much assume they are going to mark the month a special event. The Web site www.chicagopridecalendar.org has the most comprehensive listing we have found. You may also want to look at the calendar of events collected by the *Windy City Times* and *Chicago Free Press*. (See Chapter 18 for these and other media outlets.) Highlights of the month include the following:

Andersonville's Midsommarfest
When: Second weekend in June
Where: Andersonville, silly!

This street fair (on Clark Street between Foster and Balmoral)—featuring food, drink, music, arts and crafts booths, and lots of strolling eye candy—unofficially kicks off the summer season. See www.andersonville.org for details.

Bailiwick Repertory's Pride Series, with GLBT-themed plays all month long. Check out www.bailiwick.org, call 773/883-1090, or see page 167 for more on Bailiwick.

Gay Day at Six Flags Great America

Every year during Pride month, *Gay Chicago Magazine* supports an unofficial "Gay Day" at Six Flags Great America. While not officially acknowledged by the park, it's a time when we queers attend in such numbers that we possess greater freedom and comfort to fully enjoy the park's thrills. Homos on roller coasters! Imagine the delighted sibilant shrieks!

This year, our buddy Ianni made the 45-minute trek from Chicago to Gurnee, home to a huge outlet mall as well as the Midwest's largest amusement park. Ianni is Greek, and what with Sappho and Socrates, we're pretty sure the Greeks invented homosexuality, along with democracy, the Olympics, and personal lubricants. (You can't tell us that all of that olive oil was pressed just for food.) So who better to recruit as a special Field Guide correspondent?

While many of the attendees rode to Six Flags on buses hired by Chicago gay bars, Ianni drove with friends. Package deals, such as the one organized by *Gay Chicago Magazine*, represent significant savings, as a day pass to the park can run around $45, while a Gay Day ticket package including transportation was a mere $30. The cool thing is, anyone can organize a package deal as long as they have enough people signed up who are willing to pay up front. Information is on the Six Flags Web site, and if you can organize more than 50 people to go, Six Flags will even throw in a free lunch for all. Holy Batman ride, Batman! Anyone can book their own "gay day"!

But back to our intrepid field reporter. Ianni knows his ancient Greek classics, but he's not up (or down or upside down) on contemporary American amusement park rides, so off he went to experience this slice of Americana for himself. He reports that the park was *full* of GLBT people. "Maybe 10 percent, maybe 25 percent," Ianni estimated. "I'm not good at math." But he is good with faces, and he recognized a lot of Chicagoans, both folks he knows and faces familiar from the neighborhoods and bars. "No one was shy about being out," he reports. "There were a lot of public displays of affection and same-sex hand-holdings, along with innocent cruising and smiles all around." The kind of smiles, he said, "that are a silent affirmation that you are among your own kind."

Those kinds, according to Ianni, included an equal number of men and women. If you have been to amusement parks before, you know the shtick where the park automatically photographs you on the roller coasters at the moment of the most terrifying plunge, and when the ride is over you can see and purchase photos of yourself and your friends looking scared witless. Ianni was delighted to discover that many an enterprising lesbian couple, roller coaster veterans all, knew the moment when the shutter would click, and they locked lips at that crucial second, to give themselves and fellow park-goers stirring photographic evidence of woman-on-woman love.

As far as busting open his own roller coaster cherry, we're sad to say that Ianni did not convert to a fan of the genre. He liked the water rides, although he insists on calling them "water sports rides," which may indicate a lingering difficulty with the English language or perhaps a burgeoning new interest on his part. But after gamely riding the Viper, the Raging Bull, and, most disastrously for his stomach, that big wooden ship thingy that rocks back and forth in ever-wider arcs ("What was I thinking?" he moaned), Ianni was over the Six Flags experience. The next time he's outdoors on a lovely day with a bunch of friendly gays, he intends on being firmly seated and relatively motionless, the only arc in sight being the pint of Stella raised to his lips.

For Gay Day at Six Flags information, check out www.gaychicagomagazine.com. For information about the park, check out www.sixflags.com. Usually several area bars, including Charlie's, offer complete Gay Day packages with transportation and tickets. ✦

Also Sometime in June (Dates Vary)

Annual LGBT Fiction and Poetry Pride Reading
Women & Children First
773/769-9299
www.womenandchildrenfirst.com

Windy City Gay Chorus/Unison Pride Concert
773/404-9242
www.windycitysings.org

Chicago Gay Men's Chorus Pride Concert
773/296-0541
www.cgmc.org

Pride Weekend

When: The last weekend in June
Where: All over the dang place

There are enough activities of all sorts during Pride month in Chicago to fill the social calendar of every queer from here to Topeka. But the last weekend peaks, culminates (insert your own orgasmic comment here) with the prime events of the season, the "high holy days," as some of our friends call them.

Proud to Run
When: The last Saturday in June
Where: The Lakefront; check the Web site for exact locations

The Frontrunners/ Frontwalkers of Chicago (312/409-2790, www.frfwchicago.org) sponsor this annual 5K and 10K run or two-mile walk.

Dyke March.
~Photo by Mel Ferrand

Dyke March
When: The last Saturday in June
Where: Andersonville

The Dyke March started in 1995 as a response to what was seen as an epidemic of lesbian invisibility during the Gay Pride Parade, to protest the increasing commercialization of gay pride. The march grew from a ragtag assemblage of 40 or 50 women to roughly 1,000 in 2005. While that increase has included some semi-organized contingents (Chicago NOW, for example), there is no processional order, and everyone is invited to participate in the anarchic fun, with drummers, cheerleaders, lesbian moms pushing strollers, topless gals with electrical tape covering their nipples, and plenty of supportive boys. The most recent Dyke March we attended included all of the above, as well as organized chanters with a bullhorn yelling, "1, 2, 3, 4, gender roles are such a bore! 5, 6, 7, 8, we think trannies are real great! Fuck you blue, fuck you pink, fuck your gender roles, they stink!"

The Andersonville march begins at Ashland and Foster, then moves over to Clark Street, where it heads north to Bryn Mawr, before turning east to end with a rally at the lake. The rally consists of various political speakers (the Dyke March puts the politics back into Pride) and typically a musical or performance act or two. Check local Pride event schedules for the starting time and rally lineup, or log on to www.chicagodykemarch.org for info.

Backlot Bash
When: The last Saturday in June
Where: Andersonville, at 5238 N. Clark St.

What is it that makes people think lesbians want to hang out in parking lots (see also **GirlBlast**, p. 260)? In any case, this annual party, held behind Cheetah Gym

(5248 N. Clark St.), across the street from Women & Children First, runs concurrent with the Dyke March and continues on long past and into the night. The Blast offers beer and burgers for sale, and an entertainment lineup that features local queer indie bands (Three Dollar Bill played a recent Backlot Bash; see their listing in Chapter 15), with lots of scoping, cruising, and flirting opportunities thrown in. The party, while not for women only, is definitely most popular with the ladies.

Pridefest
When: The last Saturday in June.
Where: Boystown, on Halsted between Waveland and Grace.

A recent addition to Pride weekend festivities is the aptly named Pridefest, a street fair located on Halsted between Waveland and Grace, the northernmost edge of the Boystown strip on Halsted. Pridefest takes place on the last Saturday of June. Northalsted Area Merchants Association created Pridefest for two reasons. First of all, it gives the bars and merchants on that end of the strip a chance to have a street fair on their home turf, since they miss out on Northalsted Market Days a bit later in the summer. Secondly, Chicago's Pride weekend events were, to put it bluntly, lame when compared to the events at cities of a similar size or smaller. Indeed, Milwaukee's Pridefest in early June continues to be more impressive in terms of sheer celebrity star power. So the Merchants Association created this one-day festival. Robert made his first Chicago Pridefest visit recently, and after paying the $5 entry fee (a donation—you don't have to pay it) arrived just in time to see RuPaul sing her hits, which did not take that long. One good thing about a really big, tall drag queen is that you can see her from very far away. More exciting to Robert personally was the chance to see local gay rocker Jinx Titanic take the stage. Although nominally punk in attitude, Jinx and his crew depend on a crisp, clear delivery to get every word to the lyrics of such songs as "You Make Me Wanna Cum" and "Everyone Loves a Muscle Boy" across to their adoring fans. The crowds at a Jinx show love the jockstraps and Frisbees thrown to the audience, and audience participation included one lucky audience member getting his pants and underpants stripped off him in front of God and everybody, after he'd jumped up onstage to be a back-up dancer. The hand that stripped him belonged to Jinx Titanic, a cigar-puffing leather daddy with a growl that settles into your groin and stays there. (Or that's how Robert experiences it.)

Other than the music, there is not much to do at Pridefest but walk around and drink. So that's what Robert and his cronies did, with plenty of stops to chat with acquaintances. There are a few crafts booths, some nonprofits set up informational stands, and you can find some (not very exciting) food, but all of those offerings are done better at other street fairs. The lesbians linger up north at the Dyke March and its post-festivities, the gay boys all have evening plans or want to stay rested for the following day's parade, and by 7 P.M. Pridefest was about out of pride. If you can't make it to town for **Northalsted Market Days** or Andersonville's **Midsommarfest**, by all means check out Pridefest—we don't want to dissuade you. But save some energy for the big events of Pride Sunday. ✦

Pride Sunday

We don't want to even *mention* this for fear of ruining the phenomena, but it has never rained on the last Sunday in June, not in over 36 years, and certainly not during the duration of the Gay Pride parade. Be forewarned that it is usually hot. Do bring sunscreen, bottled water, and sensible footwear. Don't bring dogs, babies, or other pets. It'll be too hot, scary, and crowded. If you are in town visiting friends, they will more than likely have a pre-parade brunch. Or you might choose to eat out. We guarantee that every breakfast and brunch place in the gay hoods and beyond will be packed with homos before the big event. Check out our brunch listings (p. 115) to find a fine spot to dine.

On his most recent Pride Sunday, Robert had to go to Boystown early for a lucrative cat-sitting gig. On Roscoe Street near the parade route, a teen gay boy boisterously sang along to "Dancing in the Streets" on his front porch at 9 A.M., and it was clear the party had begun. The holiday atmosphere of Pride means that people talk to each other much more than usual on the buses and the "L." In

Jack Hoff performs at Circuit for the Chicago Kings' Pride Prom 2003.
~Photo by Spencer

restaurants and on the streets, complete strangers will greet you by saying, "Happy Pride" or "Happy Gay Day," acknowledging that on this day, we belong to a special club. Another amusing thing to watch out for on Gay Pride is what we like to call the "hetero-sexual panic clutch." Straight folks, no matter how gay-friendly and enlightened, tend to grab their significant other's hand and hold on to it like a life raft when they are sudden-ly placed into the midst of 400,000 queers. (That's how big the parade-going crowd has been estimated at in recent years.) Look for this effect next time you are at Pride or Northalsted Market Days. You'll see straight couples who have not demonstrated an iota of public affection in years holding hands like high school freshmen between classes. It's kind of cute.

Until a couple years ago, the Pride Parade kicked off at the hangover-friendly time of 2 P.M. Now it starts at noon, which explains why sensible folks cut short their party-ing the night before—that pre-parade brunch comes a lot earlier than it used to. Prime parade-viewing points get staked out at least a couple hours ahead of time. The parade traditionally runs north on Halsted at Belmont up to Grace, where it hangs a quick

U-turn and goes south on Broadway down to Diversey, and east to Lincoln Park. We are pretty sure it's a law that if you are gay or gay-friendly and have an apartment that overlooks any part of the parade route, you must have a party.

And party the people do. As the young hustler narrator "X" in Matthew Rettenmund's novel *Boy Culture* says, "Chicago has a lively parade boasting countless Midwesterners full of beer and pride and flaunting what they've got, and a little of what they don't."

While Chicago law bans drinking alcohol on the street, and Kathie and Robert would never recommend that you break the law, we have to report that about 398,000 people do indeed drink booze on the street on Pride Sunday. If you keep your drinks in plastic or paper cups and act in a responsible yet celebratory manner, you'll find Chicago's finest have more urgent priorities than worrying about the many, many beer-drinkin' queers. "We're here, we're drunk, get used to it" is one of the unofficial mottoes of the day. Ask any law enforcement officer if they'd rather be dealing with a bunch of tipsy homos or, say, some straight drunk sports fans—they'll choose the gays every time.

Pride Sunday's boozy, Mardi Gras atmosphere is one of the criticisms we've heard about the Pride Parade. It is easy for Chicagoans to get cynical about the parade: the blatant corporate advertising (woo, look, the Rolling Rock beer truck—I am so proud), the overserved crowd, the politicians who march in the parade but do not vote for gay rights, the sameness of it all year after year. But when we feel the bitter taste of the cynic in our mouths, we remind ourselves of a few things. As far as corporations go, we keep in mind that companies are made up of people, and queer employees of a given corporation have as much right to be out and proud and in the parade with their GLBT coworkers as anyone else. We also remind ourselves that 25 years ago no American corporation around would let its logo and presence be felt in a gay pride parade. Illinois governor Rod Blagojevich walks the parade route every year, shaking hands, working the crowd. Try and imagine a major public official taking a day to shake thousands of gay hands and woo thousands of gay voters 25 years ago. We have indeed come a long way. As far as boozy excess, yes, there is some of that, but the parade is not just for the queer folk living comfortably and openly in the city. It is also for the tens of thousands of visitors, some of whom have traveled many hours to be in an atmosphere where their sexuality is celebrated, their love is lauded, and they can be completely, utterly, and joyfully themselves in a massive crowd of like-minded strangers and friends. The parade is for the young lesbian couple holding hands who told Robert, "Wow, wow. You just don't understand what this is like for us. This is another planet. This is amazing." It's for the young gay boys who didn't say a thing, they just embraced on the street, and you could see from their shining faces that this was the first time they had been able to kiss each other openly and without fear. It's for everyone in attendance, when a float with a massive speaker system is pounding out a song, it's a bright summer day and everyone is dancing, the costumed people on the float, the sunburnt people on the street, everyone is dancing, the drunk and the sober, and a gigantic plume of rainbow-colored confetti blasts into the air, the crowd roars its approval, and there is a prolonged moment of pure joy in being.

Finally, we defy you to be a cynic in the face of several of the groups who march in the parade every year. A number a queer youth groups march. Look at the faces of these teens, eager and delighted, basking in the approval of the crowd, and your heart will break a little at the sight. And the group Parents, Families, and Friends of Lesbians and Gays (www.pflag.org), better known by their acronym PFLAG, never fails to put a lump in our throats. Moms, grandmothers, dads, cousins, siblings, children, and other relatives, marching with signs that say, "God blessed me with a lesbian daughter" or "I love my gay dad," all look about as ordinary and mundane as attendees at an Iowa church picnic, which is the whole point. There's drag of both a fabulous and unfabulous nature, and there's the roarigengines of the ever-popular Dykes on Bikes and the growl of the daddy-bears. The whole span and panorama of a community. Much to the consternation of one of Robert's coworkers, every year a group of queer anarchists jumps into the parade at some point, and their entry inevitably backs things up for a while. "And they don't have a permit to march!" That's what gets the coworker's goat. Those darn anarchists. If they would just follow the rules . . . Our final thought on the parade is this: if you don't feel represented, if you feel the parade is not an accurate reflection of your community, by all means, participate! Sign up to have your float, group, club, organization, candidate, corporation, foundation, members, or what have you be an entry next year. (Go to www.chicagopridecalendar.org for details on signing up and everything else Pride related.)

After an afternoon in the hot sun, if you want to continue the party, we guarantee that every bar in Boystown will have a line to get in. The messy streets, which get cleaned up astonishingly quickly by the folks with the city's Streets and Sanitation Department, will be teetering with the silly and the overserved. If you don't have an invite to a local party, our advice is to head north. **Big Chicks** always has a free post-parade barbeque, and other bars in Uptown and Andersonville, while busy, won't have the lengthy wait that you'll experience at any queer bar near the parade route.

Dragons, drag, and six-pack abs—
who doesn't love a parade?
~Photo by Gert Crispyn

A few days after the parade, Robert was sitting at the gay **Caribou Coffee** shop on Broadway, enjoying his morning java and looking out the window. One scrap of pink confetti that had somehow escaped the vacuum of the street cleaners was rising and twirling. Still dancing. ✦

GirlBlast
When: The last Sunday in June, after the Pride Parade
Where: Boystown, at 929 W. Belmont Ave.

Don't let the cover charge, the long bathroom and beer lines, the shoulder-to-sunburned-shoulder crowd of women, or the occasional drunken fight dissuade you—this is *the* lesbian party of the Pride season. Having originated years ago in the parking lot of the long-gone lesbian dance club Paris Dance, after which it moved to the now-gone Girl Bar (in the parking lot of Guitar Center!),

At GirlBlast.
~Photo by Lisa Boyle

this annual party several years ago took up its current location in the alley behind Ann Sather restaurant (929 W. Belmont Ave.). DJ-spun dance music threatens to overpower the speaker system, while sweaty, happy women and a handful of their gay male friends dance, flirt, and frolic into the night.

July

Windy City Pride Weekend
When: The first weekend in July
Where: Locations vary; check the Web site for details

This weekend celebration by and for GLBT people of color features social, literary, and entertainment workshops and events. Events are citywide but centered at a downtown hotel. Log on to www.thewindycitypride.org for more info as well as year-round resources.

The Gay Games
When: July 15–22, 2006
Where: Locations vary; check the Web site for details

GLBT athletes from all over the world converge on Chicago for a week of sports competition, from rugby to billiards and swimming to dance. A host of social, arts, and cultural happenings will accompany the advent of the Gay Games. To volunteer (Robert wants to host some soccer players!), register, find out about tickets, or get help planning your Chicago visit, log on to www.gaygameschicago.org.

Out at the Ballpark
When: Mid-July
Where: Wrigley Field

On the Gay Day at Wrigley Field members of the Gay Men's Chorus sing the national anthem, and the stands are filled with sun-soaked and beer-battered queer Chicago Cubs fans. Keep your eyes on the *Chicago Free Press* Web site (www.chicagofreepress.com) for details.

August

Northalsted Market Days
When: The first weekend in August
Where: Boystown, on Halsted Street between Belmont Avenue and Addison Street

A huge event on the city's GLBT calendar, this Halsted street fair, the largest in the Midwest, is a crowded joyful festival featuring three music stages, arts and crafts booths, food, drink, and the all-important street strolling to catch up with friends and check out the hotties. Area accommodations fill up early, all the bars are packed, and for shirtless men, scantily clad women, fried food, and beer in the hot sun, this really cannot be beat.

Eye Candy at Market Days.
~Photo by Jon Peterson

Michigan Women's Music Festival
When: Mid-August
Where: Four to five hours north of Chicago near Hart, Michigan

Whenever someone asks Kathie why she loves the Michigan Womyn's Music Festival, which takes place in mid-August, four to five hours north of Chicago near Hart, Michigan (www.michfest.com), her answer is the same: *Where else can a woman go to a dance party, dance her booty off, get tipsy, and walk home at 1 in the morning, naked, in complete freedom from any threat of violence?* This is a type of liberation that every woman should experience at least once in her life.

But isn't it all about crystal healing and drumming for the goddess within and all that bunk?

Well, Kathie answers, yes, there is a place for those things to occur at MWMF-Michigan Women's Music Festival, but nobody is going to make you participate in them if you don't want to. Actually, more than a hundred workshops take place at the fest, from yoga, financial planning, and swing dancing to (from the 2002 MWMF program) "Group Body Painting," "Reclaiming Healthy Cronehood," "Getting Pregnant: Tricks of the Trade," "Anal Sex, Pleasure and Health," "Beginning Self-Defense," "Stiltwalking," "Dianic Wicca," "Fat Women Stripping," and "Healing with the Didgeridoo."

But Kathie, the doubting Thomasina continues, isn't it just a bunch of humorless radical lesbian feminists focused solely on enforcing their ideas of political correctness and out to spoil all my fun?

Um, no. Certain behavior is prohibited in some areas. For example, there is a chem-free campsite so that women in recovery have a safe place to call their own, and there are some places—the food lines and some seating areas around the stages, for example—that are chem-free or where smoking is prohibited, but if you want to smoke and drink, you can do so all day and night anywhere else on the land except these few restricted areas. It's all a part of creating a space that meets the needs of thousands of diverse women. And for those girls who really want to party, the "Twilight Zone" has a loud and rowdy campfire that lasts well into the wee hours every night.

But Kathie, isn't it true that they make you do work shifts? Why would I want to work? I'm on vacation!

Yes, fest attendees are requested to participate in two work shifts during their stay (one shift if they stay for just the weekend). Not only does this help keep the festival itself generally affordable, it also promotes the community spirit that is an integral part of the festival experience. Work shifts are a great opportunity to participate in what goes on behind the scenes, as well as a good way to meet other festie-goers from around the globe. It's not just about you you you, baby. It's about creating a community of thousands of women for one week in the year. Think big!

But Kathie, don't you have to eat vegetarian mush every night?

It's true that the common meals are all vegetarian. Many people, Kathie among them, actually like the food they serve at the festival. But feel free to bring a camp stove or grill and as many steaks, burgers, and hotdogs or as much bacon as you want. We guarantee you will make friends with other carnivores camped nearby.

But Kathie, Thomasina presses on, aren't there women who go around topless or even (gulp) naked there?

Yes. And your point is? No, seriously, you will see women in various stages of undress (as well as gloriously dressed in fabulous costumes). Women of all shapes, sizes, and ages. Not only do you get over it pretty quickly, but Kathie thinks you will ultimately find the experience of seeing so many different body types liberating and empowering. And rest assured, plenty of people remain clothed throughout the festival, and so can you, too, if you choose to.

The Michigan Womyn's Music Festival is a great outdoor concert and camping experience. Musical and comedy acts come from all around the world to play the festival. These include the Indigo Girls, Sweet Honey in the Rock, Le Tigre, Suzanne Westenhoefer, Alix Olson, the Butchies, and old-school womyn's music stalwarts such as Cris Williamson and Holly Near. Thirty (or more) different artists will be performing at any given festival, and that's all included in the ticket price (which also includeds workshops, childcare, and three meals a day). Women also travel from around the world to attend the fest. Annual attendance ranges from 3,000 to 8,000, depending on the year. But it's more than just an extended concert without indoor plumbing. It is an oasis and a reprieve from the subliminal forces of oppression and self-censorship that women encounter so frequently that most of us have internalized them. It is a place where our experiences growing up and being female in this world are validated and celebrated. And it is an ongoing experiment, a negotiation of sorts, with different ways of living, with creating and defining our own boundaries and definitions about how to live. *And* it is a place to party, to have fun, to seriously get down. Whether you do that by joining a drumming circle around a fire pit, painting yourself in chocolate, dancing in a mosh pit at a punk show, or simply sitting in your lounge chair, drinking a beer, and watching the parade of women pass you by, is up to you.

Kathie now steps down from her biodegradable soapbox. ✦

Windy City Gay Rodeo

For more than a decade now, the Illinois Gay Rodeo Association has been raising funds for various charities, and, as they add on their Web site, "in doing this we DO TRY to enjoy ourselves as much as we can." The annual Windy City Gay Rodeo, held in mid- to late August, is ILGRA's main event, and every summer it raises much-needed monies for such worthy charities as Vital Bridges, Howard Brown Health Center, and Cowboy Dreams (which gives Chicago-area children with special needs the opportunity to ride horses). On a more informal basis, the Rodeo also promotes the wearing of Levi's, cowboy boots, cowboy hats, and large belt buckles, as well as the bowlegged swagger such attire inspires. The Gay Rodeo has grown over the years, to the point where it is nothing less than a mini-gay pride event—in a pasture. When a tall cute guy asked Robert to accompany him to the Gay Rodeo, Robert did not have to think twice about saying yes. Robert's date's gay brother's partner's hair stylist (got that?) is a board member of ILGRA, so he'd chartered a Rodeo-bound bus for his staff of gregarious straight women and his salon's best gay customers, as well as a token straight guy who smelled of patchouli and was probably open-minded enough to "experiment." In the deal of the century, a mere $20 each got the entire crew round-trip bus fare and entry to the Rodeo, as well as a continental breakfast, vodka drinks, beer, and high-carb snacks galore while en route. (This is quite a deal when you consider that the daily cost to enter the Rodeo is $10.) The busload of straight chicks, gay guys, and the token straight boy became firm, if boozy friends by the time they arrived at 6 Guns Ranch and Arena in Crete, Illinois, about a 45-minute trip from downtown Chicago. It had rained the night before, and the hot sun beating down on the damp fields made for a humid day. Robert's fellow Rodeo-goers camped out in the stands for the opening ceremonies, but the lure of shade (and the beer tent) proved irresistible. In addition to drink, plenty of food was available, both the cooked beef that you might expect in a farm setting, as well as vegetarian alternatives to the burgers and dogs. A DJ kept the dance tent yee-hawing with country favorites, while a flea market for the cowboy-inclined offered up boots, chaps, T-shirts, jewelry (lots of turquoise), and folk art. Even the drag queens dressed like they were fresh off of the ranch, with maybe a stop in Las Vegas along the way. Robert admired their ability to suppress their sweat in the heat. He did not own any cowboy boots, and it's just as well, because by the time he got home, the shoes he did wear were ruined, from mud, and worse than mud—it's a ranch, after all, so you've got to watch where you step. Fortified by further food and drink, Robert's posse decided they should try and actually watch some of the rodeo. Maybe he's spoiled by television coverage of sporting events, where all the pauses are edited out, but Robert admits that while he admired the skill of the men and women roping and riding, the pace of the rodeo seemed a mite slow to him.

The event that he (and most of the crowd) got the biggest kick from was the one event that did not require any true cowboy skills. Teams of two people race from a starting point to a tethered young goat. One person grabs the back legs of the goat, while the teammate attempts to slip a pair of whitey-tighties up over the beast's nether regions. Once the bleating goat is properly briefed, the two people dash back to their starting point, because it's a race against the clock. It sounds easy enough, right? But the field was a morass of mud and horse poo, the bleating goat was obviously more of a boxers kind of guy who didn't see the advantages to donning jockey shorts, and much hilarity and slipping in the mud ensued. Now, we are not sure if "Jockeying the Goat" is an event that happens at all rodeos, or if this is particular to a gay rodeo agenda, but what is certain is that very few entrants finished the event with their crisp Western wear in a pressed and pristine condition.

The poor goat's plight drove Robert's companions back to drink, and not long after that, the storm clouds rolled in. Although the Rodeo is billed as a "rain or shine" event, the downpour lowered the lariat on the afternoon's competition. Robert got back on the bus with his date, his date's gay brother, assorted partners and friends, and the straight girl hairdresser contingent, and they boozed their way back to the city.

The Rodeo-going crowd was more male than female, maybe a 70-30 split, and the age range tended to be 35 and up. We're not sure what keeps queer youth from donning cowboy gear, but Western wear does appear to be an enthusiasm (notice

Rodeo Rod.
~Photo by Jon Peterson

we didn't call it a fetish) that develops mainly in the gays after the age of 30. The Gay Rodeo has an official hotel fairly close to the ranch, with deals for Rodeo participants and fans, but if you are staying in the city, several area bars, including Charlie's, offer bus trip package deals to and from the Rodeo. Or you can carpool it. Driving directions and other pertinent information is offered on the Rodeo's Web site. ILGRA has managed to get airline ticket and car rental deals for Rodeo-goers as well. Check out their Web site (www.ilgra.com), or phone the Rodeo hotline (312/409-3835). If you want to find out where the Gay Rodeos are all over the dang place, you can look up ILGRA's Big Daddy organization, the International Gay Rodeo Association (www.igra.com). ✦

September

In September the first nip of fall is in the air, a lot of theater companies start their seasons, plenty of folks happily single for the summer begin looking for an autumn cuddle buddy, and all the many college and university students at Chicago institutions come back to school and reinvigorate the nightlife.

Estrojam Music and Culture Festival
When: Late September
Where: Multiple venues; check the Web site for locations and times
   This GLBT-friendly festival celebrates the art and artistry of women. The main Estrojam Festival takes place in the fall, but benefit concerts and events occur year-round. See Chapter 15 or visit their the Estrojam Web site (www.estrojam.org) for more info.

October

Night of 100 Drag Queens
When: Late October
Where: Sidetrack
   Sidetrack bar hosts this annual event, a *must* for drag enthusiasts and practitioners. The Night has proved so popular that lately it's become two nights. Expect amazement: the performers have to audition for a coveted spot on the program, and the audience for this extravaganza glams it up. Themes change yearly, but the goal—fund-raising for a worthy GLBT charity—remains the same. Sashay over to www.sidetrackchicago.com for more.

Halsted Halloween Parade
When: Not always *on* Halloween but close to it
Where: See below
   What? Dress up in some kind of costume? Halloween is always a big gay holiday, but the annual parade, right in the heart of the Halsted nightlife area, gives us an official community event in addition to all the bar contests and dances

that happen this time of year. This is a pedestrian parade (that is, people walk—and there are no floats), with prizes, performances, and fun. It kicks off at Belmont and Halsted, heading north to the judging area and stage at Roscoe and Halsted. The parade isn't *all* gay—lots of little neighborhood kids in costume participate and stare wide-eyed at the inventiveness of the adults around them. The parade is sponsored by the Northalsted Area Merchants Association (www.northalsted.com).

November

Reeling, the Chicago Gay and Lesbian International Film Festival
When: Early November
Where: Movie houses around the city; check the Web site for times and locations

A weeklong celebration and viewing opportunity for gay film. See page 201 for more info, or contact Chicago Filmmakers (773/293-1447, chicagofilmmakers.org, reelingfilmfestival.org).

The Night Before Thanksgiving
When: Wednesday night in late November
Where: Every bar in Chicago.

Maybe it's the prospect of spending the entire next day with your partner's family. Maybe it's the prospect of facing a helping of Great Aunt Minnie's infamous gray casserole with off-brand potato chips crumbled on top. Maybe some folks want one last chance to find a nice girl or boy to bring home and meet Mom and Dad. It could be just that everyone can sleep in a bit on the holiday. Whatever the reason, gay bars in Chicago—and everywhere else, we assume—are full to the brim on the night before Thanksgiving. Take this as either an invitation, or a warning.

December

Busy, busy, busy. The time between Thanksgiving and New Year's has enough benefits, balls, parties, and other functions to make a queer's head spin. The Chicago Gay Men's Chorus and Windy City Performing Arts both offer popular holiday concerts (see page 236 for more on them). Many social and service organizations mark the holidays with fund-raisers and parties, while hotels, clubs, bars, and charity groups sponsor New Year's Eve celebrations, from the upscale to the modest.

Have a Gay Holiday and a Queer New Year.
~Photo by Jon Peterson

 ROBERT AND KATHIE'S VERY QUEER DON'T-MISS-PICKS FOR ANDERSONVILLE / UPTOWN

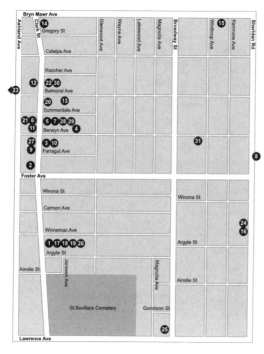

Shopping
1. Eagle Leathers, 5005 N. Clark
2. Presence, 5216 N. Clark
3. Women & Children First Bookstore, 5233 N. Clark
4. Tulip, 1480 W. Berwyn
5. Paper Trail, 5309 N. Clark
6. His Stuff, 5314 N. Clark
7. Alamo Shoes, 5321 N. Clark
8. Early to Bed, 5239 N. Sheridan

Restaurants
9. Svea, 5236 N. Clark
10. Andie's, 5253 N. Clark
11. Charlie's Alehouse, 5308 N.Clark
12. Tomboy, 5402 N. Clark
13. La Tache, 1475 W. Balmoral
14. Tanoshii, 5547 N. Clark
15. Francesca's Bryn Mawr, 1039 W. Bryn Mawr
16. Tweet, 5020 N. Sheridan

Bars
17. Clark's on Clark, 5001 N. Clark
18. The Eagle, 5015 N. Clark
19. T's Restaurant and Bar, 5025 N. Clark
20. Atmosphere, 5355 N. Clark
21. Madrigal's, 5316 N. Clark
22. Star Gaze, 5419 N. Clark
23. Joie de Vine, 1744 W. Balmoral
24. Big Chicks, 5024 N. Sheridan
25. Crew, 4804 N. Broadway

Misc. Picks
26. Man's Country, 5015 N. Clark
27. Cheetah Gym, 5248 N. Clark
28. Specialty Video, 5307 N. Clark
29. Kopi Café, 5317 N. Clark
30. Taste of Heaven, 5401 N. Clark
31. Pause Café, 1107 W. Berwyn

ROBERT AND KATHIE'S VERY QUEER DON'T-MISS-PICKS FOR BOYSTOWN

Shopping
1. Kafka Wines, 3325 N. Halsted
2. Bad Boys, 3352 N. Halsted
3. Beatnix, 3400 N. Halsted
4. GayMart, 3457 N. Halsted
5. Brown Elephant, 3651 N. Halsted
6. Equinox, 3401 N. Broadway
7. Borderline, 3333 N. Broadway
8. Windy City Sweets, 3308 N. Broadway
9. Unabridged Bookstore, 3251 N. Broadway
10. He Who Eats Mud, 3247 N. Broadway
11. Universal Gear, 3153 N. Bdwy
12. Pastoral Artisan, 2945 N. Bdwy

Restaurants
13. Nookies Tree, 3334 N. Halsted
14. Pepper Lounge, 3411 N. Sheffield
15. X/O, 3441 N. Halsted
16. Arco de Cuchilleros, 3445 N. Halsted
17. Cornelia's Roosterant, 748 W. Cornelia
18. Las Mananitas, 3523 N. Halsted
19. Angelina's Ristorante, 3561 N. Broadway
20. Ann Sather Café, 3411 N. Broadway
21. Pingpong, 3322 N. Broadway
22. Joy's Noodle, 3257 N. Bdwy

Bars
23. Berlin, 954 W. Belmont
24. Spin, 3200 N. Halsted
25. Sidetrack, 3349 N. Halsted
26. Roscoe's, 3356 N. Halsted
27. Cocktail, 3359 N. Halsted
28. Buck's, 3439 N. Halsted
29. Hydrate, 3458 N. Halsted
30. Circuit, 3641 N. Halsted
31. Cellblock, 3702 N. Halsted
32. Charlie's, 3726 N. Bdwy
33. The Closet, 3325 N. Bdwy

Misc. Picks
34. Steamworks, 3246 N. Halsted
35. Villa Toscana B&B, 3447 N. Halsted
36. Caribou Coffee, 3300 N. Broadway
37. Landmark Century Cinema, 2828 N. Clark

ROBERT AND KATHIE'S VERY QUEER DON'T-MISS-PICKS FOR WICKER PARK AND UKRANIAN VILLAGE

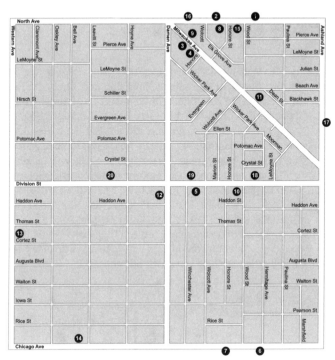

Shopping

1. Tatu Tatoo, 1754 W. North
2. Quimby's, 1854 W. North
3. Myopic Books, 1564 N. Milwaukee
4. Reckless Records, 1532 N. Milwaukee
5. Porte Rouge, 1911 W. Division
6. Alcala's Western Wear, 1733 W. Chicago
7. Tomato Tattoo, 1855 W. Chicago

Restaurants

8. Las Palmas, 1835 W. North
9. Earwax, 1561 N. Milwaukee
10. Leo's Lunchroom, 1809 W. Division

Bars

11. Davenport's, 1383 N. Milwaukee
12. Rainbo Club, 1150 N. Damen
13. Empty Bottle, 1035 N. Western
14. The Darkroom, 2210 W. Chicago

Misc. Picks

15. Global Yoga, 1823 W. North
16. Cheetah Gym, 1934 W. North
17. Cyberia Internet Café, 1331 N. Ashland
18. Alliance Bakery, 1736 W. Division
19. Jinx Café, 1928 W. Division
20. Letizia's Natural Bakery, 2144 W. Division

Acknowledgments

We would like to thank: Gary Alexander, Tracy Baim, Jennifer Blagg, Lisa Boyle, Patrick Brosnan, John Buranosky, John Cardone, Chix Mix, Neil Chudgar, Ann Christopherson and Linda Bubon of Women & Children First Bookstore, Creagh of Creaoke, Gert Crispyn, Ed Devereux and Unabridged Books, Mel Ferrand, Heather Findley and *Girlfriends* magazine, Richard Fox, Scott Free, Laura R. Gabler, Christopher Grace, Ianni Grammatis, Charles Hall, Ryan Hamlin, Kurt Heintz, Scott Jannush, Rod Lambert, Norm Lamm, Jeremy Lawson, Caldwell Linker, Martie Marro, Kyle Martin, Chandra Matteson, Adam McComber, Julie Mosier, Solveig Nelson, JT Newman, Nako Okubo, Sebastian Pinon, Chris Piss, Planet-Earth-Girl (PEG) and the Michfest BBS, Robert Prohaska, Marie-Jo Proulx, Dylan Rice, Nikki "Hot Stuff" Rinkus, Michael Sacramento, Mike Sarna, Kathy Sexton, Dave Short, Gene Skala, Richard Sparks, Spencer Photography, Kathleen Ulm, Dana Weiss, Chad Wolbrink, Sharon Woodhouse, Mike Wykowski, and everyone else who aided, abetted, encouraged, and otherwise helped us with this endeavor.

And thank you to Billy's Market Day appearance.
~Photo by Jon Peterson

D

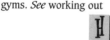

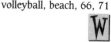

Kathie Bergquist's writing has been published in *Girlfriends* magazine, *Out,* the *Advocate, Curve,* and *Diva.* Born in Minneapolis, she moved to Chicago in 1989. She's honed her observational skills in the field, having worked at both Women & Children First and Unabridged Bookstores in Chicago, and by writing a long-running lesbian nightlife column, "The Kathie Klub" for the Chicago gay weekly *Nightlines.* Currently, Bergquist is the City Editor of the *Not For Tourists*™ *Guide to Chicago* and a regular food contributor to the *Chicago Reader.* She holds a B.A. in Creative Writing from Columbia College Chicago, and lives on the northwest side of the city with her girlfriend, Nikki, contending that Albany Park is positioning itself to be the new Andersonville. They share three frisky felines.

Robert McDonald has lived as an out gay man in Chicago for over 15 years, eight of which have been serving on the front lines of Chicago's gay community as a bookseller at Unabridged Bookstore. A self-described "theater-going, movie-watching, bar-hopping type-of-guy" when he's not out in the field observing queer culture, McDonald can be found with his nose in a book or his pen on a page. He is an avid reader and a published poet. His writing has appeared in *Publishers Weekly, Stagebill,* and the *Chicago Reader,* along with several very highbrow-type literary journals. He lives with his two interesting cats in a cute little coach house in the way-gay Chicago 'hood Andersonville. A native of Mt. Clemens, Michigan, McDonald holds an M.A. in English from Michigan State University.

Lake Claremont Press

Founded in 1994, Lake Claremont Press specializes in books on the Chicago area and its history, focusing on preserving the city's past, exploring its present environment, and cultivating a strong sense of place for the future. Visit us on the Web at www.lakeclaremont.com for new and bargain books. Or, contact us for a catalog at 773/583-7800 or lcp@lakeclaremont.com.

BOOKLIST

A Chicago Tavern: A Goat, a Curse, and the American Dream

A Cook's Guide to Chicago, 2nd Edition

The Politics of Place: A History of Zoning in Chicago

Wrigley Field's Last World Series: The Wartime Chicago Cubs and the Pennant of 1945

The Golden Age of Chicago Children's Television

Chicago's Midway Airport: The First Seventy-Five Years

The Hoofs & Guns of the Storm: Chicago's Civil War Connections

Great Chicago Fires: Historic Blazes That Shaped a City

The Firefighter's Best Friend: Lives and Legends of Chicago Firehouse Dogs

Graveyards of Chicago: The People, History, Art, and Lore of Cook County Cemeteries

Chicago Haunts: Ghostlore of the Windy City

More Chicago Haunts: Scenes from Myth and Memory

Muldoon: A True Chicago Ghost Story: Tales of a Forgotten Rectory

Creepy Chicago (for kids 8–12)

Literary Chicago: A Book Lover's Tour of the Windy City

A Native's Guide to Chicago, 4th Edition

A Native's Guide to Northwest Indiana

Award-winners

Finding Your Chicago Ancestors: A Beginner's Guide to Family History in the City and Cook County

The Streets & San Man's Guide to Chicago Eats

The Chicago River: A Natural and Unnatural History

Near West Side Stories: Struggles for Community in Chicago's Maxwell Street Neighborhood

Hollywood on Lake Michigan: 100 Years of Chicago and the Movies

Coming in 2006

Today's Chicago Blues

For Members Only: A History and Guide to Chicago's Oldest Private Clubs

From Lumber Hookers to the Hooligan Fleet: A Treasury of Chicago Maritime History